T0339759

A FATAL ADDICTION

A FATAL ADDICTION

WAR IN THE NAME OF GOD

THOMAS BLOCK

Algora Publishing
New York

Library of Congress Cataloging-in-Publication Data —

Block, Thomas.
A fatal addiction : war in the name of God / Thomas Block.
p. cm.
Includes bibliographical references and index.
  ISBN 978-0-87586-930-8 (soft cover: alk. paper) — ISBN 978-0-87586-931-5 (hard
cover: alk. paper) — ISBN 978-0-87586-932-2 (ebook) 1. Violence—Religious aspects. 2.
War—Religious aspects. I. Title.
  BL65.V55B57 2012
  201'.7273—dc23
  2012032048

Front cover: Mayan Classic Period Censer with Figure of Deity Holding Human Head
Located in the Museo Arqueologico-Sylvanus G. Morley, Tikal, Guatemala.
Credit: © Macduff Everton/CORBIS

Printed in the United States

Religion in its broadest sense must be another term for that obscurity that surrounds man's efforts to defend himself by curative or preventative means from his own violence.[1]

For my mother, Barbara Gilbert and my father, Victor Block

TABLE OF CONTENTS

INTRODUCTION

> The failure of modern man to grasp the nature of religion has served to perpetuate its effects ... We persist in disregarding the power of violence in human societies; that is why we are reluctant to admit that violence and the sacred are the same thing.[2]

TRUTH

The 20th-century activist-prophet Mahatma Gandhi (d. 1948) stated that God *is* Truth. They are the same thing.

At first glance, this looks like one of those throwaway lines about God's attributes, such as "God is Great," "God is Love" or "God is Omnipresent." Something that we hear often, yet rarely think too much about.

However, if we sit with the idea that "God is Truth" for a few minutes, it quickly becomes unsettling. Truth and our conception of reality are often very much at odds. Truth is not found by sifting through polling data or by agreeing with a generally accepted opinion. It has nothing to do with objectivity — which often simply splits the difference between opposing views — or with history, or precedent, or even our deepest held intuitions and beliefs.

Given the chasm that sometimes exists between perception and reality, Truth can be very difficult to disentangle from desire, wish, hope, political exigency and accepted objective reality. The Florentine political philosopher Niccolo Machiavelli (d. 1527) realized this dynamic, stating: "The great majority of humans are satisfied with appearances, as though they were realities, and are often more influenced by the things that seem rather than by those that are."[3]

The greatest spiritual thinkers have appreciated this difficulty. The 18th-century Jewish mystic Baal Shem Tov noted: "What does it mean when people say Truth goes over all the world? It means that Truth is driven out of one place after another, and must wander on and on."[4] And Rabbi Pinhas of Koretz (d. 1791), a Hasidic master, said: "For the sake of Truth, I served 21 years. Seven years to find out what Truth is, seven to drive out falsehood and seven to absorb Truth."[5] Very few of us have the energy and dedication to undertake this rabbi's program of discovery!

AMERICA: A CASE STUDY IN THE DIFFERENCE BETWEEN TRUTH AND REALITY

The history of the United States offers fertile ground for considering the difference between accepted fact and Truth. Contrary to the national narrative, the United States of America is anything but a peace-loving nation founded on the inalienable principles of human rights and justice for all, which it gently exports around the world to other countries.

One Truth of the matter is that the United States was founded on genocide (of the Native Americans), and stealing (of their land), and then was turned into an empire on the backs of African slaves.

More recently, the history of the United States continues to veer from its self-image as a nation of peace and gentle suasion: It has been the single most bellicose international actor since World War II. In his book *Killing Hope: U.S. Military and CIA Interventions Since World War II* (1995), William Blum outlines 55 different military actions in more than 50 countries, describing the role played by the United States in overthrowing governments, perverting elections, assassinating leaders, suppressing revolutions, manipulating trade unions and manufacturing news. The United States is the only country that has ever utilized a nuclear bomb, dropping two of them on Japan in 1945.

Yet the country has a very different self-image. According to America's most visible political leaders, the country is "exceptional" and "good." This example, one of many which will be explored throughout this book, is from a speech by then Senator Barack Obama at the Democratic National Convention in 2004. It represents the American *zeitgeist*:

> We gather to affirm the greatness of our nation not because of the height of our skyscrapers, or the power of our military, or the size of our economy; our pride is based on a very simple premise, summed up in a declaration made over 200 years ago: "We hold these truths to be self-evident,

that all men are created equal, that they are endowed by their creator with certain inalienable rights, that among these are life, liberty and the pursuit of happiness." That is the true genius of America.[6]

A recent survey by the Public Religion Research Institute and the Brookings Institution found that 58 percent of Americans agreed with the statement: "God has granted America a special role in human history."[7] And this majority of countrypersons probably don't mean to commit genocide, enslave humans and rain bombs down on countries as far flung as Yemen, Somalia and Colombia.

This book is one attempt to dig *through* all of the myth and wish that help shape America's national as well as human narratives, to honestly explore two central facets of human society: organized violence — usually known as "war" — and the yearning for the sacred, also known as "religion." Shorn of the usual political, emotional and social parameters that can separate Truth and reality, this examination will not be bound by accepted historical narratives. It explores in the clearest manner possible these central human institutions.

For if, as Gandhi maintained, God *is* Truth, then we owe it to ourselves to do our best to take an honest look at our institutions, our motivations and our failings — not as an exercise of self-flagellation but so that we might begin to live up to the maxims and platitudes that are so easily flung about in political and social forums.

ONE TRUTH

There are many painful truths that we might have a difficult time understanding and internalizing. This book is about one of them: our fatal attraction to violence and war. And even more confusing, the manner in which war and God are intertwined, in most religions and throughout all human time, even into our own.

War represents the collision of our two most basic drives: the will to live and a violent and self-destructive aspect of our nature. As the German philosopher Friedrich Nietzsche (d. 1900) explained, "Exploitation does not belong to a corrupt or imperfect and primitive society; it belongs to the essence of what lives, as a basic organic function. It is a consequence of the will to power, which is, after all, the will to life."[8]

There is no greater manner of "exploitation" than to kill another human being or be part of a force or nation that does so. In so doing, the "will to live" is taken to its logical conclusion, through denying life to another. Little is so existentially satisfying, and nothing is so stubbornly at the heart of human civilization, as this dynamic and the manner in which it plays out through war.

It is a perverse universe indeed that would fuse these two primal instincts in one being — the will to live and the need to destroy — but their centrality to the human experience cannot be denied.

A Time-Honored Truth

There are few rituals *more* basic to all states and all civilizations throughout human history than war. As the Chinese philosopher Sun Tzu (c. 500 B.C.E.) said in *The Art of War*: "Warfare is the greatest affair of state, the basis of life and death, the Tao to survival or extinction."[9]

Despite its ubiquity, it is also the most *inhuman* of human institutions. How can it still be so stubbornly central to society, even though our armaments have grown to such grotesque efficiency that thousands and even millions of people can be killed during the course of a few weeks?

What's more, as our ability to commit mass slaughter grows through technological advances, the percentage of non-combatants killed engorges to alarming proportions: from 15% in World War I to 65% in World War II, then 90% at the end of the 20th century in "low-impact" conflicts in places such as the Sudan, East Timor and the Balkans[10] and, most recently, to an almost perfect 98% of those killed being innocent victims, with the advent of pilotless drone attacks[11] in Afghanistan, Pakistan, Yemen, Somalia, the Palestinian Territories and other locales.

The stability of war as a central facet of society is undeniable. Today is certainly no different than one thousand years after the birth of Jesus, or a millennium before the birth of the Christian Messiah. For instance, during my own lifetime, the United States of America has been incessantly at war. I was born into the Vietnam War in 1963 and now, as I write this, my country is involved in various military engagements, in the Middle East, Latin America, Africa and other regions.

Additionally, members of the United States armed forces are detailed to 150 nations around the world, from Korea to Uganda to Germany to Columbia, and all points in between. Over the past 50 years, the United States military has been involved in bloody conflicts in Cambodia, Laos, Chile, Guatemala, El Salvador, Nicaragua, Lebanon, Honduras, Iran, Panama, Grenada, Iraq (twice), Kuwait, Serbia, Colombia, Pakistan and Somalia, *just to name a few*.[12] This comprises an unbroken line of American military engagements whose dead might count out the minutes that I have lived in the course of nearly 50 years.

Things are certainly not getting better. An article in the Washington Post noted:

> This is the American era of endless war . . . Today, radical religious ideologies, new technologies and cheap, powerful weapons have catapulted the world into a "period of persistent conflict," according to the Pentagon's last major assessment of global security. "No one should harbor the illusion that the developed world can win this conflict in the near future," the document concluded. By this logic, America's wars are unending and any talk of peace is quixotic or naïve.[13]

War cuts a bloody swath through all of human history with no less insistence than it has throughout my lifetime. War correspondent Christopher Hedges noted, in his gut-wrenching book *What Every Person Should Know about War*, that over the past 3400 years of civilization humans have been entirely at peace for only 268 of them.[14] The Pulitzer Prize winning historian Will Durant (d. 1981) calculated that there have been only 29 years in all of human history during which there was not a war underway somewhere in the world.[15] George C. Kohn was even more unforgiving, noting in his *Dictionary of Wars* that from roughly 2925 B.C.E. through today, an unbroken line of institutional violence can be drawn. And psychologist James Hillman stated in *A Terrible Love of War* that during the 5600 years of recorded history, 14,600 wars have been fought, more than two wars for each year of human civilization.[16]

Of course, it must also be acknowledged that war has been almost as intensively studied as it has been waged. From the first exploration of this human ritual, in Herodotus's *The Histories* (d. 425 B.C.E.), through the most recent reportage about the current war (whichever that might be as you read this), countless investigators, historians, pundits, poets and journalists have examined the causes of war in a myriad of ways. Yet all of their conclusions have failed to explain, once and for all, the genesis of this endemic human experience.[17]

This book is yet one more attempt.

A Religious People

The violent nature of our species is undeniable. As the 20th-century prophet Thomas Merton (d. 1968) pointed out: "Man is the only species besides the rat that wantonly and cruelly turns on his own kind in unprovoked and murderous hostility. Man is the only one who deliberately seeks to destroy his own kind."[18]

At the same time, the vast majority of people and societies throughout human time have considered themselves deeply religious. Even in our era, the United States is said to be the most religious industrialized nation in the world. A Washington Post article noted: "92 percent [of Americans] believe in God or a universal spirit — including one in five of those who call themselves atheists."[19]

It was this pairing in contemporary America of war and religion, spirituality and destruction, that inspired me to write this book. Shouldn't the one (religion) mitigate the other (institutional violence)? Isn't peace at the center of *all* religions? Yet the facts speak for themselves: a relationship between God and religion, not only in language but also in action, cannot be denied.

To examine the pairing of war and religion throughout human history is an academic study, but to look at it in terms of *my* country and *my* era is deeply emotional. How could it be that my nation, one of the most religious countries in the world, is also one of the most violent? Do God and war define the American spirit as much as apple pie and baseball? And if they do, how can that be? From what I have understood of religion, it leads to harmony — internal spiritual tranquility, as well as social well being between and among peoples.

The facts exhibit a different reality. With a country as religious and war-like as the United States, something else must be taking place. So I decided to delve not only into the history of war and religion, but also to examine how the inseparable pairing of these two forces impact contemporary society.

Uncovered Truth

Most religions — not only the bloody monotheistic ones with which we in the West are more familiar (Judaism, Christianity and Islam), but also many primitive religions,[20] as well as Greek, Roman, Buddhist, Sikh and Hindu creeds — have, in addition to being sacred paths preaching internal peace as well as brotherly love, less well known and bloodthirsty histories. In many cases, as I explore below, these creeds demand complete bodily commitment, sacrifice and murder to further the cause of their god. As I delved deeper into the chronicles of these major faiths, I found that few are religions of peace. And that if a religion does preach peace in a meaningful manner, it is either swallowed up from the outside by a more warlike creed, or changed from the inside, as happened to Christianity in the fourth century (see below).

The mantra "(insert name of preferred religious path) is a religion of peace" is often simply not the case. Sometimes, it is little more than a manner of papering over the violent history of a particular faith. Or, at the very least, it represents a selective view of the narrative of one's own spiritual path. Additionally, this construction has been used to justify violence against another, different religion that obviously *isn't* a religion of peace, or "they" wouldn't be forcing "us" to undertake these bellicose actions.

This dynamic is explored in detail below.

THE TRUTH SHALL NEVER DISSUADE

Human beings often do not allow facts to come between them and their deepest held beliefs. It is a dynamic that we see time and again, and one that is hidden in plain view.

Ronald Lindsay, president of the Committee of Skeptical Inquiry, was quoted in the Washington Post addressing the underlying motivation for people choosing their inklings over truth. He was discussing a question in American politics which will almost certainly be forgotten by the time you read this: whether or not President Barack Obama was actually born in the United States, otherwise known as the "birther" controversy. But this dynamic holds true for any set of deeply held beliefs, and religious beliefs are often the bedrock of a person's sense of self:

> If you have a pre-commitment to your view, and that point of view is important for your identity — if you are emotionally attached to it — your emotion is going to shape your reasoning process. You'll be presented with facts, but you'll find some way to minimize the significance of those facts.[21]

And so it is with religion: people often believe that *theirs* is a religion of peace, because they *want* to believe that they, and their god, are peaceful. Many devout people will blame anything but their own creed for the history of blood and slaughter within their sacred path, violence often committed in service to that religion.

AMERICA THE BELLICOSE

In the study that follows, I review the violence of God tradition in six of the largest religious paths practiced in our world, representing nearly 90% of the world's faith community, as well as many bellicose precursor religions in primitive societies, the ancient Near East, Greece and Rome. The one thing that all of these religious paths share is a belief in *sacred* violence — and that violence and the sacred are at times so closely linked as to be indistinguishable.

After this exploration, I turn my attention to American culture and the manner in which the violence of God tradition influences its political sphere — how the United States, as a society, goes so easily to war as "one nation under God." In exploring the language of the media, politics, religious speeches and popular culture over the decade or so since the September 11 attacks on the World Trade Center — attacks which are themselves believed by some to be exemplary acts of religious ecstasy — I found that the tendency to fuse God's will with institutionalized slaughter affected many facets of America's public discourse. Closer examination uncovered the fact that this conflation of violence and God may be traced backward in the country's history to the founding of the United States and even earlier.

The question that arose for me throughout this work — which I deal with in the epilogue — is which force is more powerful, and which *serves* which? Do religion and God exist simply to channel our aggressive impulses, with the fusion of violence and the sacred making civilization itself possible by preventing humanity from dissolving into an orgy of individual, anarchic destructive behavior? Are our sub-and pre-conscious aggressive impulses channeled through sacred violence into the institution of war, thereby protecting most of us while sacrificing the few, the warriors?

Or does it go even further than that, with war being one true human religion? With violence representing, for many, the ultimate expression, as Nietzsche averred, of the human will to live. And in this case, are God and Church sometimes subservient to our necessary, primal and genetically encoded violence?

I don't know.

But I felt that these questions must be explored — and they had to be considered honestly and openly, focusing on the facts at hand, outside of the realm of wish and dream. Often, even in books that have examined the relationship between God and religion, I feel that conclusions have been softened, holy warriors have been shunted from the center of society (referred to as "terrorists" or miscreants) and the two energies — violence and the sacred — have been teased apart, with a sigh of relief.

In those studies, the desire for a certain outcome often appeared to influence the conclusion, clouding even the most penetrating studies of violence and God. After all, a book must give the reader what he or she wants, or it risks remaining an unpublished study, considered too depressing or unmarketable to be put into print.

Chapter One: War

> No one engaged in thought about history and politics can remain unaware
> of the enormous role violence has always played in human affairs.[22]

War is violence.

Violence is endemic to the human condition.

Although philosopher René Girard noted in his seminal work *Violence and the Sacred*, "Neither primitive nor modern man has yet succeeded in identifying the microbe responsible for the dread disease of violence,"[23] a genetic basis for its expression must exist within the physical structure of the human animal. Violence, the will to express oneself in an aggressive and destructive manner, undoubtedly is tangled into our DNA like the need to eat, sleep and breathe.

Despite the fact that it might distress and even disgust some of us, the simple fact of our own violent nature must be accepted at the very beginning of this study. Any squeamishness must be overcome so that the spare facts can be appreciated and digested. No silver lining here: I will not claim that most of us, at heart, are more like Gandhi than Genghis Khan.

Political theorist Hannah Arendt (d. 1975) proposed in *On Violence* that humans' violent urges are even more powerful than other innate drives, such as nutritive and sexual instincts. She stated that nutritive and sexual drives are "activated by compelling bodily needs on one side and by outside stimulants on the other," while violent impulses "seem to be independent of such provocation. This leads to instinct frustration, to 'repressed' aggressiveness, which according to psychologists causes a damming up of 'energy,' whose eventual explosion is all the more dangerous."[24]

VIOLENCE AND SOCIETY

More than just an individual need, violence represents a central aspect of communal intercourse. It often offers a vital cohesive bond between humans, one that makes "society" itself possible. As René Girard noted: "social coexistence would be impossible . . . if violence failed to be transmitted into culture."[25] This is an even more disturbing aspect of violence: not that it merely exists as a part of the human social experience, but that it can seem to be necessary to it.

Expanding on the perceived inevitability of violence to human culture, Dr. Regina Schwartz argued in *The Curse of Cain: The Violent Legacy of Monotheism* that violence originates in identity formation, in the primal need for individuals to separate themselves from each other and the world around them. In the simple act of experiencing life as a unique person, the seeds of violence are born.[26] According to Schwartz, violence is central to personality, to existential meaning and to the fundamental experience of "being." Violence represents the first step toward consciousness.

How can this be? After all, not everyone behaves in a violent manner. Schwartz explained:

> Violence is not only what we do to the Other. It is prior to that. Violence is the very construction of the Other . . . The outsider is believed to threaten the boundaries that are drawn to exclude him, the boundaries that his very existence maintains. Outside by definition but always threatening to get in, the Other is poised in a delicate balance that is always off balance, because fear and aggression continually weight the scales. Identity forged against the Other inspires perpetual policing of its fragile borders.[27]

VIOLENCE AND SPIRITUALITY

The definition of the self, created in opposition to the other, represents the antithesis of the *spiritual* understanding of being. It is vital to highlight this difference because, as I will show, violence and religions are deeply intertwined, while violence and the *spiritual* path are antithetical to each other. This is a nuanced but central point, as the spiritual paths at the center of all religions are very similar to each other.

At the core of most religions lies the belief that the surest way to spiritual realization is to dissolve the sense of personal autonomy and individual existence into the Divine ground of all being. Far from creating the sense of self in opposition to the other, the mystical adept takes the opposite course, appreciating the interconnectedness of all beings and how the experience of selfhood grows out of ignorance.

As I work through this study, these diametrically opposed definitions of being — one, the more primal, based in separation through boundary formation (leading to violence) and the other, more spiritually mature, based on dissolving perceived differences between the self and other — will be a constant theme and one which helps explain how the deeply religious can also be terribly violent.

Because sadly, religion and spirituality do not always go hand in hand.

Violence and The Scapegoat

If individual personality formation is forged in the furnace of violence, as Regina Schwartz contends, then imagine how much more important it must be for the even more fragile construction of a society. To bring hundreds, thousands, even millions of souls together in an experience of "us," creating the basic bonds that make civilization possible, violence must be collected and channeled. Without some institutional outlet for innate human aggressiveness, the fabric of society would shred and the collection of human animals would disintegrate into the chaos of individuation, as represented in an ongoing catastrophe of violent acts leading, in the end, to the destruction of human civilization.

René Girard proposed in his beautiful study *Violence and the Sacred* that the creation of the scapegoat — some "other" upon which to vent all of the aggressive tendencies collected in the human soul — represented the beginning of society. Those of us who have followed him in thinking about civilization and violence have often found much to inspire us in Girard's seminal work. Anglican priest Jeremy Young, writing in *The Violence of God and the War on Terror*, noted:

> Scapegoating is one of the quickest and most effective means of creating a strong sense of group belonging: the differences and conflicts that may exist within a group can be ignored and projected onto another community or onto its [own] deviant members.[28]

Society is built on the creation of an "other" upon whom to vent innate murderous impulses. This is not hard to discern. We can see this in the United States with the application of its death penalty, disproportionately visited on African-American subjects, who since the time of slavery have represented the "other" against which mainstream America has often defined itself. Since the reinstitution of the death penalty in 1976, thirty-five percent of executed criminals have been Black,[29] while African-Americans make up only 12.6% of the total population.[30] More recently the scapegoat against whom many Americans define themselves has shifted, with the attacks of 9/11/2001, to Arabs and Muslims.

This dynamic is replayed on the international stage as a manner of knitting a collection of individuals into a society sharing a culture. It could be argued that the United States, more than almost any other country in the world, is desperately in need of enemies as its ethnic, cultural and religious fabric is so diverse that it is almost impossible to find shared markers *except* for a common enemy.

America's national identity germinates in war. Its textbooks are filled with stories of international engagements with heinous enemies. In each case, students are taught about the courageous and freedom-loving Americans stepping onto the international stage to safeguard God, country and the highest human ideals. Additionally, lest they come to believe that these formative events, proof of their country's goodness, are confined to the past, the United States is collectively embroiled in a series of contemporary actions with existential foes, whether terrorists, dictators, oil-hording brigands or others.

The point of relevance in both the domestic and international acts of violence is not whether an uncomfortable majority of executed citizens have darker skin than is merited by their percentage of the population (they do), or whether innocent people are put to death or not in our foreign interventions (they are). The real purpose of the death penalty in America and its wars in far-off lands is to turn its citizens' natural aggression outward onto a perceived "other" so that the countrypersons can create a sense of belonging and be part of a functioning society.

Ultimately, this need for scapegoating comes to define a central aspect of any society: keeping peace *through* violence.

> Violence, or the threat of violence, is fundamental to the creation of peace of most communities. This is clear in the case of the armed forces, who are trained in the use of violence to defend a country against both internal and external threats, or the police. The courts, the judiciary and the prison system are all systems of legal violence. The military and legal systems underlie all of our communal interactions.[31]

And in every case, the people who become tangled up within the state's system of violence (either at home or abroad) not only offer a defining boundary that helps individuals feel like part of the majority, but those scapegoats also satisfy innate aggressive needs, freeing people to live more or less peaceably within a society.

God can be a violent God.

Sometimes God *must* be, as God can demand so much violence from His creations. "God is understood in the *Torah*, Christian New Testament and the *Qur'an* to be powerful, because power is identified with violence."[32] God's covenant with the faithful often includes the promise to utterly destroy the enemy, as well as spread His word via violent acts of aggression and retribution.

What's more, God occasionally keeps His flock in line by visiting terrible and violent episodes on those who stray. "One point of undisputed agreement is that God's overwhelming character is that of a violent, punishing, pathological deity who uses unfathomable violence to both reward and punish."[33]

God is imagined in many religions as sanctioning violence and oftentimes as committing it Himself. And while I will give detailed and specific examples of pathologically violent language and action of God later in this study, it is necessary now to fix in the mind of the reader that it is not abnormal, and is sometimes even traditional, to place violence at the center of religious experience. A passage from Mark Juergensmeyer's (Director of the Orfalea Center for Global and International Studies, University of California, Santa Barbara) *Terror in the Mind of God* will suffice at this point to verify the military sheen that can affect the spiritual quest, as represented in many religions:

> Virtually all cultural traditions have contained martial metaphors. The ideas of the Salvation Army in Christianity and a Dal Khalsa (army of the faithful) in Sikhism characterize disciplined religious organizations. Images of spiritual warfare are even more common. The Muslim notion of *jihad* is the most notable example, but even in Buddhist legends great wars are to be found . . . The legendary history recorded in the Pali Chronicles, the *Dipavamsa* and the *Mahavamsa* relate the triumphs of battles waged by Buddhist kings . . . The great Indian epics, the *Ramayana* and the *Mahabharata* are tales of seemingly unending conflict and military intrigue . . . which defined subsequent Hindu culture. Whole books of the Hebrew Bible are devoted to the military exploits of great kings, their contests related in gory detail. Though the New Testament did not take up the battle cry, the later history of the Church did, supplying Christianity with a bloody record of crusades and religious wars . . . Protestant writer Arthur Wallis explained that warfare is not "a metaphor or figure of speech"

but a "literal fact." . . . Scholar Harriet Crabtree concurred, asserting that the image of warfare is attractive because it "situates the listener or reader in the religious cosmos."[34]

WAR AND RELIGION

War makes the world understandable, a black and white tableau of them and us. It suspends thought, especially self-critical thought. All bow before the supreme effort. We are one. Most of us willingly accept war, as long as we can fold it into a belief system that paints the ensuing suffering as necessary for a higher good, for human beings seek not only happiness, but also meaning. And tragically, war is sometimes the most powerful way for human society to achieve meaning.[35]

Regardless of what one might wish to believe, war and religious experience are deeply and inextricably entangled. Any person who looks you resolutely in the eye and states, "My religion is a religion of peace," almost certainly does not have a complete understanding of his or her own religious path.

I have confronted religious leaders about the violence within their own faiths. During one such meeting, at an interfaith conference at al-Azhar University in Cairo, I asked a participant, a very well-respected Catholic priest and scholar, about the Crusades, and he replied by rolling his eyes and saying: "Why do you always have to concentrate on the bad stuff?" As I am Jewish, a member of a recipient group of so much of Catholicism's "bad stuff," of course the answer should have been obvious, but my Catholic priest friend was uninterested in exploring this aspect of his faith's history, choosing to concentrate on the "good stuff" that he and other Catholic leaders were undertaking.

No doubt, there is much good being done within faith traditions. However, the unwillingness to acknowledge the difficult aspects of one's own faith can be a blind spot that only leads to more "bad stuff." Brian Daizen Victoria captured this dynamic in his important work *Zen at War*:

> Apologists for the faiths usually minimize the distress that can come with religion or that religion can produce. They want religion to be nothing but good news. You will not read about the destructive element in religions in the advertisements for the church of your choice. Yet . . . one must note the feature of religion that keeps it on the front page and in prime time — it kills.[36]

Most religious narratives are steeped in the imagery of combat, and political and even religious leaders use religion to provide justification for bellicose acts.

Violence and God, war and religion have been intertwined since the beginning of human time. Religion, after all, is about reaching into the soul to stir a consciousness beyond the limits of language and the mundane. And images of death have always been at the heart of religion's power to do just this. God and war, love and death mix together into a toxic stew, one that is accepted almost without thought by generation after generation of believers.[37]

The sacred consists of all those forces whose dominance over man increases or seems to increase in proportion to man's effort to master them. Tempests, forest fires, plagues, among other natural phenomena, may be classified as sacred. Far outranking these stands human violence — violence seen as something exterior to man and therefore as part of all the other outside forces that threaten mankind.[38]

Violence stipples the sacred texts of all religions. While many religious followers read these passages as metaphor for the personal, spiritual struggle, those who seek to justify their violence as God-sanctioned can easily find passages to support their position. And the problem is not that the people are taking the passages out of context. They are simply reading religious texts literally.

While gentler souls seek to defuse violence by asking followers of individual religious paths to "look beneath" the literal text for a second, more spiritual meaning, the fact of the matter is that religious scriptures offer some of the most perverse, violent, hateful imagery ever written — and often link this violence to the will of God.

WAR AND THE STATE

With the inclusion of the state in this human dynamic, mass murder, religion and the myth of the nation as a paternal, God-like structure come together to create the unbreakable hold of war on society. As psychologist Lawrence LeShan noted in *Why We Love War*: "War seems to be a 'natural' way of behaving for governments . . . A constant, deeply concealed pressure *toward* war may be exerted by the structure of our governments, a structure 'designed' partly for this purpose."[39]

War, religion and the state come together because the state is the closest thing to a God that humanity can comprehend. In its paternalistic relation to individual citizens, its massive size, its appearance of omniscience and ubiquity, the state represents a demigod whose purpose can easily become enmeshed with conceptions of ultimate meaning. As Carl Schmitt (d. 1985), a Catholic philosopher who became an important ideologue for the Nazis, noted:

> All significant concepts of the modern theory of the state are secularized
> theological concepts not only because of their historical development —
> in which they were transferred from theology to the theory of state where-
> by, for example, the omnipotent God became the omnipotent lawgiver —
> but also because of their systematic structure.[40]

In addition, war becomes a defining aspect of social belongingness —
a shared act that binds the disparate individuals of a land together into
a society. In war, there is a unanimous participation in the rites of collective murder, with the entire group acting in unison, either literally, as
warriors, or as accomplices, as members of the political elite, the press,
humanitarian volunteers and the general society. And the faceless form of
the enemy becomes the healing scapegoat upon whom to vent the population's innate aggressiveness, thereby unifying the citizens.

This explains the war fervor that grips a nation, accompanying a military engagement. It could be seen recently in the United States just after
the beginning of the Iraq War in 2003, when a Gallup poll concluded
that 79% of Americans considered the Iraq War was justified.

This mass psychosis is hardly something visible only in our current
age. Regina Schwartz provided a look at the Biblical underpinnings for
how war, religion and state are inseparable.

> The Bible's preoccupation with collective identity was read through the
> lens of nationalism — God's chosen people became the chosen nation . .
> . In a disturbing inversion, nationalism was authorized by the once-holy
> writ. A text that once posited collective identity as an act of God ("I will
> be your God if you will be my people") came to posit the collective iden-
> tity as the fiat of the nation authorized by God ("One nation under God").
> Nationalism has held fast to this legitimization by transcendence. Nations
> are the will of God.[41]

And if nations are the will of God, it goes without saying that so must
be their wars.

A PARSIMONIOUS GOD

Exacerbating the impetus for violence further, and providing the
perfect outlet for the discovery of a scapegoat and the warring needs of
nations and individuals, is God's parsimonious nature. Succinctly put,
there is just not enough of God to go around. According to the Abrahamic tradition, God first gave His Covenant to Ishmael through Abraham
and Hagar (Genesis 16). He then withdrew It and gave it to Isaac via
Abraham and Sarah (Genesis 21). There was not enough "God" for both
Ishmael and Isaac, so a choice had to be made.

Some time later, Christianity claimed God's promise (through Jesus) and 600 years after that, Muhammad revealed that both Judaism and Christianity had forfeited their right to the Covenant, and claimed the mantle of God. "The tendency to identify a particular people with the chosen or elect of God is endemic in the monotheistic religions . . . The combination of 'absolute truth' with the self-identification of a group as the chosen people . . . has enabled Jews, Christians and Muslims to commit the most evil atrocities in the name of God with a clear conscience."[42]

Even many non-Abrahamic faiths believe that if their God is not believed by all, then at the very least all others are in error, while in the worst (and often more normal) case, the non-believers must be eradicated so as to "prove" that theirs is the one and true God. Wars by the faithful of Hinduism, Buddhism, Sikhism and other creeds — stories that will be told in more detail — bear this truth out.

We are forced to conclude that God is not only a jealous God, but miserly, as well. Far from spreading the wealth, God is presented in most religions as a finite unit that must be claimed and then fought over. "Monotheism is entangled with particularism, with the assertion that this God and not any other gods must be worshipped, a particularism so virulent that it reduces all other gods to idols and so violent that it reduces all other worshippers to abominations."[43]

In each case, the previous "owners" of God's grace are left devoid, or at least with but one recourse to reclaim the Covenant of God: fight for it and win. Only victory can prove that God is on one's side. And this fight becomes an act of love — love for the God that has been wrested from their control and is now entombed in the clutches of a false religion. Professor Jack Nelson-Pallmeyer (University of St. Thomas, Minnesota) noted in *Is Religion Killing Us*:

> Violence is at the heart of faith. Proclaiming God "almighty" and restricting God to One whose power, if understood as superior violence, means that in monotheistic religion violence is God because violence saves God in the sense of establishing and maintaining God's credibility. The tragic legacy of violent God and violent religion rooted in "sacred" text is that religion, inevitably, if unconsciously, is reduced to violence.[44]

The simple existence of another religion becomes an existential threat. The mere presence of other gods somehow represents a denial of the truth of *your* god. Oftentimes, absolute faith isn't so absolute that the existence of other religions doesn't place in doubt the foundations of any particular creed, an admission that is usually lacking in the professed certainty of religious leaders, missionaries and warriors from all cultures and time periods.[45]

Fixing the power of the state in the Supreme Power ("One nation under God"), and making the state's God the only true God, helps create the identity of a nation, raising it out of the world of culture and politics and centering it in the realm of the divine. This ties in seamlessly with a state's need for war, as now soldiers are willing to sacrifice themselves for the continual creation of the state, believing themselves to be doing the will of the One True God. Almost without fail, political leaders will highlight the relationship between their political goals and God by calling on the omnipotence of the Divine, having Him confer credibility on the temporal authority as well as the bellicose undertaking.[46]

With not enough God to go around; with an unbreakable, destructive passion within individuals; with God, state and religion wrapped together for the simple purpose of survival, religion can become a party to state-sponsored genocide.

War and the Warrior

War cannot be fought without individuals. Without warriors, the catharsis provided to a society by institutional violence would be impossible, and the scapegoating necessary for the health of the collective would dissolve into neighbor-on-neighbor aggression.

One of the great mysteries for many people who have never been to war, nor considered going, is how individuals are compelled, seduced or choose of their own volition to go into combat. One fascinating aspect of war, one that can be difficult to fully appreciate due to its counter-intuitive conclusion, is that war counteracts the fear of death. Hannah Arendt noted this oxymoronic aspect of war, which uncovers for the soldier the fullness of life and power in the act of destruction:

> As far as human experience is concerned, death indicates an extreme of loneliness and impotence. But faced collectively and in action [in war], death changes its countenance; now nothing seems more likely to intensify our vitality than its closeness. It is as if life itself is actualized in the practice of violence.[47]

Not only does sanctioned violence allow one the "god-like exhilaration of destroying,"[48] but it also makes very clear the distinction between the living and the dead. As long as warriors stay on the correct side of that frontier, they will feel alive as they never before have.

An account by a participant — one of thousands that are written, published, blogged, spoken at poetry slams and usually ignored, as the truth is too painful — gives a sense of just how profoundly war can *positively* attract an individual:

> War may be the only way in which most men touch the mythic domains of their soul. It is, for men, at some terrible level, the closest thing to what childbirth is for women: the initiation into the power of life and death. It is like lifting off the corner of the universe and looking at what's underneath. To see war is to see into the dark heart of things, that no-man's-land between life and death, or even beyond.[49]

This is the most disturbing and confusing aspect of war: the manner in which it entices. How it satisfies so much of what we, as humans, need. In giving the "moral justification to acts of violence,"[50] acts impossible to undertake in the home society become commonplace. It is a freedom that somehow both liberates and enslaves, and brings one closest to life as death is all around.

War is Beautiful

Another of the great problems that remains hidden to the uninitiated, is how very *aesthetically* alluring war is for many of its participants. In a horrifying manner, it highlights the sensual beauty of the world, offering in its violence, destruction, unimaginable sights and sounds, echoes of what we have learned of God from the religious path.

War is beautiful.

This is the opinion of many who have gone into the war theater and written about the experience. There is too much firsthand writing about the aesthetic quality of war to deny it. In appreciating its seductive splendor, we can begin to understand the more profound, spiritual aspects of war — and why individuals have gone to and continue to go to war since time immemorial.

Even non-combatant writers have waxed more poetic about war than they ever have concerning flaxen-haired beauties. Helen of Troy, after all, launched a thousand ships; she did not stem the tide of war. It was her ability to create war that proved her beauty. The war itself represented the climax of feelings that one has for the most beautiful woman in the world, not something antithetical to this beauty. War as the ultimate act of love.

This most grotesque of human activities has been written about with the tenderness and wonder of a man remembering his first love. For instance, when for the first time a nuclear blast incinerated a major world city, disintegrating tens of thousands of human beings, "there flashed in the minds of observers images from Grunewald's resurrecting Christ and holy script from the Bhagavad Gita."[51]

As psychologist James Hillman noted in *A Terrible Love of War*: "Inside the horror is a spectacular beauty, a beauty of another order. Inside the utter chaos, there is a structure of meaning, of meaningfulness, not to be found anywhere else."[52] Of course, this horrifying truth will never become part of the public narrative of war, because the beauty and meaning it hides within it are beyond the acceptable boundaries of public discourse. We must retain the fiction that every war is absolutely necessary to bring peace, and that each will be the last.

Time and time again, warriors and those who have been enticed by Mars (the Roman god of War) have written shimmering odes to the officially inhuman institution. Ernie Pyle, an American journalist who died in combat during World War II, gushed:

> Stabbed with great fires, shaken by explosions, its dark regions along the Thames sparkling with the pinpoints of white hot bombs, all of it roofed over with a ceiling of pink that held bursting shells, balloons, flares and the grind of vicious engines. And in yourself the excitement and anticipation and wonder in your soul that this could be happening at all. These things all went together to make the most beautiful, most hateful single scene I have known.[53]

Filippo Tommaso Emilio Marinetti (d. 1944), an Italian poet and founder of the Futurist movement, wrote in the Futurist Manifesto: "War is beautiful because it combines the gunfire, the cannonades, the pauses, the scents and the stench of putrefaction into a symphony."[54] Both Christopher Hedges (*War is a Force that Gives Us Meaning*) and Glenn Gray (*The Warriors: Reflections on Men in Battle*) went even further, highlighting the eroticism of war.[55] James Hillman, writing in *A Terrible Love of War*, said that "war is spectacular . . . it becomes literature, movies and is imagined even in its midst into poems, thoughts and tales."[56]

War uncovers a beauty that is *sui generis*: available only through participation in war. It is the subconscious depths of the imagination come to life, an impossible flaring into existence of our deepest and most hidden fears and conceptions, right in front of one's eyes. War offers all of the fantastic sights and sounds of the most extreme carnival, parade, festival, party and orgy. There is nothing like it in the world and for some who go to war, nothing can ever equal its aesthetic quality.

WAR IS SUBLIME

In an exploration of war's allure, we must press on beyond the boundary of "beauty." While beauty is seductive, its power is not enough to help fuse war and God, murder and the mystic's quest. This happens somewhere out beyond beauty, in the realm of the "sublime." Beauty alone is not sublime. Beauty fused with pain is "sublime." And here is exactly where war moves from the banal into the eternal, from the horrific to the mystical.

The reason that war is sublime is not obscure. Beauty, being a representation of the highest aspects of human experience, and pain (often considered one of the most challenging), are often thought of as separate, even opposing qualities. Fusing them in war expresses the totality of experience, and can seem to offer the most potent possibility of human perception. In many respects, war offers a profundity of *being* that nothing else within the human realm can. Not even love.

Philosopher Edmund Burke (d. 1797) captured this sense of the sublime:

> Whatever is in any sort terrible . . . is a source of the sublime, that is, it is productive of the strongest emotions which the mind is capable of feeling . . . The passion caused by the great and sublime in nature is astonishment . . . that state of the soul in which all its motions are suspended, with some degree of horror . . . the mind is so entirely filled with its objects, that it cannot entertain any other.[57]

James Hillman echoed this sentiment, applying it directly to war:

> What is this euphonic simplification that war seems to offer? Is it because human responsibility has been surpassed and we have entered the sublime and are closer to the gods, and therefore beyond any considerations of good and evil? No need to consider anything except action . . . forward action justifies and purifies by forgetting.[58]

And American General George Patton (d. 1945) concurred, from first-hand experience:

> Despite the impossibility of physically detecting the soul, its existence is proven by its tangible reflection in acts and thoughts. So with war, beyond its physical aspect of armed hosts there hovers an impalpable something that dominates the material — to search for this something we should seek it in a manner analogous to our search for the soul.[59]

To marry pain with the beautiful — beauty which represents the highest possibility of universal order, a point toward which all is directed but where none can ever truly arrive — brings the universal and the particular together in the most meaningful manner. It is here in this union that war most deeply affects the human character and mimics the highest possibility of both humanity and the divine.

War is Love

> To understand war means understanding the quality, the nature of love of war, this love unlike any other and which veterans report they found only in the midst of war's terror, a love that creates a potency of one's self that is at the same time the sacrifice of one's self.[60]

More than just a sublime attraction, a beautiful addiction, war engages the participant at the highest place of his character: selfless, unmitigated love. War has now encompassed virtually all of the higher aspects of the human character, although far from uplifting them, it has brought them down into its basest experience: that of a murderer.

The power of love itself over the human mind should not be underestimated. Victor Frankl (d. 1997; the founder of logotherapy which is a form of existential analysis), writing about his time spent in the Theresienstadt Concentration Camp in World War II, said he "grasped the meaning of the greatest secret that human poetry and human thought and belief have to impart: the salvation of man is through love and in love."

Unfortunately, an echo of this love can be found in the ultimate act of destruction. Perhaps nothing reveals the universe's perversity more than this fact: in war, human love and human destruction are wrapped tightly and irrevocably together. Nobel Prize winning author Rudyard Kipling (d. 1936) noted that the love between war comrades could attain an intensity that surpassed the love for women.[61] War correspondent Christopher Hedges discussed the fusion of love and war in *War is a Force that Gives Us Meaning*:

> Love, like death, radiates outward. It battles Thanatos at the very moment of death's sting. These two fundamental human impulses crack like breakers into each other. And however much beyond reason, there is always a feeling that love is not powerless or impotent, as we had believed a few seconds before. Love alone fuses happiness and meaning.[62]

A Love of Killing

Love in war is a terrifying experience, one that strips humanity bare (instead of uplifting) and scrubs all action of morality, leaving only spare, primal emotion. In war, any and every action can become emblematic of love. "Love can be found inside of war, a love of the most profound sort.

And also of the ugliest sort — necrophilia, sadism, exuberant murder, morbid prurience."[63]

Love, even, of the act of destruction flowers in the dark night of the war theater. An article in the Daily Mail (U.K.) detailed the passionate adoration of killing that developed in one American Iraq War veteran:

> "Killing becomes a drug, and it is really addictive," Charles Whittington [a veteran of combat in Iraq and Afghanistan] wrote. "I had a really hard time with this problem when I returned to the United States, because turning off this addiction was impossible . . . When I stick my blade through his stomach or his ribs or slice his throat, it's a feeling that I cannot explain, but feels so good to me."[64]

Hardly confined to American society, another piece in the *New Yorker* shared a firsthand account of the joys of being on the happy end of the slaughter in Rwanda (1994). Girumuhatse , a Rwandese participant in the slaughter, told his story to writer Philip Gourevitch:

> I had always been told that Girumuhatse killed with a machete, but he said that he had preferred to use a *masu*, a nail studded club. "When I killed, it was like communal work duty." Nothing seemed to have troubled him when he went to work with his club, and I wondered whether he had enjoyed it.
>
> "Yes. For me, it became a pleasure to kill. The first time, it was to please the government. After that, it became a pleasure for me. I hunted and cut with real enthusiasm. It was work, but work that I enjoyed . . . I was very excited when I killed. I awoke every morning excited to go into the bush. The genocide was like a festival . . . There were no limits anymore. It was a festival. We celebrated."[65]

Horrible, revolting, inhumane — and deeply and passionately appealing.

This love extends even to the implements of destruction, those same apparatus that many of us who do not understand, and look at with horror.

> The weapon is another Hephaistian instrument holding beauty and violence in a permanent embrace . . . You can hold the gods in your hand, carry death in your purse . . . God is in the gun, and the passionate love for these weapons may express less a love of violence than a mystical protection against it.[66]

The weapon is a lover's "red, red lips," or the alabaster turn of a youthful bosom. It is the tangible proof that there is a God, and that one man or woman can make a difference and achieve mystical meaning in a mundane world.

No matter how much we talk about war, theorize, understand, quantify, fight against, demand better, march in protest, write letters, gnash our teeth and rend our garments, until we (humans) can honestly face the pure joy of killing in war, we can never come to terms with the institution, let alone begin to cure the illness of state sponsored mass murder.

War as Mysticism

> War is a mythical happening; those in the midst of it are removed to a
> mystical state of being . . . the love of war tells of a love of the gods . . .
> where else in the human experience, except in the throes of ardor — that
> strange coupling of love with war — do we find ourselves transported to
> a mythical condition and the gods most real?[67]

The fusion between war and the human yearning for immanence is complete. War *is* mysticism. As Barbara Ehrenreich noted in *Blood Rites: Origins and History of the Passions of War*, war occasions "the highest and finest passions humans can know: courage, altruism, and the mystical sense of belonging to 'something larger than ourselves'."[68]

War *mimics* the mystic's path, while replacing the mystic's goal of Divine union with the basest of actions: institutionalized slaughter. Mysticism, generally defined, is the personal search for a meaning beyond the particular, an individual experience of the Divine oneness. Within religious traditions, this search takes place in the quietude of meditation, prayer and healing action. It is centered on reflection and self-awareness. Mystics in all traditions are gentle, open-minded and deeply cognizant of the bonds that tie all of God's creation into a seamless whole.

Mystical experience is not a fantasy. Andrew Newberg (Director of Research at the Myrna Brind Center for Integrative Medicine at Thomas Jefferson University Hospital and Medical College) explored the neurological effects of spiritual practice in his book *How God Changes Your Brain*:

> Using brain imaging studies of Franciscan nuns and Buddhist practitio-
> ners, and Sikhs and Sufis — along with everyday people new to medita-
> tion — Andrew Newberg asserts that traditional spiritual practices such
> as prayer and breath control can alter the neural connections of the brain,
> leading to "long-lasting states of unity, peacefulness and love."[69]

Humans have what the Roman mystic Plotinus (d. 270) called an "amphibious nature," and we must integrate the desire for individuation with the need to belong. Meditation and mysticism are examples of one approach, but it is an arduous one. A second, easier way to assimilate these needs is war. Or, as Leo Tolstoy described it in *War and Peace*: "Every general and every soldier was conscious of his own insignificance, aware of being but a drop in that ocean of men, and yet at the same time was conscious of his strength as a part of that enormous whole."[70]

Spiritual feeling, as it is attained in war, echoes the profundity of experience found in mysticism, while offering an easy -to- achieve and hollowed out version that stems from destruction, not the quietude of understanding. As Helmuth von Moltke (d. 1891), chief of staff of the Prussian Army for thirty years, noted: "War fosters virtues of man: courage, self-denial, obedience to duty and the spirit of sacrifice."

These virtues define almost exactly the mystic's path — every single one of them is demanded for the individual devoting him or herself to spiritual understanding and a complete devotion to God. Few Sufi mystics or Christian ascetics would deny that each and every one of these is central to his or her pathway to realization.

However, war is not mysticism. As war correspondent Christopher Hedges noted, to achieve the institutional juggernaut of an army, the most basic aspect of the mystical search must be overcome — and it is in this subtle omission of the mystic's path that war turns warriors to the ecstasy of destruction and away from the creative energy that represents humanity's highest spiritual possibility. "To achieve corporate action, self awareness and especially self-criticism must be obliterated."[71]

War gives humans the illusion that they are fighting for a greater power, with a "mystical sense of belonging to 'something larger than ourselves'" (Ehrenreich, above). Before this power, "all bow and become one."[72] These exact words could easily be applied to the mystical path toward divine realization, which leads an aspirant to an appreciation of and respect for the God-nature hidden in everything, both living and inanimate. However, the issue tips when we look at just how war accesses this ultimate meaning — it does so by *bypassing* the rational thought process and accessing the animal aspects of the human psyche.

Where war bleeds irrevocably into the lower strata of human nature is represented in the statement that war "obliterates self awareness and especially self-criticism" (Christopher Hedges, above). Self-critical thought is the only thing that truly separates us from animals — without it, we are little more than dexterous rats, killing machines with ever more efficient tools of destruction.

Virtually all mystics from all major systems propose that the path to God leads directly through the self. Confucius said: "Attack the evil that is within yourself; do not attack the evil that is within others."[73] The Prophet Muhammad stated that the first stage of worship is silence. The

Jewish Kabbalists believed that humans are literally the microcosm of God — and that the surest way to learn about God is to learn about oneself. As the 13ᵗʰ century Kabbalistic text *Sha'are Emunah* stated: "Blessed is he or she who knows that within and above are synonymous."[74]

Bypassing the self-critical thought is the antithesis of mystical appreciation, and the beginning of chaos.

War is Holy

> If the god is nothing more nor less than the massive violence that was expelled by the original act of generative unanimity, then ritual sacrifice can indeed be said to offer Him portions of His own substance.[75]

Virtually all wars were holy wars. And even today, many wars are presented as holy wars by political leaders. Young men and, more recently, women volunteer to risk death or, even worse, a psycho-spiritual maiming, as a way of proving their love of God. In war, they find some echo of the universal force, an addictive power that reminds them of God, but is not.

This is not to say that political and social issues aren't at the forefront of the stated reasons for a particular conflict. But if we peel away the layers of socio-political impetus — be it boundary invasion, energy needs, fighting against a dictatorship or whichever specific motives newspapers and political leaders offer — the underlying impulse for individual warriors to join the cause is often religious and even spiritual. The social catharsis provided by the scapegoat (the enemy) belies the deeper spiritual release provided by the violence. Additionally, the language of war is almost always couched in religious and spiritual terminology.

This veiled holy war aspect is based in the shared, quasi-mythical experience that war engenders in a society.

> The way that people begin to perceive reality in the period typically preceding the outbreak of war is seductive . . . We cease to structure our world in our customary way and turn to the ways of a fairy tale or myth . . . . During a mythic war, God, history and destiny are on one's side.[76]

Christopher Hedges stated: "Lurking beneath the surface of every society, including ours, is the passionate yearning for a nationalist cause that exalts us, the kind that war alone is able to deliver."[77]

Holy war — or most wars, as nations rarely undertake a war that they don't consider holy — becomes a metaphor for the struggle between God's will and the forces of resistance. It is more than a nationalistic calling. It is a moral obligation to actively assist in establishing the rule of

God here on Earth.[78] Both sides in the carnage act with God on their side. All citizens fight to protect the greater good against the forces of evil and chaos. This dynamic will be explicitly explored further along in this book, as I examine the language of the leaders in the United States and of its stated enemy, Osama bin Laden, both of whom used virtually the same religious idiom to describe their fight against the other.

In the end, we are left with these words from Christopher Hedges, stitching the last suture into place between war and the spirit:

> Once we sign on for war's crusade, once we see ourselves on the side of the angels, once we embrace a theological or ideological belief system that defines itself as the embodiment of goodness and light, it is only a matter of how we will carry out murder.[79]

The fusion between war and God is complete. They are not only inseparable but interchangeable. For many people in human civilization, war *is* God. A God demanding ever-more human sacrifice, blood which knits the survivors together into a cohesive society, one nation under war.

Chapter Two: From the Beginning of Humanity

> If war is a primordial component of being, then war fathers the very struc-
> ture of existence and our thinking about it: our ideas of the universe, of
> religion, of ethics . . . we think in war-like terms, feel ourselves at war
> with ourselves and unknowingly believe predation, territorial defense,
> conquest and the interminable battle of opposing forces are the ground
> rules of existence.[80]

Our greatest fear as a species has always been of chaos. But chaos lies
within the human soul, not outside of it. Religion developed, at least in
a sociological sense, to deal with the ungovernable madness at the heart
of the human being.

Violence and religion grew into human experience together, two
aspects of the very same drive — two manners of channeling the chaos at the center of our species. Perhaps they can be viewed as Yin and
Yang, the two necessary halves that make the whole, but they are inextricably linked and were part of human society at the very beginning of
civilization.

Original Human

We can now appreciate the atmosphere of terror that accompanies the
primordial religious experience. When violent hysteria reaches a peak,
the monstrous double looms up everywhere at once. The decisive act of
violence is directed against this awesome vision of evil and at the same
time sponsored by it. The turmoil gives way to calm, hallucinations vanish
and the détente that follows only heightened the mystery and hallucina-

tion of the whole process. In an instant, all extremes have met, all differences fused.[81]

It is vital to note that the "monstrous double" emerges from within
the human being, much in the same way that God and religion do. They
are created together in the human soul, perhaps even from the same impetus, but then separated when projected onto the world outside. This
is *not* to say that there isn't immanence, that there isn't a God. It simply
expresses the idea that the *concept* of God that we hold comes from the
darkest place within, and may or may not have something to do with the
ineffable power at the heart of all being.

In primal society, where the human being was only semi-conscious,
believing that even voices from within his or her own head might come
from without, everything was a potential danger including the impulses
and voices that arose from within. Julian Jaynes (d. 1997; an American
psychologist), posited in *The Origins of Consciousness in the Breakdown of
the Bicameral Mind* that ancient people were not "conscious" in the sense
that we are today. Unable to introspect, they experienced auditory hallucinations, voices of gods as seen in ancient texts from the Iliad to the
Torah, which, coming from the brain's right hemisphere, told a person
what to do in circumstances of novelty or stress.[82]

These original voices of God, experienced by the primal human as
originating from outside of him or herself, though with access to the in-
nermost sanctum of the individual's mind, became the basis for religion
— and the fusion between humanity's own pathology and that of the
gods. The projection of humanity's psyche onto the immanence of being
can be explained simply by a consideration of the manner in which early
humans experienced reality and their need for an immanent structure to
underpin their strange and horrifying experience of semi-consciousness.

PRIMITIVE RELIGION AND THE BIRTH OF THE VIOLENT GOD

In primitive societies the risk of unleashed violence is so great and the
curse so problematic that the emphasis naturally falls on prevention. The
preventative measures fall within the domain of religion, where they
can occasionally assume a violent character. Violence and the sacred are
inseparable.[83]

For humanity to change from a completely animal character to some
form of collective society, the innate violent tendencies at the heart of
his limbic system had to be dealt with in some manner. With a growing intelligence and ability to control the world around him, man had

an increasing ability to vent his personal violent impulses in ever more extreme ways.

By ritualizing violence, by sequestering it within the religious impulse, it could be controlled, pointed outward, prevented from completely destroying the nascent human civilization.

> In assuming a mythico-ritual character, violence tends toward the exterior, and this tendency in turn assumes certain sacrificial characteristics; it conceals the site of the original violence, thereby shielding from this violence . . . the elementary group whose very survival depends on the absolute triumph of peace. Groups agree to never be completely at peace, so that their members may find it easier to be at peace among themselves.[84]

Without systematizing violence, and giving it a sacred tint, human civilization itself might not be possible. In this construction, war can be considered the foundation for every painting ever painted, every opera sung, every piece of theater acted. It is in war — and, even more importantly, God-sanctioned and even God-initiated conflict — that the seeds of human civilization are sown.

The Stone Age (c. 3 million years ago to 500,000 years ago) ethos of warfare and sacrifice has shaped human culture.[85] Higher civilizations have been grafted onto this initial impetus. The founding text of the Abrahamic religions — the *Torah* — certainly has more in common with the original, sacrificial and violent impulses of the earliest humans than with any New Age dream of one world and one mind. We have built God, religion and society onto an original "sacred-violence" foundation. We have not evaded or superseded it. Even today, most of human society is fated to follow the primordial impulse to offer up their young, just as they are fated to accept the necessity of war.[86]

SACRIFICE

As Bruce Chilton (Bernard Iddings Bell Professor of Religion at Bard College) noted in *Abraham's Curse*, before war, even, the violence of God was satisfied through human sacrifice. Only later on, as civilizations grew and urbanized, was the violence turned outward, and the "healthier" option of war was founded. It should be noted, however, that human sacrifice as a religious rite lasted within human society up until the dawn of the Enlightenment, in the Americas, with the Aztec civilization in particular (c. 15–16th centuries).

> The end of the Stone Age saw the first urban communities and, in some cases, the institutional killing of children . . . the urban temple, the foundation of the whole city, had to be seen as holier and more powerful, more

attractive to gods, than any other altar. Human sacrifice emerged as the price required to assure divine favor in building a city, the means of making the urban temple the ultimate altar. Several ancient myths depict the founder king of a city sacrificing his own child, by slaughtering him on the foundation stone of the city in order to secure prosperity.[87]

This dynamic of sacrificing a human to God was still central to religion up until the very threshold of recorded history. The Neanderthals (c. 110,000 to 35,000 years ago), who emerged from the long era of the Stone Age, buried both animal and human skeletons near hearths that played a religious function. Remains of young children have been found near the Knossos Palace on Crete dating from 4000 years ago, their little bones charred and nicked in the same manner that the ancient Minoans prepared their sheep and goats for ritual slaughter.[88]

The Greek historian Diodorus Siculus (c. 60–30 B.C.E.) reported on the ancient practice of human sacrifice in Carthage (c. 1000 B.C.E.; a Phoenician center in what is today Tunisia), detailing one event in which 200 children were selected for sacrifice in a time of war and another 100 were volunteered by their parents for "participation" in the rite. Diodorus also situates human sacrificial rites within the Egyptian (c. 3150–30 B.C.E.), Celtic (c. 800–100 B.C.E.) and Messenian Greek (c. 1300–150 B.C.E.) cultures.[89]

Ritual slaughter of the most powerful member of a society was systematized in the Babylonian creation myth.

Babylonian Religion: Creation from Destruction

In the beginning, Apsu and Tiamat (the sweet and saltwater oceans) bear Mammu (the mist). From them also issue the younger gods, whose frolicking makes so much noise that the older gods cannot sleep and so resolve to kill them.[90]

One of the first creation myths, the first stories attempting to understand the world and our place within it, comes from the Babylonians (c. 2nd millennium B.C.E.). Inheriting many ideas from the even earlier Sumerian civilization (c. 4th millennium B.C.E.), the Babylonian creation myth was influential to the stories told in the Jewish Bible and thence to the nearly three billion practitioners of the Abrahamic faiths (Judaism, Christianity and Islam) today.

The Babylonian creation myth placed horrific violence at the heart of the human experience. "Human beings are created from the blood of a murdered God. They originate in violence and are all too prone to resort to violence and so, have to be kept under control by the exercise of violence."[91]

A synopsis of the Babylonian creation myth will help us appreciate the intersection of violence and God, chaos and religion:

> This plot of the elder gods [to kill the noisy children] is discovered, Ea kills Apsu, and his wife Tiamat pledges revenge. Ea and the younger gods in their terror turn for salvation to their youngest, Marduk. He exacts a steep price; if he succeeds, he must be given chief and undisputed power in the assembly of gods. Having extorted this promise, he catches Tiamat in a net, drives an evil wind down her throat, shoots an arrow that bursts her distended belly and pierces her head. He then splits her skull with a club and scatters her blood in out-of-the-way places. He stretches her corpse full length, and from it creates the cosmos.[92]

It does not suffice to simply inform the audience that Marduk was successful in his task — the slaughter of the older God (who happened to be his mother) — but the complete, violent recitation of the act is detailed. It is also interesting to note that Marduk "split her skull with a club," which is the exact same action that our Rwandese murderer Girumuhatse employed, utilizing a *masu*, or nail-studded club, in his "government work."

The act of creation was violence itself. They myth of the gentle god who created the universe out of love is simply wishful thinking, something stretched across the truth like a gauze so as to make it more palatable to general society. René Girard extrapolated from the matricidal beginnings of the universe, replete with billy clubs and split skulls: "All the signs seem to suggest that the gods, along with the community itself, owe their origin to internal and unanimous violence and to a victim who is a member of the community."[93]

Tiamat, not only a "member of the community" but the literal mother of the community, played just this primal role.

In the Babylonian creation myth, we can see how violence and religion emerged together. Father Jeremy Young, in his book *The Violence of God and the War on Terror*, explained how chaos, violence, humanity and religion fused to form the basis of the human experience of God:

> Because the cosmos is made from the body of Tiamat [a murdered God], who represents chaos, in the world represented by the [Babylonian creation] myth, chaos is prior to order. This means that the potential for chaos has not actually been eliminated by the act of creation; instead, it has been incorporated into the foundation of the created order and is always threatening to break out again. Consequently, chaos needs to be repeatedly controlled by force and intimidation.[94]

Many scholars believe that the Jewish Bible was first codified and written down during the Babylonian exile (597 B.C.E.–515 B.C.E.), when Jews lived under Babylonian rule and became acquainted with the Mesopotamian gods and religion. As such, they set their God up against Marduk, the powerful creator of the Mesopotamian universe, while still borrowing some of the Mesopotamian ideas and iconography. A look at the actual moment of creation in both myths shows possible influence of the earlier, Babylonian, tale on the religion of Israel:

> And God said: "Let there be a vault in the midst of the waters, and let it divide from water." And God made the vault and it divided the water beneath the vault from the water above the vault, and so it was. (Genesis 1:5-7)

> The Lord rested; he gazed at the huge body, pondering how to use it, what to create from the dead carcass. He split it apart like a cockleshell; with the upper half he constructed the arc of the sky, he pulled down the bar and set a watch on the waters, so they should never escape. (*Enuma Enish,* fourth tablet)[95]

Further comparison of the first chapters of Genesis with the fifth chapter of the Babylonian creation story (where Marduk creates the universe out of the body of his mother) shows many similarities, not only in imagery but also in specific language.

The fundamental dynamic of a violent God was set with the ancient Mesopotamian creation myth, which then influenced the Jewish Bible and, hence, nearly half of today's world population.

> Although the official names given to the gods and dominant mythologies have changed since Babylonian times, the myth of redemptive [and even creative] violence has continued to exist and to exert its influence on subsequent societies down to our day.[96]

THE GREEK AND ROMAN RELIGIONS

> The ancient Greeks linked war and love. Aphrodite, the goddess of love, became the mistress of Ares, the god of war.[97]

Western civilization is founded on the philosophy, political structure, culture and, to a lesser extent, religious mythology of the Greek (c. 750–150 B.C.E.) and then Roman (c. 400 B.C.E.–400) societies. Many aspects of the Abrahamic faiths can be traced back into ancient Greece and Rome.

> In the Western tradition, an awareness of Greek religion was kept alive in three ways: through its presence in ancient literature and in all litera-

ture formed on that model, through the polemics of the church fathers and through its assimilation in symbolic guise to Neo-platonic philosophy.[98]

Here, as well, we find that the strong fusion of violence and the sacred. War in ancient Greece was woven into the society at all levels. In ancient Crete (c. 3000–1100 B.C.E.) and Lacedaemon (c. 1000–100 B.C.E.; also known as Sparta), the system of education and the greater part of the laws were framed around the central unifying activity of war.

GREEK GODS AND WAR

For the Greeks, violence was entwined with divinity. As René Girard (b. 1923; a French historian, literary critic, and philosopher of social science) noted, concerning the quality of *kudos*, a Greek term signifying the ultimate power available to both humans and gods:

> The epithet *kudos* signifies an attitude of triumphant majesty, a demeanor characteristic of the gods. Man can enjoy this condition only fleetingly and always at the expense of other men. To be a god is to possess *kudos* forever, to remain forever a master, unchallenged and unchallengeable.[99]

It is interesting to note here that man could only enjoy *kudos* at the expense of other men — as if there were a finite amount of this god-like power, which had to be fought over. This is in keeping with the idea of the parsimonious God who will give His covenant to only one people — be they Jewish, Christian, Muslim, Sikh, Buddhist or other — while all others are in error, outside of the protecting aura of the one true God. Perhaps the idea of a god that must be gathered into the community *at the expense of other men* began in this long-ago time, when the earliest Greeks were warring over the gods' *kudos*, and even then could only enjoy the unchallengeable power "fleetingly."

Zeus, the Greek father of gods and men, won his power in much the same manner as did Marduk, the Mesopotamian god, who perhaps influenced the Greek understanding of the deities.

> Zeus had had to win his power through struggle and defend it against revolt . . . once Zeus had come of age, he led the gods in war against the Titans: sky, earth, sea and underworld were all convulsed in battle, but Zeus emerged victorious. He is seen by the Greeks in two images: as the boldly striving warrior and as the figure enthroned with scepter in his hand.[100]

He was hardly the only war-like figure in the Greek pantheon. The ideal of temporal, human war became attached to a specific god, Ares, whose aggression was considered sacred. What's more, violence in war led to the "altered states of the battlefield,"[101] a concept which still informs the contemporary warrior's mythical love of war. Ares was represented as a "brazen warrior whose war chariot is harnessed by fear and terror; he is overwhelming, insatiable in battle, destructive and man-slaughtering."[102]

GOD AND SACRIFICE

Violence and the sacred went further than the gods in ancient Greece. They were stitched together into the quilt of human society. Early in Grecian civilization, dating back to Crete (c. 3000 B.C.E.), the blood-thirst of the gods was satisfied by human sacrifice. As was noted, the Knossos included a crypt with a deposit of children's bones showing clear evidence that they had been ritually killed.[103] One sacred building dating to about 1700 B.C.E. has been identified as a temple with the relics of human sacrifice.[104]

The poet Hipponax (sixth century B.C.E.) provided a first-person account of a human sacrificial ritual. He related that a man was chosen on account of his ugliness and was fed figs and other delicacies. After this, he was whipped with a fig branch on his *membrum virile*. He was then burned and his ashes scattered in the sea. Other eyewitness accounts portray the *Pharmakos* (scapegoat, or healing object) as being simply driven out of the community after a period of humiliation and whipping.

Many such descriptions exist:

> On dire occasions such as plague . . . a poor man was offered pure and costly food for a year, then, decked in boughs and sacred vestments, he was led around the whole town amid curses and finally chased away. From the cliffs of Leukas a condemned criminal was plunged into the sea every year.[105]

Lest we grow too smug about what great strides we have made since the time of ancient Greece, we must remember that in the 21st-century United States, there is a similar ritual, called "execution." In this sacrificial rite, a criminal, sometimes with darker skin than the majority in the country, is chosen from a pool of prisoners and subjected to a gruesome death after languishing for years and sometimes decades in a solitary holding cell. It is a solemn occasion, presided over by a high priest and signed off by the controlling civil authority — a ritual that mimics almost exactly the *Pharmakos* of ancient Greece.

Unlike Americans, however, the ancient Greeks did move beyond human sacrifice, ultimately settling on animals to provide the literal scapegoat upon which the society could vent its destructive urges. Walter

Burkert described the manner in which the animal would play this vital social role: "The heart is torn still beating from the body before all else. To taste the entrails immediately is the privilege and duty of the inner-most circle of participants. The inedible remains are then consecrated."[106]

It is interesting to note how closely this tracks the manner in which the Aztecs were sacrificing their human virgins to appease their gods, as Hernán Cortés and his band of conquistadores subjugated that ancient civilization (c. 16th century). Hernán Cortés related in his *Letters*:

> They have a most horrid and abominable custom . . . and this is that, when-ever they wish to ask something of the idols, in order that their plea may find more acceptance, they take many girls and boys and even adults, and in the presence of these idols they open their chests while they are still alive and take out their hearts and entrails and burn them before the idols, offering the smoke as sacrifice.[107]

ARISTOTLE AND PLATO

No two ancient philosophers have had a deeper influence on Western thought than the Greek thinkers Plato (d. 347 B.C.E.) and Aristotle (d. 322 B.C.E.). Among the many subjects they taught and wrote about was, of course, war and the sacred. These Greek thinkers codified the link between the two within a philosophical structure that was to influence later theologians in all three Abrahamic faiths.

Plato, although he was certainly no believer in wholesale violence, lay down the markers for what would become 20th-century fascist govern-ments in Italy, Russia, the Middle East and elsewhere. Benito Mussolini had a strong attachment to his works. And no wonder: in *The Republic* (c. 380 B.C.E.), Plato advocated a system of elite minority rule by highly educated, intellectual rulers called philosopher kings, who were allowed to exercise total control over the politics and security of a society. Isn't it likely that Mussolini, as well as Stalin, Hitler, Mubarak, Saddam Hus-sein, Assad and others felt they were just such chosen leaders.

Another recurring point in Plato's Dialogues was that war should not be considered apart from justice. In this sense he is one of the originators of the ""just war"" idea.[108] He also said: "The state control is religion . . . belief in the gods is proclaimed as a duty to the state."[109] This is an idea that fits in today with the idea of the nation-state, and its massive social and even spiritual presence.

Aristotle, twenty years Plato's junior, further developed the concep-tion of a ""just war"," which influences religious and nationalist thinking to this day. Here, the murders committed in certain types of war became qualified as righteous. When the state itself was righteous (as, of course, all states consider themselves to be), then the war itself was just.

> War provided a natural form of acquisition for the state . . . It could legiti-
> mately be deployed in self defense, to prevent the state's enslavement, to
> obtain an empire to benefit the inhabitants of the conquering state, or to
> enslave non-Hellenes deserving of enslavement . . . In his *Politics* (VII: 14),
> Aristotle insisted that "War must be for the sake of peace."[110]

Since "state control is religion" (Plato) and when the state is righteous, the war is just (Aristotle), we can see how war, religion and god quickly came together nearly 2500 years ago to set the stage for a never-ending series of bellicose campaigns in the name of God and the state, which have helped to define human civilization to this day.

In Plato and Aristotle's thinking, we see the foundation for every Christian ""just war"" from the time of St. Augustine (d. 430) until George W. Bush's campaign in Iraq. Is it simply coincidence that a couple learned men in ancient Greece would characterize war thusly, thereby affecting human history ever after? Or did Plato and Aristotle simply state the obvious, setting the foundation stone for ""just war"" in a species that cannot live without it?

ROME

Roman culture and society grew out of ancient Greece, an extension of that empire which moved the pivot of Western civilization across the Adriatic Sea. Following the markers laid down by earlier Greek thinkers, Romans declared that a war could be just when it was "carried out in conformity with the proper set of religious laws . . . Deliberations about war were expected to pass through a college of priests, who had special responsibility for maintaining peaceful relations among Latins, who would seek a judgment of the gods about the justice of the proposed course of action."[111]

In addition to war, Ancient Rome, like the 21st-century United States, found other ways of collective scapegoating to focus the human aggressive urges, using these manners to bring the rest of society together. In the United States, for instance, we have a whole menu of violent restorative options including executions, the intensive torture of "terrorists" or other enemies of the state ("waterboarding," chaining internees to walls and the floor, forcing them to sleep naked, etc.), solitary confinement for those designated "a risk to the state" and other perverse methods of focusing our innate hostilities on some "other," thereby making the one nation under God possible.

Bruce Chilton described Roman antecedents to American social behavior in *Abraham's Curse*:

> The seal of Rome's power — capital punishment for criminals of most classes, especially slaves and non-citizens — might include throwing victims to beasts, setting them on fire, forcing them to drink molten lead that burned out their insides, crucifying or beating them to death, sewing them into sacks with carnivores prior to drowning, hurling them from the height of a cliff, or condemning them to become gladiators in the arena. Rome coveted the display of pain, humiliation, and death as much as the punishment of death itself.[112]

The only difference between the behavior in ancient Rome and that of today's United States is that the Romans were open and gloating about their cult of violence, while the citizens of the United States hide the executions behind prison walls, claim to be horrified by the practice of torture, and generally take a schizophrenic attitude toward the human need for catharsis through institutionalized violence.

MARS

The Romans assimilated Ares into their pantheon and turned him into their own God of war: Mars. In keeping with the history of linking war and regeneration, Mars was also an agricultural guardian. He was second in importance of the Roman gods to Jupiter (king of the gods and the god of sky and thunder).

Mars represented military power as a way to secure peace and was a father *(pater)* of the Roman people. In the mythic genealogy of Rome, Mars was the father of Romulus and Remus, the founders of the city. His love affair with Venus (the Roman goddess of love, beauty and fertility) deeply fused the destructive power of war with the highest aspects of the human character.

It is also important to note that the original impetus for war — to channel the innate aggressive and self-destructive tendencies of the individual, so that the civilization could cohere and thrive — was explicitly stated vis-à-vis Mars:

> The force [of Mars] had to be held from exploding into civil life . . . The Romans felt Mars to be a collective danger and for their own security, placed his cult outside the city walls in the "field of Mars" . . . The geographical placement of Mars outside the city walls in a field of his own

literalizes the psychic wall between the more human and inhuman areas of our being.[113]

Of course, I disagree with that last statement. Throughout this book I propose that war is as natural to human experience as other, more acceptable aspects of our character. The placement of Mars outside the city walls simply represents the desire to separate ourselves from this central facet of our own psyche. In a social sense, we do this by institutionalizing this aspect of our being through war, and by choosing surrogate murderers (warriors) to act out our own primal, destructive desires, thereby freeing the rest of us to live in a "civilized" state.

This, to me, is the meaning of the exile of Mars.

CHAPTER THREE: JUDAISM

> The violence-of-God traditions that lie at the heart of the "sacred" texts of Jews, Christians and Muslims are rooted in images of God featured centrally in the Hebrew Bible . . . The Bible speaks of God as compassionate and merciful, but it depicts God's power . . . as violent, coercive, punishing, threatening and deadly.[114]

Although Judaism is not the oldest major religion currently practiced — that designation is reserved for Hindus (c. 2000 B.C.E.) — the Jewish scriptures underpin religious practice in the West, and certainly in the United States, where the Judeo-Christian heritage is touted by politicians and most citizens alike as America's spiritual foundation. And it is in the Jewish Bible that we find the specific seeds of the pathologically violent God that often rules in our era, as well as much of the impetus for contemporary violence centered on the State of Israel.

This chapter, like the subsequent overviews of Christianity, Islam, Hinduism, Buddhism and Sikhism, does not represent *the* definitive study of violence within this religious path. Rather, it offers an overview, examining the deep affiliation of violence and the sacred. A definitive tome covering the violent strains in all of these religions would weigh in at thousands of pages. The purpose of my book is not to exhaust the subject, but to introduce it into the public square and political conversation, so that we might reconsider war, spirituality, religion and nationhood — and perhaps to begin the difficult task of untangling these human institutions from one another.

The Abrahamic faiths (Judaism, Christianity and Islam) are centered in the stories, prophets and monotheistic deity of the *Torah* (the Jewish Bible). With its succession of violent stories, this book has helped spawn the European millennia of wars, Islam's *dar al harb* (world at war), the Crusades, the Inquisition, World Wars I and II, the Holocaust, the creation and utilization of the nuclear bomb, *jihad*, the perfection of the suicide bomber, pilotless bomb attacks by "drone" aircraft, terrorist plane attacks, religiously-based oppression, biblically-infused murder and various other manners of destroying human souls in spiritually sanctioned combat. Additionally, Judaism today continues its Biblical prescription with religiously based oppression seen in the Israeli–Palestinian conflict, as well as by providing a flashpoint for violence that affects the world from Malaysia to New York City.

Israel, the religion and the nation, was founded in blood. The name "Israel" itself means "El does battle," and the Jewish God was the warrior "El," after whom the nation styled itself.[115] Even given the muscular spirituality of the gods that came before in Mesopotamia, Greece and other ancient locales, the God of Israel rivaled the worst that humanity has ever endured in an irrational deity:

> The invasion and conquest of Canaan [Book of Joshua] is a story of unprovoked aggression and genocide, both of which are attributed to the direct command and intervention of God . . . If God were a human being, He would be tried and found guilty of war crimes . . . The God of the invasion of Canaan is the moral equivalent of any of the great perpetrators of genocide in the 20th century, such as Hitler, Stalin, Mao, Pol Pot and Saddam Hussein. The story of the dispossession and genocide of the Canaanites is central both to the Jewish and Christian religions and their respective beliefs in the active intervention of God on behalf of His chosen or elect people.[116]

JEWISH SCRIPTURE

> The Lord is a man of war; The Lord is His name . . . Thy right hand, O Lord, glorious in power; Thy right hand, O Lord, dasheth in pieces the enemy. (Exodus 15)[117]

While most Jews would assure you that God is merciful, loving, just and fair, the truth, as represented in the *Torah*, resides far from this image. The God of the Bible is a murderous, capricious, hateful, petulant, jealous deity who gives and takes, supports or slaughters at His whimsical pleasure, often with no rhyme, reason or forethought whatsoever.

Story after story, passage after passage is rife with God-sanctioned thievery, skullduggery, murder, incest, adultery and all other manner of human ills, often rewarded, while the Ten Commandments loom over all, arbitrarily applied at the whim of the Great Master. It is outside the scope of this book to detail every instance of the pathology, narcissism and capricious hatred of the Jewish God's behavior, but an objective overview of a few of the stories, apart from the myth and belief that they have spawned, will suffice to illustrate the unsound moral foundation upon which the Abrahamic faiths are built. For further review, I point you to any edition of the *Torah*, available in approximately 2400 languages.

In Deuteronomy (7:1-2), God instructs His People on how to enter into a land promised them by the Creator:

> When the Lord your God shall bring thee into the land whither thou goest to possess it, and shall cast out many nations before thee, the Hittite and the Girgashite, and the Amorite, and the Canaanite, and the Perizzite, and the Hivite, and the Jebusite, seven nations greater and mightier than thou, and when the Lord thy God shall deliver them up before thee, and thou shalt smite them; then thou shalt utterly destroy them; thou shall make no covenant with them; nor show mercy unto them . . .[118]

A bit further along in the same Book of Deuteronomy, concerned that compassion might enter into the hearts of His People and weaken their resolve, God clarifies His wishes for His armies as they move into the lands He has identified for them:

> Howbeit of the cities of these peoples, that the Lord thy God giveth thee for an inheritance, thou shalt save alive nothing that breatheth, but thou shalt utterly destroy them.[119]

God waxes positively micromanager as He continues on to describe exactly how Israel should wage war. He intones: "Thou shalt not destroy the trees thereof by wielding an ax against them; for thou mayest eat of them . . . Only the trees that thou knowest are not trees for food, them thou mayest destroy and cut down."[120]

From trees, the Lord their God moves on to outline which enemy women might be taken as chattel (Deuteronomy 21:10):

> When thou goest forth into battle against thine enemies, and the Lord thy God delivereth them into thy hands, and thou carriest them away captive, and seest among the captives a woman of goodly form, and thou hast a desire unto her, and wouldst take her to thee to wife, then thou shalt bring her home to your house, and thou shalt shave her head, and pare her nails; and she shall put the raiment of her captivity from off her, and she shall remain in thy house, and bewail her father and her mother for a full month, after that, thou mayest go in unto her, and be her husband . . .[121]

In the Book of Joshua, we read:

> So Joshua smote all the land, the hill-country and the South, and the Lowland, and the slopes, and all their kings; he left none remaining; but he utterly destroyed all that breathed, as the Lord, the God of Israel, commanded.[122]

A bit further along in the same passage of Joshua (11:19-20), we find another example of the Jewish God's violent demands:

> There was not a city that made peace with the Children of Israel, save the Hivites the inhabitants of Gibeon; they took all in battle. For it was the Lord to harden their hearts, to come against Israel in battle, that they might be utterly destroyed, that they might have no favor, but that they might be destroyed, as the Lord commanded Moses.[123]

Major prophets also get into the destructive spirit. In the Book of Isaiah (c. 8th-6th centuries B.C.E.), the first 39 chapters prophesize doom for a sinful Judah and for all the nations of the world that oppose God. Within the text, we find many instances of violence, destruction and a living hell-on-Earth, such as this one (Isaiah 13:9, 15-17):

> Behold, the day of the Lord cometh, cruel and full of wrath and fierce anger; to make Earth a desolation . . . Every one that is found shall be thrust through; and every one that is caught shall fall by the sword. Their babies also shall be dashed in pieces before their eyes; their houses shall be spoiled, and their wives ravished.[124]

An Atmosphere Pervaded with Violence

These are but a spare few of the violent, hateful and triumphal passages that stain the Jewish Holy Book. Biblical scholar Raymond Schwager pointed out six hundred passages of explicit violence in the Hebrew Bible, one thousand verses where God's own violent punishments are described, a hundred different passages where God explicitly commands others to kill and a handful of stories in which God is represented as killing, or trying to kill, for no apparent reason.[125]

This collection of stories teaches a debased, twisted and capricious version of morals. At times, though perhaps not violent, the tales and their message fly in the face of the concept of "morality" itself, regardless of what religion. For instance, in Genesis 21, we see the Lord exhorting Abraham to take a concubine (Hagar) to bear a son, Ishmael (his wife Sara was, at that time, barren) to continue the Abrahamic lineage. When Ishmael was thirteen years old, God changed his mind, had the ancient Sara (then 99 years old) bear a son (Isaac) and allowed Sara to throw Hagar and Ishmael out of the house and into the wilds. Abraham, in the attitude of every Jewish husband since, quietly acquiesced to his wife's demands.

In Genesis 22, God, ever the erratic omniscient power, told Abraham to sacrifice his and Sara's son, Isaac, to the Lord, to prove his fealty. With Ishmael long gone by this time, this would have ended the covenant initiated by God (Genesis 15), leaving Abraham with no one to carry on his lineage. However, showing all the courage of a half-drowned worm, Abraham lied to his son and took him up to Mount Moriah, fully intending to destroy his own progeny on the orders of the increasingly perverse and unstable deity. In keeping with His fickle character, however, God rescinded the demand at the last second.

In the story of Esau and Jacob (Genesis 25-27), twin brothers struggled over Isaac's birthright. Though legally the Abrahamic covenant belonged to Esau, as he was the first born of the two, Rebekah, Isaac's wife, ordered Jacob to fool the blind old man (Isaac) into giving him the birthright instead of Esau. Rebekah sent Jacob to his father dressed in Esau's garments, laying goatskins on his arms and neck to simulate Esau's hairy skin. Jacob lied first about how he had returned so quickly from the appointed hunt ("Because the Lord your God arranged it for me"). Then when asked point-blank, "Are you really my son Esau?" Jacob responded simply, "I am." Isaac then blessed Jacob with the dew of the heavens, the fatness of the earth and lordship over many nations as well as his own brother. His punishment for breaking several of the Ten Commandments was to successfully take over the Abrahamic covenant and be renamed "Israel" by an angel.

The Jewish Scriptures are rife with examples of incest, to the point that even sex between a father and his daughter was not explicitly forbidden. In Genesis 19, after the destruction of Sodom and Gomorrah (from which Lot was saved, as the single worthwhile man in the city), Lot was tricked into getting drunk and then having sex with both of his daughters to preserve the family line. Ironically, this story took place shortly after they had fled from the cities that were destroyed by God for their immorality.

In the next chapter, Abraham married his half sister, Sara (Genesis 20; which might explain the difficulties in conceiving, by the way), while earlier we had learned that Abraham's brother Nachor married his niece, Melcha (Genesis 11). In other passages, we read of a brother raping his sister (II Kings 13); Moses's great aunt marrying her own nephew (Exodus 6), and in Genesis 38, Judah, the fourth son of Jacob (he of the stolen birthright), mistook his daughter-in-law Tamar for a prostitute while she was veiled, and had sex with her.

The Jewish text is sprinkled with further examples of murder, infidelity, thievery and other immoral behavior, sometimes even on the part of God Himself. What is most disturbing, however, is that there is no clear moral reaction to these events. In some cases, actors are punished for their immoral and illegal (against the Ten Commandments) behavior, while in others they are rewarded.

The collection of stories leads to the conclusion that if one has God's approbation, one may do as he or she pleases — and the surest way to know that one has God's approval is simply BY noting whether one can get away with the action or not. To our day, this bizarre law of consequence reigns, and individual and state actors often view their perverse and murderous actions as "just" on the basis of whether they are powerful or lucky enough to pull it off without obvious social or geo-political consequences.

The Jewish God and His Battered Spouse

> God's violence is relentless throughout the Jewish Bible. God orders Moses to kill disobedient children, adulterers, a man who "lies with a male as with a woman," and to stone to death those who gather sticks on the Sabbath. God "blotted out every living thing that was on the face of the ground, human beings and animals and creeping things and birds in the air" in the genocidal Flood (Genesis 7:23) . . . God reduced a disobedient people to cannibalism (Lamentations 4:10). God sent two she-bears to maul forty boys because they insulted a prophet (II Kings 2:23-24).[126]

Through this series of oppressive, aggressive and self-righteously violent stories, an image of the Jewish God emerges that is anything but kind, loving and merciful. "On the contrary, the Hebrew Bible depicts the God of Israel as a narcissistic character who requires constant adoration or He flies into a rage. He is violent above all other characteristics."[127]

Growing out of this was a perverse relationship between God and his People (Israel), which can best be likened to the abusive relationship between a battering husband and his spouse.

> A number of prophets (Hosea, Jeremiah, Ezekiel) employ the metaphor of marriage to describe the covenant relationship. The use of this metaphor attributes to God all of the rights belonging to a husband in a patriarchal society . . . including the right to chastise and beat his wife when she has been disobedient or unfaithful. These prophets present Israel as an unfaithful wife who is both disobedient and sexually promiscuous . . . and God as an aggrieved husband who in his anger and humiliation repeatedly

> acts in controlling and abusive ways toward his wife, including extreme
> physical violence . . . The violence in God's relationship with Israel begins
> with Israel's unfaithfulness as a wife.[128]

Israel is always held responsible for the violence that God inflicts upon her.

> God is described as an abusive husband who batters his wife, strips her
> naked and leaves her to be raped by her lovers, only to take her back in the
> end, insisting that when all is said and done, Israel the wife shall forever
> remain the wife of an abusing husband.[129]

SACRIFICE, MARTYRDOM AND THE WILL OF GOD

As with the god of most early religions, the Jewish God thirsted for blood, first of humans and later for animals. We see in Genesis 22, in the story of Abraham's call to sacrifice his son Isaac, God's desire:

> What Abraham is called to do in Genesis 22 is, from a Biblical standpoint,
> monstrous. He trudges up Moriah to prepare human flesh for God's con-
> sumption, although the law of ancient Judaism explicitly forbids treating
> people as food, committing murder, approaching human blood or engag-
> ing in infanticide . . . Sacrifice binds a community together, while offering
> a person, making a child a sacrificial victim, threatens the community's
> existence. Yet healing and destruction seem to have become inextricably
> entwined.[130]

God did rescind the demand *once he became convinced that Abraham was willing to carry it out.* Regardless of the horrible psychological scars this must have left on father and son, the perversity of the moment, the utter torturous inhumanity, must never be overlooked or diminished. It should also be noted that God did need blood in the end, and a sacrificial ram appeared and was immediately destroyed.

Bruce Chilton, in *The Curse of Abraham*, noted how this central Abra-hamic story has affected the three faiths that Abraham spawned:

> Uniquely among the religions of the world, the three that center on Abra-
> ham have made the willingness to offer the lives of children a central vir-
> tue for the faithful. Child sacrifice is not merely a possibility; it is incorpo-
> rated within the pattern of faith, not as a requirement of literal ritual, but
> as an ethical virtue that every believer should be prepared to emulate.[131]

I can almost hear your "pooh-poohing" from here! After all, you say: "I'm a believer in [insert Abrahamic faith here] and I certainly *don't* believe in child sacrifice! How barbaric!"

Would that these protestations had merit . . . but in interpretations of this Abrahamic story, as well as the wars it has helped sanction, it has spawned a cult of "sacrifice" for young warriors everywhere. The Abrahamic religions have persistently pushed their believers and, most importantly, their children to sacrifice themselves in the name of the Lord.[132] The average age for an American soldier enlisting in the U.S. Army in 2008, for instance, was 21. The average age of a Muslim suicide bomber in Israel in 2005 was the same.

This sacrifice — both in the American army or as a Palestinian suicide bomber — often is presented as a form of "martyrdom," a virtue held in the highest regard in all Abrahamic faiths, though traced back into the earliest Jewish narratives. Within Judaism, the "blood covenant" (the Ten Commandments were described as *dam habberit*, the "blood of the covenant"[133]) coupled with the story of Abraham on Mount Moriah, fused together into a call to sacrifice oneself in the name of the Lord.

> The imperative to become a martyr and join the armies of the suffering . . . is an intrinsic dimension within the Abrahamic tradition that derives from a specific, formative moment in the history of Judaism . . . The Maccabees (c. 2nd century B.C.E.) motivated themselves — and their children in particular — with the example of Abraham's offering of Isaac . . . and constructed their ideal of martyrdom in direct response to the politics of their period . . . According to the Maccabean theology, there was no middle ground between true belief and the powers of this world; the choice was not between remaining faithful and compromise, but between martyrdom and collaboration with the enemies of Israel. This remorseless standard — applied specifically to children and woman as well as men — makes the willingness to die the litmus test of true faith.[134]

What's more, these second century B.C.E. revolutionaries played a central role in codifying Jewish practice for later believers. Their scribes copied or wrote the last books of the Hebrew scripture, allowing them to set into the Holy Writ the ideals of martyrdom and self-sacrifice. From here on, self-sacrifice in the name of God became a standard virtue, and within a spare few centuries, this ideal would become central to another militant faith: Christianity.

To get a sense of how this belief still influences us to this day, an article about an American warrior killed in Afghanistan echoes the exact elements proposed in the Maccabean narrative more than 2200 years ago:

> Engaged in a frenzied firefight and outnumbered by the Taliban, Navy Lt. Michael Murphy made a desperate decision as he and three fellow SEALs fought for their lives on a rocky mountainside in Afghanistan's Kunar Province in 2005. In a last-ditch effort to save his team, Murphy pulled out his satellite phone, walked into a clearing to get reception and called for reinforcements as a fusillade of bullets ricocheted around him. One of

the bullets hit him, but he finished the call and even signed off, "Thank you." Then he continued the battle.

Navy Cmdr. Chad Muse, commanding officer of SEAL Delivery Team 1 in Hawaii, noted one of Murphy's favorite books was Steven Pressfield's "Gates of Fire," an account of outnumbered Spartans and their epic battle against hundreds of thousands of invading Persians nearly 2,500 years ago at the Battle of Thermopylae. Like the Spartans, who were ultimately slaughtered, Murphy had a spirit that didn't give up. "It's about sacrifice — and valor and heroism in battle," Muse said.[135]

Ultimately, the ideal of self-sacrifice became completely entangled with the sacred virtues of worship and war, bringing them together explicitly in manners that have reverberated through the centuries down to our era:

For ancient Israel, war is a continuous, highly expanded sacrifice. The cult was not simply an important feature of warfare or a set of rituals attending it; rather, warfare was an important feature of the cult. Holy war was one centrally important way in which Israel worshipped Yahweh.[136]

Israel: God, Land and the Other

The thing about war, sacrifice and the sacred is that an "other" is necessary to complete the dynamic. The sacred love of God as evidenced in the willingness to sacrifice oneself occasions the need for a strong and present force to perform the ritual slaughter. This force is the enemy.

Identity is the basis of this separation between us and them, while the scarcity of God completes the necessary formulation to bring God, war and sacrifice together. I touched on God's parsimonious nature earlier, but the idea is worth revisiting, as it exists within each individual religion, and helps define the opposition as the sacrificial agent. The "other" plays a sacred role, as they have assumed the mantle of the Divine Hand, sacrificing His Own Child as part of the hallowed rite.

For Judaism, identity is originally forged from an idea of purity.

In the Hebrew Bible the foreigner is often seen as a source of potential pollution, and the exclusion or annihilation of the foreigner is frequently advocated by Biblical writers or commanded by God . . . This racism is an unavoidable concomitant of covenant theology, and especially the idea that the Children of Israel are the chosen people.[137]

The Jewish holy book is oft cited as the beginning of monotheism, and the other two religions look approvingly on its creation of a unitary deity. However, the flip side of this equation is that the Jewish scriptures also inaugurated the conception of the miserly God, One who only has love for a single people, with the rest operating outside of the orbit of His love and protection.

No other holy scripture prior to the Jewish Bible identified a specific ethnicity as the sole focus of God's love and attention. With Judaism, the idea of us and them was cemented in a particular way. The "other," now imagined as tribes and countries somehow standing between Jews and their God, became enemies to vilify and destroy. This schema, laid down in the ancient Holy Scriptures, came to affect the two subsequent Abrahamic religions, Christianity and Islam, both of which claimed to take over the covenant, and often turned their wrath on those who didn't accept their claim to the original Abrahamic promise.

> Society is encoded in the Bible as a principle of Oneness (one land, one people, one nation) and in monotheistic thinking (one deity), it becomes a demand of exclusive allegiance that threatens with the violence of exclusion.[138]

This destructive dynamic has moved beyond the Abrahamic religious sphere to help define secular ideas of state and nationhood.

> Through the dissemination of the Bible in Western culture, its narratives have become the foundation of a prevailing understanding of ethnic, religious and national identity as defined negatively, over and against others . . . When this thinking is translated into secular formations about peoples, "one nation under God" becomes less comforting than threatening.[139]

With the "other" in place, and with this force considered diametrically opposed to not only the God of the one true religion, but also the people who have received the covenant, a state of perpetual war is inaugurated. And going to war becomes the highest form of prayer — sacrificing oneself as a blood offering to God, in affirmation of His reality, as well as the warrior's love for Him.

"Just War"

> The Book of Daniel insisted that God was waging a battle with the forces of evil in heaven. This war was mirrored by and influenced earthly events.[140]

The Jewish God and his Biblical protégés had no need for a "just war" theory, such as those developed by the later Abrahamic faiths. War was waged at God's command and whimsy, with little rhyme or reason and as was shown time and again, need not fit into any controlling moral schema. God's violence was inexplicable and ever-present, and the Israelites needed little more provocation than an oblique sign or a simple desire to launch into an all-out, genocidal military campaign.

However, for political and legal reasons, a "just war" theory was developed within Judaism in post-Biblical times, as the direct communication with God faded over the centuries and Israelites had to divine His messages encoded in the *Torah* and through prophetic utterances. Rabbi Dr. Asher Meir (a member of the Ethics Committee of the Prime Minister of Israel's office) explored contemporary Jewish "just war" theory in his syndicated column "The Jewish Ethicist":

> Judaism is founded on a vision of brotherhood among all peoples. Yet in an imperfect world, war is sometimes a necessary means to realize this vision. When we are facing a ruthless enemy who will have no mercy on us, we must do whatever is necessary to overcome them in order to bring about an end to ruthlessness and cruelty. But to the extent that we face enemies who don't play by the rules, we must remember the priest's original admonition: to keep in mind that we are fighting enemies, and not brothers, and that these individuals will not display any mercy toward us. In this case we may have to adjust our norms in order to overcome the forces of cruelty and inhumanity. Yet even in this case, we have to keep in mind that the conflict of war is only a means to bringing about a peaceful future world where conflict is obsolete.[141]

It's important to acknowledge that in this case, the "ruthless enemy" of whom the Rabbi speaks is the Palestinian people, and that this column is simply justification for the abhorrent treatment of this oppressed people. He notes: "we face enemies who don't play by the rules," but does not acknowledge that the rules are set by the Israelis, often with Biblical and religious justification (as this column surely means to be), and leave absolutely no room for a fair or even fight. Sometimes it appears as if Israeli justice is as arbitrary and violent as that of the God of the Jewish Bible.

Rabbi Dr. Meir situates this Jewish "just war" theory within the Biblical past, stating: "a realistic objective for a war conducted with humane norms is the civil war between Judah (the southern kingdom) and Israel (the northern kingdom) recounted in II Chronicles chapter 28." However, the subtext is contemporary geo-politics, and the justification for Israel's one-sided treatment of the people with whom they share the land.

Orthodox Rabbi Norman Solomon, in his "Judaism and the Ethics of War," not only situates Jewish "just war" theory in the scriptures, but chooses one of the most vile passages, Deuteronomy 20, which intones (among other things): "Howbeit of the cities of these peoples, that the Lord thy God giveth thee for an inheritance, thou shalt save nothing alive that breatheth, but thou shalt utterly destroy them."[142] Rabbi Solomon, basing his ideas on this and other passages in the Biblical chapter, notes that Deuteronomy lays down several constraints and conditions for "normal" war:

> The war is to be fought only by those who are courageous, possessing faith in God . . . an offer of peace is to be made to any city that is besieged . . . should the city refuse the offer of peace the males are put to the sword, the females and small children taken captive and the city plundered.[143]

It is not difficult to envision how we get from these rules of engagement to the Gaza War (2009), in which up to 1500 Palestinians were killed (and 13 Israelis), most of whom were not specifically determined to be combatants. According to Jewish "just war" theory, the incursion could have been much worse, with a complete "plundering" of Gaza, whose inhabitants were viewed as refusing an offer of peace. Undoubtedly, some religious Israelis (and members of the government) felt that they let the Gazans off easy, while much of the rest of the world saw a one-sided battle that veered into a slaughter of the innocents.

It should also be noted that Jewish law allows for a blanket indemnification for the perpetrators under the guise of "God issued instructions." This is especially problematic in current day Israeli politics, as many Settlers and others in the hyper-religious community most definitely do believe that they have received instructions from God to undertake everything from stone throwing (often by Settler children as young as four years old) to Baruch Goldstein's opening fire on innocent civilians at a mosque (1994; Cave of the Patriarchs in Hebron, killing 29 Muslims at prayer and wounding another 125), spraying 111 bullets into the holy space. Basing his actions on passages in the book of Esther, Goldstein believed that "by mowing down Arabs that he thought wanted to kill Jews, [he] was reenacting part of the Purim story."[144]

Today, Goldstein's gravesite has become a pilgrimage site for Jewish extremists. A plaque near the grave reads "To the holy Baruch Goldstein, who gave his life for the Jewish people, the *Torah* and the nation of Israel."[145]

To find justification for his acts, Goldstein could look to recent commentators such as Tzvi Yehuda (d. 1982; a Rabbi and leader of religious Zionism), who stated that the "establishment of Jewish sovereignty over *Eretz* [the land of] Israel is a commandment of the *Torah*."[146] In 2010, Jewish settlers were criticized because during celebrations of Purim they sang songs praising Baruch Goldstein's massacre demonstratively in front of their Arab neighbors. A phrase from the song read "Dr. Goldstein, there is none other like you in the world. Dr. Goldstein, we all love you . .

. he aimed at terrorists' heads, squeezed the trigger hard, and shot bullets, and shot, and shot."[147]

It is important to note — and this applies to the Gaza incursion in 2009, as well as "just war"s in all other religious cultures — that *jus in bello* demands that non combatants be spared. Unfortunately, as Barbara Ehrenreich noted in *Blood Rites: Origins and History of the Passions of War*, in today's "low-intensity" wars, civilians constitute 90% of the dead[148] — making a true ""just war"" impossible.

JUDAISM TODAY — MORE OF THE SAME?

Judaism today shows no evidence of changing from the primal dynamic of us versus them set down more than 5000 years ago in the earliest narratives from Genesis and the other four books of the *Pentateuch* (five first books of the Jewish Bible). Even more damaging is the manner in which Israel has become set up against many in the world as a flashpoint for religiously inspired war, both for and against the Jewish state.

Often, we find actions or reactions flowing from those who seek to protect the ancient nation — such as the United States and, to a lesser extent, Europe — and those that want to destroy it. Add the oppression that the Israeli state visits on citizen and non-citizen Palestinians, its illegal possession of nuclear arms and its bedrock belief that Israel, as a state, is sanctioned by the violent God of the Jewish Bible, and the world is left with an ongoing religio-virulent infection that metastasizes throughout the Middle East and, indeed, throughout the world. Too often, these political battles are couched as a war between the tripartite division of God, with the monotheistic deity of Abraham having split in three, and now — often centered on the ancient land of Israel reborn — Abraham's progeny must fight to the death to see which people have the true covenant, and which are the pretenders.

Israeli politics sometimes seems to emerge directly from the vicious narrative of the Jewish Bible. Perpetrators of Jewish violence in our era have often justified their deeds with pious language, using Jewish theology, historical precedents and Biblical examples.[149]

A series of contemporary Israeli religious and military leaders situate their actions within the Jewish religious tradition. Rabbi Meir Kahane (d. 1990; an ordained Orthodox rabbi who later served as a member of the Israeli Knesset) founded the militantly anti-Arab Kach party. The party's platform called for the annexation of all conquered territories and the forcible removal of all Palestinians. He helped develop what would become a recurring theme in Israeli politics: that of the religious Zionist, who fuses spirituality and violence in the name of the Chosen People.

> In using violence against cosmic foes [represented in Kahane's thinking by the Palestinians], Rabbi Kahane indicated that the lives of individuals targeted for attack were not important . . . Any individual who was part of a group deemed to be the enemy might justifiably become the object of a violent assault. In a spiritual war there is no such thing as an innocent bystander . . . The idea was that the Messiah will come in a great conflict in which Jews triumph and praise God through their successes. This was Kahane's understanding of the term *Kiddush ha-Shem*, "the sanctification of God."[150]

Although this conception of religion, violence and the "other" is primitive, it continues to affect followers of Kahane. Baruch Goldstein, whose atrocities were outlined earlier, has had a shrine erected to his "heroism," and is buried across from the Meir Kahane Memorial Park. Today, Jewish tour guides explain the religious importance of Goldstein's act, as well as underscoring how the Biblical land and sites on the West Bank are sacred, and that Jews are under God's requirement to occupy them.[151]

Yigdal Amir, the Bar Ilan University student who assassinated Yitzhak Rabin in 1995 (putting a bullet through the nascent peace process as well), was quoted as saying that he had "no regrets" for his actions, adding that he had "acted alone and on orders from God." In his mind, the slaughter was justified by a "pursuer's decree," which morally obligates a Jew to halt someone who presents a "mortal danger" to Jews.[152]

Even as recently as the Gaza incursion (2009), the military's Chief Rabbi, Brigadier General Avichai Rontzki, made this message crystal clear: "We are the Jewish people, we came to this land by a miracle, God brought us back to this land and now we need to fight to expel the non-Jews who are interfering with our conquest of this Holy Land." Rabbi Rontzki took a quotation from a classical Hebrew text and turned it into a slogan: "He who is merciful to the cruel will end up being cruel to the merciful." The information was included in a booklet handed out to the soldiers, containing a rabbinical edict against showing the enemy mercy.[153]

HOW THE JEWISH BIBLE AFFECTS CHRISTIANITY

> The account of Exodus can be considered the most important story in the Bible . . . According to many liberation readings, God is a powerful, anti-imperial Deity who takes sides with slaves, destroys superior armies and delivers God's chosen land . . . God's violence and human violence done in

> God's name are the legitimate and preferred means to justice. God's is a liberating violence.[154]

The Jewish scriptures are foundational texts for both Christianity and Islam. Far from superseding the ancient Israelite teachings, both religions simply built on top of them. They accepted the narratives, prophets and teachings, and then added theirs on top, while insisting that they had received God's covenant which the earlier religion(s) forfeited.

As such, the idea of holy violence present within Jewish history was accepted in its entirety by the other two Abrahamic creeds. One elegant outcome of this has been that all three religions point their "holy wars" at the other two, using the originally Jewish conception of holy war to justify their destruction of those from the other two faiths. While I will explore each Abrahamic cousin separately in the following two sections, it is nonetheless instructive to briefly examine the manner in which religious thinkers in both Christianity and Islam accepted the violence of God theories elaborated in the Jewish scripture.

Gratian (d. 383), a Roman Emperor who favored Christianity over the traditional Roman religion, situated the novel conception of Christian warriors in the Hebraic past, using the example of Moses killing the Egyptian as an example of "courage at war."[155] St. Augustine (d. 430) crystallized the Christian "Just War" theory, presenting it in a form that influences us to this day. He made it clear that the Old Testament idea of war, commanded by God, was a continuing warrant for the use of military force to punish wickedness.[156] As Robert Holmes (author of *On War and Morality*) outlined in "A Time For War? Augustine's "Just War" Theory Continues to Guide the West":

> Augustine insists that one can kill only under the authority of God, as communicated by direct or implicit command from God, or by a legitimate ruler who carries out God's intent to restrain evil on earth. Augustine further suggests that one who obeys such a command "does not himself 'kill'." He acts only as an instrument of the one who commands. Augustine concludes, "The commandment forbidding killing was not broken by those who have waged wars on the authority of God, or those who have imposed the death-penalty on criminals when representing the authority of the state, the justest and most reasonable source of power" . . . Thus Augustine fashioned what is now called the ""just war" theory," which over the centuries has become a complex set of criteria to govern both the recourse to war in the first place and the conduct of war once begun.[157]

A cottage industry of later Christian theologians emerged to interpret Augustine's concept of the Hebrew holy war precedent. Building on his ideas, they religiously justified the Crusades, Inquisition, the 15th–18th-century genocide in the Americas, the religious wars in Europe throughout the Middle Ages and modern era and even the massive World Wars of the twentieth century.

For instance, both Heinrich Bullinger (d. 1575) and William Cardinal Allen (d. 1590) held that religion permits the righteous to go to war against adherents of other faiths, as religious difference itself was a sufficient threat to the "true religion, justifying bellicose reactions." Both of these Christian thinkers based their judgments of the justice of holy war on examples drawn from the Old Testament.[158] Luis de Molina (d. 1600) used Deuteronomy 1:7 to justify the actions of warriors as "God's executioners."[159]

SACRIFICE

Christianity also appropriated ideas of sacrifice as worship, to inspire young men to fight the state's and religion's battles. The new Abrahamic creed situated the need for individuals to wage war in the necessity of sacrifice and the "blood covenant," originally sealed between Moses and God with the Ten Commandments (see above).

> During the second century C.E. both Judaism and Christianity argued vehemently that God *desired and accepted* human sacrifice . . . Did Genesis 22 [Abraham's aborted sacrifice of Isaac] foreshadow Christ's gruesome death on the Cross, as Christian interpreters maintained, or did Abraham really hack his son apart on Mount Moriah, as some Rabbis taught? Either way, the Divine approval of human sacrifice remains, and many texts on both sides of the Jewish-Christian divide call attention to that approval rather than attempting to soften it in any way.[160]

Building on the Abrahamic story of the willingness of the father to sacrifice his son, an entire literature of martyrdom grew up in Christian history, glorifying those who gave — or still give — their lives as ritual offerings to please God.[161] Within this Judeo-Christian construction, "we speak of human death as 'sacrifice,' as parties in armed conflict frequently do."[162]

To appreciate how war language explicitly borrows from this lexicon of sacrifice and faith, we need only read the words of a man considered by many to be an American hero, Senator John McCain (b. 1936; R-AZ). Senator McCain eulogized a soldier fallen in Afghanistan:

> He loved his country, and the values that make us exceptional among nations, and good ... Love and honor oblige us. We are obliged to value our blessings, and to pay our debts to those who sacrificed to secure them for us. They are blood debts . . . The loss of every fallen soldier should hurt us

lest we ever forget the terrible costs of war, and the sublime love of those who sacrifice everything on our behalf.[163]

AND ECHOES IN ISLAM

The ideas of martyrdom, *jihad* ("A religious war with those who are unbelievers in the mission of Muhammad . . . enjoined especially for the purpose of advancing Islam and repelling evil from Muslims"[164]) and self-sacrifice are central within Islam, as well. Even more so than in contemporary Judaism and Christianity, it seems that the Islamic religious value of suicide in the name of God has reached a very high spiritual station.

Although the "suicide attack" dates back to the 17th century (the first documented examples are by Dutch warriors in the Far East as well as Europe[165]), the sacrificial act is currently associated with Muslims, and deservedly so. Since the first Islamic suicide attack of our current era in the early 1980s, suicide bombing has become the archetype of violence by Muslim extremists.[166]

While there are no exact data on just how many Muslim suicide attacks have taken place over the past 30 years, the Christian Science Monitor documented 2200 such events over this period, most of which occurred in the home countries of the attackers, often killing Muslims in addition to their foreign targets.[167] Suicide bombers are assured by some of their religious leaders that their actions are religiously sanctioned, and that they will be well-compensated for their acts of martyrdom, with up to 72 virgins in a paradisical after-life. In fact, many, if not most, Islamic scholars disagree — suicide being illegal within traditional Islam — but there is enough religious precedent flowing through the Judeo-Christian-Muslim heritage, and enough recent theological scholarship, to assure Islamic suicide bombers that their actions are pure and moral.

CHAPTER FOUR: CHRISTIANITY

> The theological structure of Christian belief promotes the appalling record
> of violence, persecution, hatred, intolerance, bigotry, abuse and hypocrisy
> associated with the Christian churches over the past two millennia. This
> is because it encourages believers to deny or repress their doubts, sins and
> failures in order to be acceptable to God who, Christian doctrine declares,
> will condemn those whom He finds unacceptable to eternal punishment.
> Consequently, the faithful are liable to project the negative features of
> their characters, beliefs and behavior onto scapegoats who are blamed for
> them and excluded, persecuted or attacked in order to preserve the "good
> consciences" of Christianity.[168]

Cut from the very flesh and blood of Judaism, founded by an apostate
Rabbi, Christianity was simply grafted onto the ancient Abrahamic faith,
accepting fully the earlier scriptures and then superseding them with Jesus's message of love. Growing quickly from an oppressed collection of
deeply peaceful worshipers into a state religion that stretched from one
end of the globe to the other, Christianity claims more than a billion adherents today. Additionally, it is the *de facto* state religion of what many
consider to be the contemporary world's most dangerous superpower:
the United States.

Similar to Islam — which separates the world into *dar al-Islam* (the
House of Islam) and *dar al-harb* (the House of War, i.e., all others) — the
New Testament is dualistic, positing that humans have no choice but to
be ruled by God (the Christian God, that is) or by the forces of evil, those
that oppose their God.[169] Like believers of all religions, Christians can
and do justify killing the "other," as those who have not accepted Jesus

as their Lord and Savior are *already* dwelling in the realm of darkness, and death (as was the case during the Inquisition) can save their souls. If the individual is lost, at the very least these murders can help purify the Earth.

Jesus — a Message of Peace?

> To negate violence in the New Testament, one must deliberately forget Luke 22:36: "whoever has no sword, let him sell his tunic and buy one." They also purposely forget Matthew 10:34: "I came not to bring peace, but the sword." They pass over the fact that Matthew 23 is a page full of verbal violence unique in all literature of all time. And most of all, they pass over the fact that according to John 2:14-22, Matthew 21:12-13, Mark 11:15-17 and Luke 19:45-46, Jesus used physical violence to drive the traders from the Temple.[170]

Perhaps one of the greatest religious myths that we have to contend with is that the Christian Bible, known to its followers as the New Testament, is a peace document. How many times do we hear the exhortation to "turn the other cheek," as if this were Christianity's only message of how to deal with conflict? How many well-meaning Christian peace workers, gathering over donuts and coffee in church basements, assure each other that their path represents that set out by Jesus, and that martyrdom for Christians takes place in quiet suffering, hands at the side and fully accepting of one's fate?

Alas.

Violence is inescapable in the New Testament. The most important Christian image is the crucifixion, testament to the centrality of human sacrifice to worship. Human blood is the ineradicable centerpiece of the Christian message of redemption. Christianity was founded on an act of extreme violence. The New Testament states frequently that Jesus was sent to die, that his death was both intended and required by God.[171]

Uncovering violence within the Christian scriptures (leaving aside, for now, the body of violence-justifying exegesis that has expanded the ideal of Jesus's religion from the fourth century until today) is not difficult at all. I will not quote all of these passages — they are far too numerous — I will simply give a representative sampling to show that Jesus's exhortation to "turn the other cheek" is but one of a series of conflicting messages emanating from the Christian Holy Writ. Violent imagery and language abound in the New Testament:

Matthew

And if thy right eye offend thee, pluck it out, and cast it from thee . . . And if thy right hand offend thee, cut it off, and cast it from thee: for it is profitable for thee that one of thy members should perish, and not that thy whole body should be cast into hell. (5:29-30)

And the brother shall deliver up the brother to death, and the father the child: and the children shall rise up against their parents, and cause them to be put to death. (10:21)

Think not that I am come to send peace on earth: I come not to send peace, but a sword. (10:34)

Then Jesus began to denounce the towns in which most of his miracles had been performed, because they did not repent . . . "I tell you that it will be more bearable for Sodom on the Day of Judgment than for you." (11:20-24)

The master of that servant will come on a day when he does not expect him and at an hour he is not aware of. He will cut him to pieces and assign him a place with the hypocrites, where there will be weeping and gnashing of teeth. (24:50-51)

Mark

If your hand causes you to stumble, cut it off. It is better for you to enter life maimed than with two hands to go into hell, where the fire never goes out. And if your foot causes you to stumble, cut it off. It is better for you to enter life crippled than to have two feet and be thrown into hell. And if your eye causes you to stumble, pluck it out. It is better for you to enter the kingdom of God with one eye than to have two eyes and be thrown into hell, where "the worms that eat them do not die, and the fire is not quenched.' Everyone will be salted with fire." (9:43-49)

He that believeth and is baptized shall be saved; but he that believeth not shall be damned. (16:16)

Luke

But I will show you whom you should fear: Fear him who, after your body has been killed, has authority to throw you into hell. Yes, I tell you, fear him. (12:5)

The master of that servant will come on a day when he does not expect him and at an hour he is not aware of. He will cut him to pieces and assign him a place with the unbelievers. "The servant who knows the master's will and does not get ready or does not do what the master wants will be beaten with many blows." (12:46-47)

Those enemies of mine who did not want me to be king over them—bring them here and kill them in front of me. (19:22-27)

John

Whoever believes in the Son has eternal life; whoever does not obey the Son shall not see life, but the wrath of God remains on him. (3:36)

Those who do not believe in Jesus will be cast into a fire to be burned. (15:6)

Then Jesus said unto them, "Verily, verily, I say unto you, Except ye eat the flesh of the Son of man, and drink his blood, ye have no life in you. Whoso eateth my flesh, and drinketh my blood, hath eternal life; and I will raise him up at the last day." (6:53-54)

Acts

And it shall come to pass, that every soul, which will not hear that prophet [Jesus], shall be destroyed from among the people. (3:23)

Immediately, because Herod did not give praise to God, an angel of the Lord struck him down, and he was eaten by worms and died. (12:23)

Romans

Without understanding, covenant-breakers, without natural affection, unmerciful: who, knowing the ordinance of God, that they that practice such things are worthy of death, not only do the same, but also consent with them that practice them. (1:31-32)

Therefore, just as sin entered the world through one man [Adam], and death through sin, and in this way death came to all people, because all sinned . . . (5:12)

1 Corinthians

If anyone destroys God's temple, God will destroy that person; for God's temple is sacred, and you together are that temple. (3:17)

Nor let us act immorally, as some of them did, and twenty-three thousand fell in one day. Nor let us try the Lord, as some of them did, and were destroyed by the serpents. Nor grumble, as some of them did, and were destroyed by the destroyer. (10:8-10)

Ephesians

And walk in the way of love, just as Christ loved us and gave himself up for us as a fragrant offering and sacrifice to God. (5:2)

The book of Matthew is particularly egregious and has given plenty of ammunition to everyone from fourth -century Roman rulers to Pat Robertson (b. 1930; a television evangelist and ex-Baptist minister who politically aligns himself with the Christian Right) to justify Christian violence:

> The Gospel writer known as Matthew frequently places threatening and
> hateful words on the lips of Jesus . . . Matthew can't seem to imagine peo-
> ple doing the right thing without warnings of violent judgments hanging
> over their heads, including threats of hell . . . Matthew's Jesus consistently
> uses heavily apocalyptic imagery when warning the people of imminent
> judgment to come.[172]

There are many more instances of explicit violent language, threats
and behavior, culminating in the Book of Revelation, which details the
Armageddon and, far from the loving and redeeming religion that many
wish Christianity to be, represents the creed as one of destruction, murder and holocaust.

It must also be noted that the Christian weekly liturgy offers a blood-
bath of imagery and language. The Christian Eucharist presumes the
punishing violence of God. The language "body" and "blood" of Christ
places the Lord's Supper in a human sacrificial context. Christian rituals
and hymns are saturated in violent images of God, often masquerading as
themes of liberation or atonement.[173]

Lastly, lest you think that these scriptural passages are to be read as
metaphor, or with subtle nuance, here is a quote from a recent Papal encyclical, *Dominus Iesus*, issued on August 6, 2000, in the name of Cardinal
Joseph Ratzinger (b. 1927), who became Pope Benedict XVI on April 19,
2005:

> For Holy Mother Church relying on the faith of the apostolic Testaments,
> whole and entire, with all their parts, on the grounds that, written under
> the inspiration of the Holy Spirit . . . they have God as their author, and
> have been handed on as such to the Church Herself. [These books] firmly,
> faithfully and without error, teach the truth which God, for the sake of
> our salvation, wished to see confided in the Sacred Scriptures.[174]

The Early Church Fathers

> The essence of virtue is not to be found in inflicting injury but in prevent-
> ing it.[175]

Oddly enough, given the violent language and imagery embedded in
the Christian Holy Writ, plus the bloody history of the religion, Christianity *did* begin as a genuinely peaceful religion. The early church fathers
argued that any participation in worldly affairs of statecraft, and specifically war, was unethical and contrary to the teachings of Christ.

Tertullian (d. 220; called the Father of Latin Christianity) had this to
say about participating in the wars of his era:

> The question now is whether a member of the faithful can become a soldier and whether a soldier can be admitted to the faith even if he is a member of the rank and file [soldiery] . . . There can be no compatibility between an oath made to God and one made to man, between the standard of Christ and that of the devil. The soul cannot be beholden to two masters, God and Caesar.[176]

The standard of separating the early Christian believer from everything having to do with the civil authority was unwavering. Tertullian stated: "We either refuse offices in order to avoid falling into sin or we must undergo martyrdom in order to be freed from obligations."[177]

Origen (d. 254; one of the most distinguished writers of the early Church) addressed the carnage of the Jewish Bible, which underpins so much of today's Christian fusion of temporal war and the spirit, relegating it to the realm of metaphor, assuring that physical conflict had no place within the church:

> Unless those carnal wars [of the Old Testament] were a symbol of spiritual wars, I do not think that the Jewish historical books would ever have been passed down to the apostles to be read by Christ's followers . . . The Apostle, being aware that physical wars are no longer to be waged by us but that our struggles are to be only battles of the soul . . .[178]

Leader after leader from this era assured that there was no place in war for a true Christian. Lactantius (d. 320) stated:

> It is not right for those who are striving to stay on the path of virtue to become associated with . . . wholesale slaughter. For when God forbids killing, He is not only ordering us to avoid armed robbery, which is contrary to public law, but He is forbidding what men regard as ethical. Thus, it is not right for a just man to serve in the army since justice itself is his form of service.[179]

Lactantius' belief that Christianity "forbids what men regard as ethical," i.e., killing in war, would certainly strike a discordant note today. There is little doubt that the majority of Christian followers in contemporary America draw a thick distinction between "murder" and "killing." I have had numerous devout Christians explain to me in quiet tones how the Ten Commandments forbid "murder," but not killing *per se*.

Ergo, the majority of American Christians today can strongly support war, the death penalty, torture and other forms of violence, and even consider them divinely ordained, provided that they do not consider them "murder." Even worse, a majority of Christians in America (more than 60% in a recent Gallup poll) believe that killing of *civilians* in war is sometimes justified![180]

The early church fathers would strongly disagree with this conception: "Thou shalt not kill *unless you want to or need to or have been told to or believe it is the right thing to do.*" But as we will see, the idea of divinely ordained slaughter emerged into Christianity more than 1500 years ago, and by now has a very solid collection of church thinkers' and saints's writings to back it up.

MARTYRDOM

> Christianity has been a primary force in shaping our acceptance of abuse. The central image of Christ on the Cross as the savior of the world communicates the message that suffering is redemptive ... Those whose lives have been shaped by the Christian tradition feel that self-sacrifice and obedience are not only virtues but the definition of a faithful identity. The promise of resurrection persuades us to endure pain, humiliation and violation of our sacred rights to self-determination, wholeness and freedom. Our internalization of this theology traps us in an unbearable cycle of abuse.[181]

The rejection of *instigating* violence by the early Christians in no way freed the religion from violent imagery and actions — it just pointed the violence inward onto the believer, as a manner of echoing Christianity's original creative act: that of God sacrificing His own Son. During this early era, the "soldier of Christ" was an individual at war against the sinful desires latent in his own urges and behavior.[182] The enemy lay within.

These ideas built on beliefs from the parent Jewish religion and fused with the story of Christ. Bruce Chilton noted in *Abraham's Curse* that what Abraham and Isaac did on Mount Moriah was but a foreshadowing of what Jesus revealed: God's desire to destroy his own child in a single, supreme, all-forgiving sacrifice.[183] The New Testament's "Book of Hebrews" (12:24) dates the thirst for sacred blood even earlier than the story of Abraham and Isaac, stating that the true Christian's dedication for eternal sacrifice is one "whose blood speaks better than Abel's."[184] The "Book of Hebrews" (c. 95) made the willingness of the believer to become a martyr a religious duty, mimicking the sacrifice of God's son to Himself.[185]

Self-sacrifice and martyrdom became the highest form of worship for these early Christians. By the second century, Christian teachers assured that the ultimate act of faith was to give up one's life for the creed. Self-denial, from austere asceticism to suicide for faith, was presented as the surest way to attain union with Christ, dying with Him so as to be raised to Him. Martyrdom was necessary to bring Jesus's Crucifixion alive to new generations of believers.[186]

Ignatius of Antioch (d. 117; a student of John the Apostle) intoned:

> Let fire and cross, struggles with beasts, dissections, slicings, rackings of bones, cutting up of limbs, grinding of the whole body, cruel tortures of the devil come upon me, only that I attain Jesus Christ.[187]

This impulse has had a profound effect on Christian nations over the past two millennia. Countries with a deep history of Christianity have displayed a capacity to mobilize their youth on a massive scale in times of crisis, and put them in harm's way. This self-sacrificing reflex feeds easily into the European and American cultures of bloodshed,[188] where serving the nation as a warrior is conflated with serving Christ and God in sacrifice. Ultimately, as Bruce Chilton (Bernard Iddings Bell Professor of Religion at Bard College) noted:

> In its detail, in its persistence, in its long-lasting effects for centuries after Roman persecution came to an end, and above all in its capacity to be re-tooled in the service of nationalistic propaganda of martyrdom that encourages sacrifice on behalf of country, the Christian veneration of martyrs has proven to be the single most influential incentive to self-sacrifice among world religions over the centuries.[189]

THE FIRST COUNCIL OF NICAEA AND THE FALL OF CHRISTIANITY

> The wars of religion to which we are heir and are still fighting today began in the battle of Milvian Bridge (313). There, Constantine, soon to be the Roman Emperor, had his soldiers before battle inscribe on their shields the Cross and the phrase: "in this sign, you shall be victor."[190]

Christianity could not repress for too long through martyrdom the violence seething within the human soul. By the fourth century, enough people had converted to Christianity that the latent destructiveness within humanity boiled to a point that it had to be pointed outward. Not all new Christians believed that the only true path to Jesus lay in self-mortification. More and more believed that the sword should be turned on pagans and unbelievers, to prove God's power and inflict His wrath in the civil world of politics and war.

The Roman Emperor Constantine I (d. 337), who had learned of the power of Christ at the Battle of Milvian Bridge prior to his ascension to the throne, definitively fused Christianity and war. In 313 he issued the Edict of Milan legalizing Christian worship. The emperor became a great patron of the Church, and set a precedent for the position of the Christian Emperor within the Church. In 325, at the Council of Nicaea,

Constantine avoided a church rupture over the nature of Christ, issuing a decree that Jesus was both fully human and fully God. From that time on, Christianity was the religion of the European emperor (called the "Holy Roman Emperor," a position that existed for nearly 1500 years, to Napoleon in the 18ᵗʰ century).

Constantine's conversion to Christianity and his actions at the Council of Nicaea began a new chapter in the religion, providing religious justification for wars of state.

> When the power of the empire became joined to the ideology of the church, the empire was immediately recast and reenergized, and the church became an entity so different from what had preceded it as to be almost unrecognizable. Constantine's conversion led to the militarization of the Christian movement. No longer guided by the compassionate teachings of Christ, but spearheaded by the emperor's goals of conquest.[191]

Christ's temporal power had a new meaning. One could be noble and serve the spiritual realm through commanding attention and respect on Earth. In fact, civil success in the world of violence *proved* God's power, and His love of Jesus and Christianity. Prominent Christian leaders, turning away from three centuries of self-mortification and a militant passivity, embraced the model of a state-sanctioned religion. Far from demanding removal from worldly affairs, the greatest Christian thinkers now approved the use of violence, urging devout Christians on to attack their competitors. The state power had been baptized as religious power.[192]

Even the concept of the Christian martyr underwent a noxious change — another innovation that would infect Christian societies into our era. The martyr was now not simply a passive victim, suffering pain and violence in the name of Christ. After the Christianization of the Roman Empire, the martyr became a soldier as well, a warrior-victim who fought in the name of Christ. New hagiographies were written in which the stories of these new murderer-martyrs were told alongside earlier church fathers, who had died quietly under the persecutions of the previous centuries.[193]

> As the Roman Empire became Christian, Christians introduced a fateful shift in the identity of the martyr. Once the Roman Empire could call on Christian soldiers for its defense, the benefit of martyrdom could accrue even to those who risked their lives by engaging in violence on behalf of their faith in Christ. Martyrs became executioners as well as victims, while laying claim to the virtue of victimhood the whole time.[194]

By the middle of the fourth century an institutional understanding of how to apply "restorative" violence came into being. Bruce Chilton explored how far the conception of religious violence went:

> Later in the fourth century, in Callinicum on the Euphrates River, a local Bishop had encouraged the plunder and arson of a synagogue by a mob of unruly Christians . . . The Emperor Theodosius (d. 395) directed that the Bishop rebuild the synagogue at his own expense. Bishop Ambrose in Milan confronted Theodosius personally, arguing that the mob consisted of overly enthusiastic but good-hearted people, childlike martyrs in their immature but vigorous faith. Ambrose got his way. Mob violence had become virtuous, on the argument that Christ was witnessed in these acts as martyrs had once witnessed Christ. Having made his [successful] case to Theodosius, Ambrose described himself as feeling as if he had entered into paradise.[195]

And thus began one of the most pernicious periods of one religion's treatment toward the believers of another religion, as over the next 1600 years Christian Europe would subjugate its Jewish citizens to expulsions, pogroms, Crusades, Inquisitions, mass slaughters and, finally, the Holocaust, the attempted destruction of every single follower of the Jewish creed—often in the name of Jesus Christ.

A disgusting narrative, but not one you will often hear from followers of the religion of the Lamb. As my priest friend said to me, "Aw, man, why do you always have to focus on the negative stuff? There's so much good in Christianity . . ."

"Just War"

> It is the iniquity on the part of the adversary that forces a "just war" upon the wise man.[196]

There are few more powerful personalities in the history of God and war than St. Augustine of Hippo (d. 430). He spilled much ink, most of which turned to blood, in defense of the idea that war could and did fit within the structure of the Christian religion. While Constantine discovered the power of the Cross at Milvian Bridge in 313, it was Augustine who situated the idea of a just and righteous war within the Christian tradition, a legacy that continues to influence the faith of Christ.

St. Augustine was convinced that war fulfilled the useful purpose of reminding humans just how weak and dependent they actually are. Institutional violence occurred in obedience to the will of God in order to "rebuke, humble or crush the pride of man."[197] He used verbal gymnastics to situate mass murder within the pantheon of Christian activities.

> Waging war and extending the empire by subduing peoples is viewed as
> happiness by the wicked, but as necessary by the good. But because it
> would be worse if wrongdoers dominated those who are more just, it is
> not inappropriate to call even this necessity "happiness."

Augustine went so far as to outline the specifics of war strategy that
could be utilized in the name of God. "Such things as ambushes are legitimate for those who are engaged in a "just war". In these matters, the only
thing a righteous man has to worry about is that the "just war" is waged
by someone who has the right to do so."[198]

For Augustine, war was undertaken as an extension of Christian
teachings. He advocated the use of the Roman military against Christian
heretics and schismatics.[199] Implicit in this understanding of "just war"
was that each Christian victory on the battlefield "proved" the righteousness of the campaign, as well as the power of God. This pathological conception of "just war" metastasized over time to become "manifest destiny," with Christian Europeans believing that they had the God-given
right to take whatever they wanted and kill whomever they pleased, as
it was God's will that they should rule the world. And their temporal
successes proved it!

Augustine continues to be the single most influential theologian
within Christianity for helping canon lawyers, theologians, politicians
and a vast array of modern Christian thinkers formulate their ideas on
war. Many modern thinkers reverentially refer to St. Augustine when
talking about war, and use his language and ideas.[200]

Error Has No Right

Augustine developed another insidious theory which, when coupled
with the divine right of the political leader to use war as a religious tool,
essentially made all Christian wars religious in nature. Called "error has
no right," it situated the perceived enemies of Christianity in a judicial
no-man's land. The simple fact of their disagreement with Christians and
Christianity removed all of their legal rights, opening to them the necessity of Christian judgment in the form of extirpative war:

> The doctrine [of "error has no right"] was developed by St. Augustine to
> justify the use of state coercion to suppress his heretical opponents. Be-
> cause they are radically in error, they have no right to express or hold their
> beliefs. Ever since, the doctrine has been put to similar use as the principle
> behind every use of coercion, especially state coercion.[201]

Coupled with ideas of violence in the name of God, as well as the
infallibility of the Christian church, Augustine's "error has no right" doc-

trine became an impetus for a millennium of religiously sanctioned wars, slavery and other oppression in Europe, the Americas, Africa and the Near and Far East.

THE HOLY ROMAN EMPIRE

> The best condition of the human race depends on a unity of wills. But this cannot be unless there is one will dominating all the others and directing them all to one goal . . . Nor can this will be one unless there be one ruler over all, whose will can dominate and direct all others.[202]

Constantine's desire to bring God and country, war and ultimate justice together had the effect of creating the European theocracy known as the Holy Roman Empire, which existed for nearly 1000 years in Central Europe. The first Holy Roman Emperor is generally considered to have been Otto I, King of Germany, crowned in 962; while the final Holy Roman Emperor was Francis II, who abdicated and dissolved the Empire in 1806 during the Napoleonic Wars. Others, however, date the founding of the Holy Roman Empire to the year 800, when Pope Leo III crowned Charlemagne emperor of Europe on Christmas Day.

Charlemagne brought the Christian holy war to a new, more violent level.

> Charlemagne's activities stand as the most brutal pages in Christian missionary efforts. For Charlemagne . . . the Resurrection Cross of Christ symbolized the power that protected them in warfare and led them to victory. Priests "traveled with the army and carried gold and jewel encrusted crosses mounted on standards in procession through the troops."[203]

The new holy warrior ethos permeated all aspects of religious observance. The theologian Paschasius (d. 860) recast the daily Eucharist, in which the body and blood of Christ are eaten in the form of wafer and wine, not as a celebration of the resurrection but as a re-enactment of the Crucifixion, the killing of the bleeding Christ. Communicants were to stop considering the event as hopeful and life affirming. They were now asked to focus on Jesus's suffering and dying. In political-military terms, over time the death theme came to mean that killing in warfare was a source of thanksgiving.[204]

From this time onward, *all* European wars were presented as holy wars, even when fought against other Christians! In the case of internecine battles, each side would simply brand the other as the mistaken party ("error has no right"), and then do their best to prove their Godly credentials through victory on the battlefield, showing that God loved them more and that the adversary was in error.

This act of "thanksgiving," undertaken through slaughtering those in error, became fused with the idea of sacrifice, which also echoed the Crucifixion and tightened the connection between a bloody death and Christ's dying for all of humanity's sins. Now, anyone going to war could become a little Christ, taking on the sins of all humanity in their violent act of thanksgiving.

> Patristic theology insisted on the importance of the martyr's self-sacrifice, including very young martyrs, to an extent unprecedented among the major religions in antiquity. That happened because the [church] fathers ratcheted up the ethical imperative found in Hebrews — its demand that believers pursue their devotion to Christ "until blood" (Hebrew 12:4), that is, to the death.[205]

AUGUSTINIAN INFLUENCE ON LATER CHRISTIAN THINKERS

> It is indeed better that men should be led to worship God by teaching, than that they should be driven to it by fear of punishment or pain . . . However, many have found advantage in being first compelled by fear or pain, so that they might afterwards be influenced by teaching.[206]

The Augustinian infection burrowed deep into Christianity's soul, turning a once-peaceful creed into one of the most bloodthirsty in the history of humankind. Throughout the Middle Ages, the greatest Christian thinkers looked to Augustine to situate wars of passion, aggrandizement and just plain slaughter within the Christian tradition. For instance, the 12th-century Bolognese monk Gratian (acclaimed as the Father of the Science of Canon law) stated:

> Do not think that none can please God while serving in arms . . . Therefore keep this in mind first of all, when you prepare to fight, that your valor, including your bodily courage, is a gift of God . . . be therefore peaceful while you wage war.[207]

This 12th-century monk also assured that "those who waged wars ordered by God never acted against the precept 'Thou shalt not kill,' as a soldier who kills a man in obedience to power under which he has been legitimately constituted cannot be accused of homicide."[208] To his credit, however, Gratian did draw the line at priests bearing arms, averring: "priests may not take up arms themselves; but they are allowed to exhort others to do so in order to defend the oppressed and to fight the enemies of God."[209]

Within fifty years of Gratian's pronouncement, the Pope himself urged prelates into battle. Pope Innocent IV (d. 1254) assured:

> Any prelate, if he has temporal jurisdiction, could legitimately take up arms against disobedient subjects as long as he has the legal authority to declare war. And even if he does not have the right to declare war, as long as he has the jurisdiction he may take up arms, because in such cases, it is not properly called "war," but rather "justice."[210]

With the church's highest authority guaranteeing that even a man of God could take up arms, and when he did so it was to administer justice and not commit murder, the floodgates opened to validate all manner of deleterious behavior. Remember: already in the fourth century a Christian mob had been exonerated of sin for marauding through a Jewish synagogue and neighborhood, their only fault being an excess of faithful zeal. So as the idea of sacred violence expanded and became settled within the Church canon, it only stood to reason that it would encompass all actors and virtually allviolent situations.

Hostiensis (d. 1271; one of the most important canonists of the thirteenth century) guaranteed: "Whoever by a legitimate judicial authority free of error attacks another, attacks justly, whereas the one attacked defends himself unjustly." St. Thomas Aquinas (d. 1274; held in the Catholic Church to be the model teacher for those studying for the priesthood) quoted Augustine with these reassuring words:

> Augustine says: "Beware of thinking that none of those can please God who handle warlike weapons" . . . Now religious orders are established in order that man may please God. Therefore nothing hinders the establishing of a religious order for the purpose of soldiering.[211]

Far from being peripheral members of the Christian Church, these voices were central to building the theological structure of the medieval church, and are still studied by Catholic laypersons and priests alike. Though many Christians will cringe at these ideas and assure that they want to "concentrate on the good stuff," many others will point to these thinkers as they build a religious basis for state-sponsored violence. I will explore this contemporary dynamic in depth in a later chapter, *"War as Love,"* where I examine the religious language used in the justification of American interventionism, and specifically since the 9/11/2001 assault, an attack that was itself justified within the Islamic religious tradition.

From these 12th and 13th-century church elders, Renaissance Christian thinkers — those who gave justification to the genocide and wars of aggrandizement in the Americas — took their spiritual sustenance. Christine de Pizan (d. 1431), a Venetian-born woman and a highly regarded poet in her day, challenged the stereotype of the peace-loving female with this comment: "Wars undertaken for a just cause are permitted by God. We have proof of this in several places in the Holy Writ."[212]

The Italian Cardinal Thomas Cajetan (d. 1534) went further, imputing an almost God-like role of giver of justice to the ruler who waged a "just war":

> He who has a "just war" is not a party, but becomes, by the very reason that impelled him to make war, the judge of his enemies. For it is not a perfect commonwealth if it lacks the ability to exercise vindictive justice, either against internal or external disturbances.[213] It is the enemy's own fault if he reduced himself to that state where foreigners can exercise vindictive justice against him, for it was in his power to offer satisfaction earlier.[214]

THE PRINCIPLE OF DOUBLE EFFECT

Like the Jewish scripture before, this Papal legate detailed how the victorious religious warrior might consider all goods of the conquered people as his own:

> All of the losses resulting from a "just war", not only for the soldiers, but also for any member of the [vanquished] commonwealth against which there is a "just war" are devoid of sin and entail no duty of restitution on the part of those who inflicted the losses, even if by accident innocents should be injured . . . strictly speaking, one justly receives [the booty], even though another innocent person accidentally suffers unjustly, for what happens by accident falls outside of the rules.[215]

This idea that those fighting "just" wars could injure the innocent with impunity was called the "principle of double effect." This is a set of ethical criteria that Christians used for evaluating the permissibility of acting when one's legitimate act would also cause an effect that would normally be inadmissible.

Francisco de Vitoria (d. 1546; Catholic philosopher, theologian and jurist considered as the father of international law), elaborated on just how far the Christian warrior would be covered by this principle:

> It is occasionally lawful to kill the innocent not by mistake, but with full knowledge of what one is doing, if this is an accidental effect . . . This is proven, since it would otherwise be impossible to wage war against the guilty, thereby preventing the just side from fighting.[216]

Francisco Suarez (d. 1617; generally regarded to be among the greatest scholastics after Thomas Aquinas) assured that "if the end is permissible, the means necessary are also permissible and hence it follows that in the whole course, or duration, of the war hardly anything done against the enemy involves injustice."[217]

These church fathers were building on earlier precedent, where St. Thomas Aquinas (d. 1274) had devised an ingenious theory that exonerated warriors from their responsibility in causing "collateral damage," and the killing of innocents. He developed this "principle of double effect," assuring that Christian warriors were not responsible for foreseeable, yet unintended side effects of their bellicose campaigns, in the same way that the blood of Christ protected them from any guilt for harms directly intended.

Later Christian thinkers, from Cajetan down to our era, have used this idea to allow for causing "collateral" damage within the construct of a religiously sanctioned "just war",[218] ultimately resulting in our contemporary statistics, where up to 90% of all damage done in today's "low-impact" wars is "collateral," with only 10% representing targeted enemy warriors.

Protestant War

Martin Luther (d. 1546), who founded Protestantism when he broke with the Catholic Church after posting his "95 Theses" in Wittenberg (1517), still found much to love about the Mother Church's attitude toward war. After all, now that he was right and the Catholic Church was wrong, it would undoubtedly have to be punished, and what better way than to be subjected to a Protestant war? "What else is war but the punishment of wrong and evil?" Luther intoned. "Why does anyone go to war except that he desires peace and obedience?"[219]

Going even further in the direction of earlier Catholic war apologists, he stated:

> In a war of this sort it is both Christian and an act of love to kill the enemy without hesitation, to plunder and burn and injure him by every method of warfare until he is conquered . . . In such a case, let the proverb apply, "God helps the strongest."[220]

Leaving aside Jesus's statement that the meek shall inherit the earth, Luther's "proverb" still lends itself to completely reductionist and terrifyingly dangerous reasoning. The only manner of proving who is "strongest" is through warfare, the general society barely even noticing true spirituality, which is based in humility. Additionally, this reasoning may be applied retroactively to any bellicose campaign fought and won — which is the exact dynamic we have seen in Christian countries from the time of Augustine right through the United States' adventures in Europe, the Far East and most recently the Middle East.

THE CRUSADES

> Jerusalem is the center of the earth . . . She seeks and desires to be freed, and ceases not to implore your aid . . . Therefore, undertake this journey for the remission of your sins, assured of the imperishable glory of the Kingdom of Heaven.[221]

The Crusades represent the bloodiest period in the history of European Christianity, provided that one is willing to overlook the Inquisition (1478–1834), the genocide of the indigenous people of the Western Hemisphere (1492–1890), the War of the Roses (1455–1485), World War I (1914–1917), World War II (1939–1945) and the Holocaust (1938–1945).

Earlier justifications and even demands for war as an act of fealty to God led to some ultimate and obvious conclusions. One of them was the incredible carnage of the Crusades, a series of religiously inspired military campaigns, waged by much of Roman Catholic Europe. The specific crusades to restore Christian control of the Holy Land were fought between 1095 and 1291, while other campaigns in Spain and Eastern Europe continued into the 15th century.

Anselm of Aosta (d. 1109), who became Archbishop of Canterbury in 1093, crystallized the religious foundation for the Crusades with the phrase: "Peace by the Blood of the Cross." This became the rallying cry for the warrior-penitents. Those who shared in partaking of the body of Christ through the Eucharist incurred the obligation either to convert or kill those who did not share in this ritual. According to the Archbishop, killing and being killed imitated the "gift" of Christ's death.[222]

The centuries-long campaign began in 1095, when Pope Urban II (d. 1099) called for Christians to retake the Holy Land from the infidel Muslims. Urban offered a reward for the present as well as the future, absolving all participants of their sins, releasing them from the hardships of religious observances such as fasting and mortifications and giving them a license to kill, plunder, steal and indulge any other sensual appetites, forgiven in advance for all sins committed in the name of Christ.[223]

Urban made the Crusade his life's work, touring throughout France during his final years to preach the holy battle, assuring that the bloodshed would purify the faithful and be pleasing unto God.[224] As he stirred up Christians to "liberate" Jerusalem from the Saracens, their devout passion rose to such a fevered pitch that they could not possibly await arrival in that far-off land before embarking on God's work. They slashed their way through the Jews of the Rhineland en route to their date with destiny, stating: "You are the children of those who killed our object of veneration and He Himself said, 'There will yet come a day when my children will come and avenge my blood.' We are His children and it is obligatory for us to avenge Him."[225]

Ultimately, this side work against the Jews far exceeded the carnage of the Crusades themselves.

> Campaigns against defenseless Jews punctuated the violent progress of the Crusades, finally far exceeding the Crusades themselves in duration, violence and body count. During the 12th century, the primordial logic of the *cherem* [excommunication] and the vocation of self-sacrifice in imitation of Christ fused to produce a genocidal campaign, consigning its Jewish victims to hell on earth and to the devil in death. The plague of sacrificial violence against Jews, perfected during the Crusades, continued in Europe until the 20th -century Holocaust and its future remains uncertain.[226]

The Pope's promises and exhortations worked their magic, and in 1099 the holy warriors did indeed retake the sacred city of Jerusalem from the Muslims. Raymond of Aguilar gave a firsthand account of the spiritual joy of the Christian conquerors:

> In the temple our men were wading up to their ankles in enemy blood; some 320 corpses were set ablaze as a burnt offering. The slaughter began on Friday at the ninth hour, the same time that Jesus was crucified. The Crusaders gathered for mass in the place of Jesus' burial, while the blood of their victims was still on them, so that the devotion was enhanced by the blood that had been shed: their victims', their comrades', their own and Christ's.[227]

The Christian penitents slaughtered virtually all the Muslims and Jews found in the Holy City, including women and children.[228]

The Crusades were the prototypical religious war. Warriors took religious vows before departing for the campaign. New religious orders of knights were founded for the purpose of fighting Christianity's enemies.[229] The Crusades developed a new conception of the warrior-monk, pledged to lifelong chastity as well as to war. In this perverse new creation, military monastic orders such as the Knights Templars and Knights Hospitaliers developed the idea of the "chaste and chivalrous knight" who was as holy as the cloistered monk.[230]

Professor James Turner Johnson, in *The Holy War Idea*, explained how deeply affected were all Christian leaders by the new ethos:

> After the proclamation of the First Crusade by Pope Urban II in 1095, religious and clergy of all levels spread the word throughout Christendom and enlisted volunteers. St. Bernard of Clairvaux, a monk who went on to found one of the strictest religious orders in the Western church, strongly supported the founding of the military order of the Templars and was a vigorous public advocate of the Second Crusade . . . Many clergy and monks accompanied the armies of the Crusades . . . Individual monks or priests sometimes bearing arms and sometimes not, took the lead at the head of the armed forces and personally authorized them.[231]

More than a century after Urban II initiated the bloody pogrom, Christian leaders were still situating the slaughter within the Lamb of God's works. Pope Innocent IV (d. 1254) reassured:

> The Pope may declare war and grant indulgences to those who occupy the Holy Land, which the infidels illegally possess. All this has a good cause, for the Pope acts justly when he strives to recover the Holy Land — which is consecrated by the birth, life and death of Jesus Christ.[232]

While no one can say with accuracy how many were slaughtered (the enemies) and sacrificed (Christians) throughout the two centuries of the Crusades, estimates range from one to nine million souls. At the upper estimate, this represents exactly 50% of the total population of Europe at the time!

THE INQUISITION

The history of Christian extirpation is so rich that it offers far too much material for a volume such as this one. As such, I will deal briefly with but one of the gruesome religio-savage events of the past half-millennium. The various Inquisitions (1231–1860), instituted in Spain, Italy, Portugal and other locales in Europe, were battles against "heretics" by the church. Even before the "official" beginning in 1231, the righteous work began in the 12th century, with the introduction of torture for the persecution of heresy.

The Inquisition was focused on all manners of enemies of the church, from Jewish and Muslim *conversos* (those who converted or pretended to convert to Christianity under duress) to heretics within the religion. The church fathers charged with protecting the faith invented every conceivable device to inflict pain by slowly dismembering and dislocating the body. Many of these devices were inscribed with the motto "Glory be only to God." Here is a list of just a few of the sacred contraptions that were devised to help people understand how deep was Christ's love for them, and how profoundly Jesus' helpers here on earth wanted them to realize this:

> *Judas Cradle* - The victim was seated on a triangular-shaped seat that was inserted in his or her anus or vagina. He or she was slowly impaled.
>
> *Brazen Bull* - When a victim was placed inside the brazen bull, he or she was slowly burned to death. A complex system of tubes added an aesthetic quality by making the victim's screams sound like an infuriated ox.
>
> *Rack Torture* - The torturer turned the handle causing the ropes to pull the victim's arms. Eventually, the victim's bones were dislocated with a loud crack; some of the limbs were torn apart.
>
> *Exposure* - The victim was buried up to his neck in the earth, allowing animals, insects or other people to kill him slowly.
>
> *Chair of Torture* - Spikes covered the back, armrests, seat, leg rests and footrests. Two bars pushed the arms against armrests for the spikes to penetrate the flesh even further.
>
> *Pear of Anguish* - A pear-shaped instrument was inserted into one of the victim's orifices. The instrument consisted of four leaves that slowly separated from each other as the torturer turned the screw at the top.
>
> *Head Crusher* - With the chin placed over the bottom bar and the head under the upper cap, the torturer slowly turned the screw pressing the bar against the cap. This resulted in the head being slowly compressed. First the teeth were shattered into the jaw; then the victim slowly died with agonizing pain, but not before his eyes were squeezed from their sockets.

Please note that these are but a spare compendium of the rigors that awaited the lost soul. Although according to Pulitzer Prize winner Will Durant in *The Reformation (The Story of Civilization VI)*, only 32,000 people were actually murdered over the full course of the Inquisition, French writer Victor Hugo (d. 1885) estimated that about five million people were tortured throughout the Inquisition's history.

CHRISTIANITY TODAY

> Christians have used Christianity to justify slavery of Africans and the removal to reservations or death of Native Americans. In the American Civil War, the North acted with God's "terrible swift sword," and the Southern cause came to be "baptized in blood." Afterwards, Protestants in the Ku Klux Klan employed chaplains, read Bibles and mounted crosses as they set out against blacks, Catholics and Jews.[233]

The unbreakable link between God and war has hardly waned with the "secularization" of Western society. The twentieth century saw no easing of the Christian dynamic of sacrifice and slaughter. In fact, it was by far the bloodiest hundred years in the history of our species, with 160 million people dying in wars, representing about half of the population of the United States at the end of that bloody span.

As James Hillman pointed out in *A Terrible Love of War*, Western Christianity's God comes to the fore when war is in the air.

> In World War II, God was a co-pilot on bombing runs, as one book title declared, and a popular song turned a chaplain into a "helluva gunner." In World War I, "clergymen dressed Jesus in khaki and had Him firing machine guns." The Bishop of London exhorted his fellow Christians to "kill the good as well as the bad . . . kill the young man as well as the old . . . kill those who have shown kindness to our wounded as well as those fiends."[234]

Douglas MacArthur, in his farewell address to the United States Congress, said that it had been his sacred duty to "carry to the land of our vanquished foe the solace and hope and faith of Christian morals."[235]

And George Weigel, a Catholic theologian who is Distinguished Senior Fellow of the Ethics and Public Policy Center, has argued that classic Christian doctrine did not treat war as a social and political anomaly that had to be "justified" by theological thinking, but simply as a "moral category" of its own, a neutral instrument of statecraft and international affairs that could be used for good or ill.[236]

The intersection between Christianity, war and the United States will be explored in more depth in the chapter *War as Love*.

CHAPTER FIVE: ISLAM

> The problem of Islam and violence is not limited to incompatible texts but
> is rooted in the overwhelming preponderance of passages in the *Qu'ran*
> that legitimize violence, warfare and intolerance. Violence in service to
> Allah is both justified and mandated by Allah or Muhammad under the
> sanction of divine threat.[237]

Islam, like most of the world's religions, was founded on and then expanded in blood. Echoing Moses's "blood covenant" sealed with God, the Islamic pact brought divinity and violence together. The Prophet Muhammad was himself a general and warrior, commanding forces in battle on nearly forty separate occasions. After his death, the wars of Islamic domination that he spawned killed hundreds of thousands over the next several centuries, throughout Arabia, the Middle East, North Africa and southern Europe. The Muslim military policy was to kill all those who resisted Islamic domination.[238]

Islam has always represented a political as well as religious structure. "It offers government by immutable law, and provides the believer not only with a revelation of Divine will, but also a highly detailed legal code which regulates all aspects of human behavior."[239] Given how deeply intertwined violence and worship are within this final Abrahamic religion, Islam is an extremely dangerous path. It fuses the violent and sacred impulses within the human spirit, making them indistinguishable for some Muslims.

EARLY ISLAM

> Fighting is prescribed upon you, and ye dislike it. But it is possible that ye dislike a thing that is good for you . . . Allah knoweth and ye know not.[240]

With a warrior-prophet as its founder, a policy of aggressive territorial advancement at the edge of the sword and a conception of holy obligation (*jihad*) that many read, and continue to read, as an obligation to commit murder in the name of God, Islam hardly lived up to its name. The word "Islam," after all, comes from the same root as "Salaam," or "peace," and may be translated as "achieving peace through submission to God's will."

Unfortunately, this "submission" has often involved slaughtering the "other" in God's name. Bruce Chilton noted:

> The Muslim doctrine of the "Four Swords" emerged during the early centuries of spectacular triumph. "*Allah* gave the Prophet Muhammad four swords: the first against the polytheists, which Muhammad himself fought with; the second against apostates, which Caliph Abu Bakr fought with; the third against the People of the Book [Jews and Christians], which Caliph Umar fought with and the fourth against dissenters, which Caliph Ali fought with." This teaching of Al-Shaybani (d. 804) helps explain what motivated the enormous success of Muslim raiders.[241]

Muhammad learned his lesson well from Jewish antecedents as represented in the *Torah*. It is vital to remember that Islam, like Christianity, hardly turned its back on Abrahamic history: Muhammad accepted all the Jewish prophets and stories of the Jewish Bible. However, he claimed to supersede them, due to Jewish iniquity, and said that he was perfecting the way of Abraham and Moses as the final prophet in the lineage dating back to the Genesis narrative.

Although illiterate, Muhammad was obviously aware of the Jewish prophets and their stories. And the Jewish wars of conquest in Deuteronomy were rehearsed in Muhammad's own life. Joseph Montville (Distinguished Diplomat in Residence at American University), writing in the volume *The Crescent and the Couch*, discussed Muhammad's final and definitive battle at Mecca, with the Jewish Qurayza clan:

> Muhammad drew the line with the Qurayza . . . several hundred men were executed, the women and children enslaved and the property divided among the Muslims.[242]

This passage sounds as if it were taken almost verbatim from the Jewish Bible! In Numbers 31, we read:

> And they warred against Midian, as the Lord commanded Moses, and they slew every male . . . And the children of Israel took captive the women of

Midian and their little ones, and they took for the spoil all their cattle and all their flocks and all their goods.[243]

We are left with a Muslim Holy Book that, far from exhorting believers on to peaceful means of worship, sometimes seems to egg them on to commit violence, or perhaps even suffer it, if they cannot live up to the harsh demands of an unrelenting deity:

> Spiritual violence is central to the Qur'an . . . It is embodied in Muhammad and Allah's unrelenting threats of hell and fire, used to condition human behavior . . . the tidy and simplistic view of life is based on God's absolute power and on rigid distinctions between good and evil, between belief and disbelief. It can fuel conflict, encourage intolerance and justify violence whenever historical reality doesn't conform to expectations that flow from the theology and worldview of the Qur'an.[244]

SCRIPTURES

> Those who reject Our Signs, we shall soon cast into the fire; as often as their skins are roasted through, we shall change them for fresh skins. That they may taste penalty: for Allah is exalted in power and wise . . .[245]

Within the Qur'an, as within all of the other Holy Books that humankind has ever penned, one can find numerous passages either exhorting followers on to sacred carnage, or glorifying successful battles, with victory provided by God. These passages are no less vile within the religion literally named after "peace" than any other human creed. Jack Nelson-Pallmeyer in his book *Is Religion Killing Us?* noted the pervasive violent exhortations and imagery that infuse the Islamic text:

> The Qur'an begins each *Surah* [chapter] with comforting words: "In the name of *Allah*, the Beneficent, the Merciful." It is surprising, therefore, that the actual text of nearly every *Surah* uses images of a wrathful, punishing God to condition human behavior . . . God's violence or threatened violence often spills over into human violence done in service to God's will.

In this respect, the Muslim God sounds similar, if not identical, to the wrathful, petulant and violent God of the Hebrews. Far from recasting or diminishing the violence inherent in Judaism's Holy Spirit, the Islamic scriptures simply reinterpret it in a new language, sharing it with a novel and much larger audience and unleashing anew the sacred hostility that lies latent, and all-too-often blatant, within the human conception of God and worship.

Although all religions base their theoretical idea of God and His relationship with man on love, the truth of the matter is far different. All three Abrahamic holy texts liberally utilize the fear of God as an important, if not the main motivator for following religious law, and worshipping the sacred presence. Islam is no different:

> Almost every *Surah* in the *Qur'an* presents fear of God's wrath as the foundation for belief and action. Muhammad, like Matthew, seems unable to imagine people behaving ethically or living out what he understands to be God's will without the threat of God's sanction . . . Muhammad's *Allah* advocates specific actions and threatens people guilty of noncompliance with an "awful doom" or "grievous penalty."[246]

It is not difficult to find specific passages in the *Qur'an* that bear this out. In *Surah* 9:5 (from the chapter "Repentance"), the *Qur'an* states:

> And when the sacred months are passed, kill those who join other gods with God. Wherever you shall find them; and seize them, besiege them and lay wait for them with every kind of ambush.[247]

In the "Cow" *Surah*, we read these lines (2:191-193):

> Kill them wherever you find them. Drive them out of the places from which they drove you. Idolatry is worse than carnage. But do not fight them within the precincts of the Holy Mosque, unless they attack you there; if they attack you, put them to the sword. Thus shall the unbelievers be rewarded . . . Fight against them until idolatry is no more . . .[248]

Implicit in the message is that God is never wrong. Any evil that befalls unbelievers is due to their own iniquities. Leaving aside the psychodynamic that it sets up for the faithful — as no human beings can be perfect to any institutional spiritual system, regardless of how hard they believe or try — the manner in which it shifts blame for the violence to the victim is truly perverse. From the point of view of the religious practitioner, it always justifies *after the fact* any ill that befalls a person.

> How many towns have We destroyed? Our punishment took them on a sudden by night or while they slept for their afternoon rest. When Our punishment took them, no cry did they utter but this: "Indeed we did wrong."[249]

JIHAD

> The bi-partition of the crowd in Islam is unconditional. The faithful and the unbelieving are fated to be separate forever and to fight each other. The war of religion is a sacred duty and thus, though in a less comprehensive form, the double crowd of the Last Judgment is prefigured in every earthly battle.[250]

As painful as it is to acknowledge, *jihad* as holy war was wrapped into Islamic observance from the beginning of the religion. Ann Lambton (d. 2008; a leading British scholar on medieval and early Islamic political theory) stated: "The first duty of the Islamic world is to exalt the word of God until it is supreme. Hence the only proper relationship to the non-Islamic world is one of perpetual warfare . . . The duty of *jihad* is imposed on the follower until the whole world is converted or submits to Islam."[251]

Muhammad, understood from the point of view of many devout Muslims, was a prophet of fighting and war, advocating an expansion of temporal power to represent the expansion of *Allah's* sphere of influence.[252]

Many commentators argue that the true meaning of *jihad* is the internal struggle for spiritual purification. Professor Abdulaziz Sachedina (Frances Myers Ball Professor of Religious Studies at the University of Virginia) stated that the concept of *jihad* as a war to increase the sphere of Islam originated later than the Qur'an, with interpretation by the classical jurists. He was building on ideas from such Muslim historians as Cheragh Ali (d. 1895) who, writing in "A Critical Exposition of the Popular *Jihad*," noted: "*Jihad*, as signifying the waging of war, is a post-Qur'anic usage."

The effort to define the term continues. For instance, a *hadith* (saying of the Prophet Muhammad) that is in circulation states: "Upon his return from battle Muhammad said: 'We have returned from the lesser *jihad* [war] to the greater *jihad* [i.e., the struggle against the evil of one's soul]'." However, as even a cursory web-search will uncover, this *hadith* does not stand up to the rigorous vetting that sayings of the Prophet must withstand, and it is not considered as part of the accepted canon of the Prophet's utterances. In all probability, it was penned long after the death of Muhammad to try to take the edge off of the Islamic prescription to fight (literally) for the faith.

Regardless of how one *might* interpret *jihad*, many Muslims accept the idea of an ongoing Holy War at the center of their religion. That not all agree with the call to arms is irrelevant to the present discussion. Those within Islam who choose to link violence and the sacred can point to thirty-six different appearances of the word violence or one of its derivations in the Qur'an, in each case employed for the practice of warfare.[253]

Like the God of Israel, *Allah* is represented in the Qur'an as a holy warrior.

> The Qur'an presents *Allah* as an all-powerful holy warrior. David slew Goliath "by *Allah's* will" (2:251). Those who fight on behalf of *Allah* defeat armies "twice their number" because *Allah* doth support with His aid whom He pleaseth (3:14) . . . [and] "There is no victory except from *Allah*" (3:126; 8:10).[254]

Later commentators agreed, deepening the linkage between violence and the sacred within the Islamic creed. The medieval Islamic jurist Ahmad ibn Taymiyyah (d. 1328) articulated a definition of *jihad* that made it the pinnacle of Islamic practice:

> The head of the affair is Islam, the central pillar is the *salat* [prayer] and the tip of the hump is the *jihad* . . . Now it is in *jihad* that one can live and die in ultimate happiness, both in this world and in the hereafter.[255]

However, before we grow too breathless with the bellicosity of Islam, especially in the current political climate of Islamophobia, it is important to point out how this same language simply echoes that of the other two Abrahamic faiths.

A violent quote by a Christian purist, basing his ideas on the Old Testament, exhibits how widespread *jihad* is within all of Abraham's spiritual progeny. William Gouge (d. 1653; a Puritan clergyman) expressed his belief in God's approval of wars fought by the "just" against unbelievers:

> The wars of Israel "extraordinarily made by the express charge from God" are those with the "best warrant there could be. Maintenance of Truth and purity of Religion" moved Israel to make war. "Saints" such as Abraham and Joshua, some of the Judges and the "best of the Kings" are cited as having waged war with God's approval. Gouge notes that priests went to war among the Israelites, that "God is said to teach men's hands to war and fingers to fight." Moreover, God himself fights in such wars: "God Himself is styled a man of war."[256]

A Blood Covenant

As has been variously noted, the original covenant between Moses and God, signified by the two tablets of the Ten Commandments, was called a "Blood Covenant." The blood covenant, however, takes many more forms than death. In all religions, various types of self-mortification prove the deep faith of the supplicant. Islam is no different. And a gory eyewitness account from the work of 20th-century essayist (and Nobel Prize Laureate) Elias Canetti recounted one scene of Islamic self-flagellation, the "Day of Blood" in Tehran:

> 500,000 people, seized with madness, cover their heads with ashes and beat their foreheads on the ground. They want to give themselves up to torture, to commit suicide in groups, or to mutilate themselves with a refined cruelty . . . A great silence descends. Men in white shirts advance in hundreds, their faces turned ecstatically to heaven. Of these men, several will be dead by evening, and many more mutilated and disfigured; their shirts, red with blood, will be their shrouds. They are beings who have already ceased to belong to this world . . . With steps of automata they ad-

vance, retreat and move sideways in no apparent order. In time with each step, they strike their heads with their jagged swords. Blood flows and their shirts become scarlet. The sight of the blood brings the confusion in the minds of these voluntary martyrs to a climax. Some of them collapse, striking themselves haphazardly with their swords. In their frenzy they have cut through veins and arteries, and they die where they fall . . . The martyrs take off their shirts, which are now regarded as blessed, and give them to those who carry them . . . No destiny is accounted more beautiful than to die on the feast day of *Ashura*.[257]

Ironically, the holiday is based on Jewish lore. *Ashura* was an ancient Judaic feast day of celebration and atonement. Moses fasted on this day to demonstrate his gratitude to God for the deliverance of the Israelites from Egypt. According to Sunni traditions, Muhammad fasted on this day and encouraged others to fast. It is better known these days for mourning the martyrdom of Hussain ibn Ali, the grandson of the Islamic prophet Muhammad, who was killed at the Battle of Karbala (Iraq) in the 680 (61 AH). Mourners congregate for sorrowful, poetic lamentations performed in memory of the martyrdom.

What better way to honor a fallen martyr than to become one yourself?

ISLAM TODAY

In light of the collective weight of violence-legitimizing passages in the *Qur'an*, it seems something less than forthcoming to speak of Islam [today] as being hijacked by extremists. Passages (from the *Qur'an*) could reasonably be interpreted to justify or even require violence, terrorism and war against enemies in service to *Allah*, or in pursuit of "Islamic justice."[258]

Jihad is problematic today. Many mainstream Muslims want to distance themselves from Osama Bin Laden and *mujahideen* ("strugglers" or "people doing jihad"; the word is from the same Arabic root as *jihad*) in general, but the facts remain clear: for many in Islam, religious war and violence against the "other" are spiritual duties. It is the obligation for all Muslims to fight against disorder and strife caused by unbelief (i.e., lack of acknowledgment that Muhammad is the final prophet, and Islam is the only true religious path) in the world.[259]

The following statement by Osama bin Laden is the kind of thing that is disavowed by mainstream Muslims as *not* representing the true religion, or the concept of *jihad*:

Our encouragement and call to Muslims to enter *jihad* against the American and Israeli occupiers are actions that we are engaging in as religious obligations. *Allah* most high has commanded us in many verses of the *Qur'an* to fight in His path and to urge the believers to do so. These are

His words: "Fight in the path of *Allah*, you are not charged with the responsibility except for yourself, and urge the believers, lest *Allah* restrain the might of the rejecters, and *Allah* is stronger in might and stronger in inflicting punishment."[260]

As much as Islamic practitioners who don't agree with this statement might like to disavow it, as well as the tremendous destruction it has wrought, it is hardly a peripheral interpretation of the Islamic path. Dr. Abdul Aziz Rantisi (a founder of Hamas) expressed a similar appreciation for the holy spirit of justified violence against unbelievers, when he used the word *istishhadi* instead of "suicide bomber" to describe the young men and women littering Israel and other parts of the Middle East with corpses (including their own). "It means self-chosen martyrdom," he averred, adding: "All Muslims seek to be martyrs."[261]

During the Iran–Iraq War (1980–1988), the Iranian government employed suicide bombers against heavily armed Iraqi army positions. The volunteers were acting on their religious duty, to repel the advance of the secular Iraqi army and protect the *dar al-Islam* (the Islamic nation). Death was embraced as an outcome of participating in *jihad*, based on the model of Saladin's (d. 1193) warfare against the Christian Crusaders in Jerusalem.[262]

Holy warriors can point to many contemporary scholars to back their claims. Not only spurious Islamic leaders such as Osama bin Laden but respected, mainstream leaders interpret the many bellicose passages in the Qur'an, and their calls to holy war, in a literal manner. Egyptian theorist and revolutionary Abd al-Salam Faraj (d. 1982) argued that the Qur'an and the *hadith* were fundamentally about warfare. The concept of *jihad* was meant to be taken literally, not allegorically. Faraj regarded anyone who deviated from the moral and social requirements of Islamic law to be targets for *jihad*.[263]

Sometimes the call for holy war is couched within the lexicon of non-violence, confusing matters even more. According to Sheikh Omar Abdul Rahman (b. 1938, a leader of *Al-Gama'a al-Islamiyya*, a militant Islamist movement in Egypt), a Muslim can never call for violence, only for love and forgiveness. However, "if we are aggressed against, if our land is usurped, we must call for hitting the attacker and the aggressor to put an end to the aggression."[264]

In *The Neglected Duty: The Creed of Sadat's Assassins and Islamic Resurgence in the Middle East*, Professor Johannes Jansen explored the contemporary justifications for waging *jihad*, noting that "each Muslim has not only the individual duty to wage *jihad* against threats to Islam but also the individual competence to choose which of many threats he or she is to direct such *jihad* against."[265]

A "JUST WAR"

At the heart of this Islamic "just war" theory are the rulings that provide the impetus and religious cover for the violent acts. A *fatwa* is a written legal decree issued by an Islamic scholar with the breadth of knowledge of *shari'a* (Islamic religious law) to be considered a *mufti* (official religious leader). Most of these opinions cite precedents from decisions by earlier religious scholars, as well as from the body of *hadith* (sayings of the Prophet Muhammad) and the Qur'an.[266]

The principles of Islamic "just war", as represented in violent *jihad*, are based on central Islamic legal judgments that echo a pre-Abrahamic conception of justice. *Mu'amala bil-mithl* (repayment in kind) echoes Hammurabi in the first code of laws ever written (c. 1700 B.C.E.): "an eye for an eye; a tooth for a tooth and a soul for a soul." This idea is accepted within Islamic jurisprudence, with the reservation that the value of a Muslim life is greater than that of a non-believer, being worth up to ten times more. In tabulating the Muslims around the world who have been killed by Americans and their allies, some radical religious leaders have utilized this logarithm to justify the killing of at least four million Americans, up to half of them children.[267]

As Shmuel Bar related in "*Jihad* Ideology in Light of Contemporary *Fatwas*":

> The rise of the modern Islamist *jihad* movement in the last two decades of the 20th century has coincided with the rise of a growing body of *fatwas* that declare *jihad* as a legal religious obligation and define clear guidelines for the waging of *jihad*. These *fatwas* therefore provide moral and legal sanction for acts of terrorism.[268]

It should once again be noted that these rulings are not coming only from peripheral, extremist religious leaders. For instance, the *Fatwa* committee of al-Azhar University (founded in 972; the chief center of Sunni Islamic learning in the world, representing 80% of Islamic practitioners) has issued a wide range of rulings legitimizing suicide terrorism.[269]

Sheikh Ali Gomaa (b. 1952), the Grand Mufti in Egypt and "one of the most widely respected jurists in the Sunni Muslim world,"[270] issued a ruling that runs contrary to his image as an important moderating force in today's Islam, as well as an interfaith pioneer:

> The civilian who occupies land in a state of war is a *harbi* (person from the state of war). Everyone in Israel is *ahl al-qital* (warrior). It is permitted to kill an Israeli traveling abroad because he is a *harbi* and a *harbi* "spreads corruption throughout the face of the earth."[271]

Sheikh Hammoud bin al-Uqlaa al-Shuaibi (one of the leading scholars in the Arabian Peninsula), writing a spare six days after the attacks on the World Trade Center in the United States, took the chance to retroactively justify the action, as well as to call more Muslims to the *jihad*:

> Democratic participation justifies killing civilians . . . due to the fact that they bear responsibility for the decisions made by their elected leaders . . . Similarly, the attacks of 9/11 were justified because "every decision made by the *kafer* (disbeliever) state, America, particularly those which relate to war, is based on public opinion through referendum and/or voting in the House of Representatives or Senate. Every American, having participated in this opinion poll and having voted regarding the war, is considered a combatant or at least a party to the war."[272]

Ultimately, as Shmuel Bar notes:

> The role of the *ulama* [Islamic scholars] and their *fatwas* in legitimizing terrorism is a pivotal element in the social and political legitimization of terrorism and in the motivation of its supporters. The rulings analyzed above are not merely political manifests aimed at motivating followers, but serve as an important tool in the battle pitched between radical and mainstream Muslims over the future of Islam.[273]

He continues on to note that legal counter-attacks are few and far between from moderate scholars and *mufti*. This is due, Bar claims, to the deference that mainstream *ulama* feel toward the radicals as "quintessential believers." The problem is exacerbated by an unwillingness to take any stances that might cause internal divisions within the Islamic nation.[274]

Islamic violence and terrorist acts are situated within that creed's Holy Writ and history. Violence as religious practice is normative Islam. This is *not* to single out this religion in any particular way, for as we shall see in the final section, it is sacred violence within Christianity *today* which is as great a threat to world peace and the continuation of the human species, as that found within Islam or any other of the sacrificial cults that we call "World Religions."

CHAPTER SIX: HINDUISM

> I am time grown old, creating world destruction set in motion to anni-
> hilate the worlds; even without you, all these warriors arrayed in hostile
> ranks will cease to exist. Therefore, arise and win glory! Conquer your
> foes and fulfill your kingship! They are already slain by me. Be just my
> instrument, the archer at my side.[275]

The violence of God tradition is certainly not sequestered within the
Abrahamic faiths, or the West. The Eastern creeds as well harbor a dark
secret. Religions considered steeped in interior and exterior peace such
as Hinduism, Sikhism and even Buddhism are awash in sacred blood
spilled in the name of God.

Hinduism is the predominant religious tradition of South Asia and
with nearly one billion adherents worldwide, is the third largest religion
in the world (after Christianity and Islam). It is formed of diverse traditions and has no single founder.

Unlike virtually all religions that postdated the ancient Indian creed,
Hinduism is not based on the teachings of a single inspired leader, but
on a collection of ancient and more recent texts. It has evolved over the
millennia based on these scriptures, through a back-and-forth conversation between diverse interpretations and practices. Even the name of the
faith, "Hindu," is foreign to it. Muslim invaders first used the appellation
in the eighth century to refer to the customs and beliefs of these people[276]
that they considered infidels.

Among Hindu texts, the *Vedas* (the world's oldest sacred texts) are
the foremost in authority, importance and antiquity. Other major scrip-

tures include the *Upanishads* (of which more than 200 are known), the *Mahabharata* (epic narrative of the Kurukshetra War, which took place in the ancient past), the *Ramayana* and finally the *Puranas* (history of the universe from creation to destruction). The *Bhagavad Gita*, a treatise from the *Mahabharata*, is of special importance.

The *Mahabharata* itself is a massive work of special significance to world spirituality. Weighing in at 1.8 million words — larger than the *Iliad* and *Odyssey* combined — it has been has compared in importance to the Bible, the writings of Shakespeare, the works of Homer, Greek drama, and the *Qur'an*.[277]

This epic account is centered on war and glorifies armed conflict as the highest spiritual activity:

> The rituals of warrior life and the demands of sacred duty define the religious and moral meaning of heroism throughout the *Mahabharata* . . . The distinctive martial religion of this epic emerges from a synthesis of values derived from the ritual traditions of the Vedic sacrificial cult combined with loyalty to a personal deity.[278]

The Hindu concept of religion is expressed by the Sanskrit term *dharma* (sacred duty), which refers to the moral order that sustains the universe. Within Hindu culture, it generally means religiously ordained duty.[279] However, given the foundational importance of the martial class and war, it comes as no surprise that duty can often take a violent turn. The Hindu religion gives high value to its warrior caste[280] and it justifies and requires warfare and violence, as can be seen in its sacred text, the *Bhagavad Gita*.[281]

BHAGAVAD GITA

> If you fail to wage this war of sacred duty, you will abandon your own duty and fame only to gain evil. People will tell of your undying shame, and for a man of honor, shame is worse than death . . . If you are killed, you win heaven; if you triumph, you enjoy the earth; therefore, Arjuna, stand and resolve to fight the battle.[282]

The *Bhagavad Gita* (Song of God) is the best known of the Hindu scriptures, one that you will find the Hare Krishna (a Hindu religious movement founded in New York City in 1966) giving away on street corners, and which you will likely read if you take an "Introduction to World Religions" course during your university years.

The narrative forms around counsel by Lord Krishna (who is considered to be a manifestation of God) to Prince Arjuna (Krishna's dear friend and brother-in-law) during the Kurukshetra War (dated as early as 6000 B.C.E.; a conflict between two groups of cousins of an Indo-Aryan tribe).

At times referred to as the "manual for mankind," it has been highly praised by not only prominent Indians such as Gandhi but also by Aldous Huxley, Albert Einstein, Ralph Waldo Emerson, Carl Jung and Hermann Hesse. Although the *Bhagavad Gita* clearly encourages war, and a holy one, at that, Gandhi reinterpreted it "to be a spiritual message requiring human beings to struggle against the violence within in order to nonviolently transform the world without."[283]

While Gandhi's is certainly a noble sentiment, it is also another example of how well intentioned religious followers deny the specific meanings of their own faith's texts, not countering the violent narrative but simply avoiding it. As we see time and again, this denial does little to stem the gruesome tides of religiously sanctioned violence, only marginalizing these thinkers from the mainstream of their own religions.

In Gandhi's case, his non-violent approach led a fellow Hindu to kill him, shooting him three times at point-blank range. It was the Hindu fanatic (who could not forgive Gandhi for his belief that Muslims had equal value to Hindus and no-one was better than anybody else) who perhaps had best heeded Krishna's counsel, and not the international peacemaker.

The context of the *Gita* is a conversation between Lord Krishna and the Pandava prince Arjuna taking place on the battlefield before the start of the Kurukshetra War. Far from providing counsel of peace and forgiveness, this central Hindu scripture lays out explicitly the nexus between obedience to God and the necessity of war. They are represented as the same thing. And, coming from what many to believe to be the oldest remaining scriptural text still in use today, the *Bhagavad Gita* provides a scrim through which to view all other religions, as they fuse violence, the sacred and obedience to God into a unbreakable, deeply destructive dynamic.

The premise of the *Gita* (as it is affectionately known) is that in relinquishing attachment to the fruits of action and giving oneself to God, one attains true peace.

> A man who relinquishes attachment and dedicates actions to the infinite spirit is not stained by evil, like a lotus leaf unstained by water. Relinquishing attachment, men of discipline perform action with body, mind, understanding and the senses for the purification of the self. Relinquishing the fruit of action, the disciplined man attains perfect peace.[284]

The explicit message of Krishna's counsel is that the highest form of action is that of the warrior. The *Bhagavad Gita's* subtitle is: "Krishna's Counsel in a Time of War," and the premise is that Arjuna, reluctant to engage in an armed conflict with his own kin, must be cajoled into undertaking the battle. Lord Krishna assures: "He incurs no guilt if he has no hope, restrains his thought and himself, abandons possessions and performs actions with his body only."[285]

The *Gita* also makes the same claim that some Buddhist warriors would millennia later: that as the individual person truly has no "personhood," killing is not possible, and the only aspect of the slaughter that matters is the obedience to the religious precepts. "The self embodied in the body of every being is indestructible; you have no cause to grieve for all of these creatures, Arjuna! Look to your own duty . . . nothing is better for a warrior than a battle of sacred duty."[286]

In the end, Krishna is explicit about his demand that Arjuna fight his kin — advice that Gandhi's assassin certainly could have had in mind while pulling the trigger.

> Our bodies are known to end, but the disembodied self is enduring, indestructible and immeasurable; therefore, Arjuna, fight the battle. He who thinks this self a killer and thinks it killed, both fail to understand; it does not kill nor is it killed.[287]

Krishna goes on to note that human beings cannot exist without action — that non-action is impossible, and therefore, circumstances define the actor's possibilities, not the actor himself. "No one exists for even an instant without performing action; every being is forced to act by the qualities of nature."[288] Therefore, it is disciplined action that defines the highest good — action performed without attachment to the fruit of the action, fueled by obedience.

Arjuna finally gives in completely to the wise counsel of Lord Krishna. He comes to appreciate the inevitability of his own actions, realizing that by performing his warrior duties with absolute devotion, he can unite with Krishna's cosmic purpose and free himself from the crippling attachments that bind mortals to eternal suffering.[289] Krishna goes so far as to insist that Arjuna's objections to killing his relatives are based in the same subjective, worldly desire that blinds his foes.[290]

If you hear echoes of a later religion, Buddhism, in aspects of this exposition — concerning devotion, inevitability, attachment to desire and "self" — then your ear is finely tuned. The Buddha lived in what is now the border area between India and Nepal, not far from the lands where the *Bhagavad Gita* emerged. The Buddha was born into a Hindu family, and his religious beliefs were an extension and recasting of the ancient Indian religion.

The *Gita* is honest in one very important respect. By bringing violence and the sacred together explicitly, humanity's violent tendencies can at least be separated from the center of social interaction and channeled into action against the "other," those who exist outside of the social unit. As translator Barbara Stoler Miller (Samuel R. Milbank Professor of Asian and Middle Eastern Cultures, Barnard College) noted:

> Though much of Krishna's teaching seems remote from the moral chaos that Arjuna envisions will be a consequence of his killing his kinsman, Krishna's doctrine of disciplined action is a way of bringing order to life's destructive aspect. When the puzzled Arjuna asks: "Why do you urge me to do this act of violence?" Krishna . . . identifies the real enemy as desire, due to attachment, an enemy that can only be overcome by arming oneself with discipline and acting to transcend the narrow limits of individual desire.[291]

Unfortunately, what we find in virtually all societies and time periods is that although individual warriors attempt to overcome their own personal sense of self and desire and fuse into something greater (i.e., the army), the leaders who command the armies never do. Religion becomes a way for leaders reeking of "desire and attachment" to cause the spiritually desperate to perpetrate mass murder. Time and again this dynamic plays itself out. And as we will see in the last section of this study, even today in the United States, this exact same formulation set forth nearly 5,000 years ago in northern India remains as powerful and central to society as it was then.

Violent Imagery

With a religious text based on a sacred war, much violent imagery is utilized. Krishna's exposition of the relationship between death, sacrifice and devotion highlights the Hindu idea that one must heroically confront death in order to transcend the limits of worldly existence.[292] If one is unfortunate enough to not be confronting death at that moment, one must nonetheless imagine the horrors of the physical destruction of the self to help him or her attain greater spiritual understanding and detachment.

When Arjuna finally comes to understand that his participation in this war and slaughter of his family members is a divine duty, he is able to see Krishna in his entirety. What he discovers is hardly a comforting sight:

Seeing the fangs protruding from your mouths like the fires of time, I lose my bearing and I find no refuge . . . Rushing through your fangs into grim mouths, some [past warrior kings] are dangling from heads crushed between your teeth . . . As moths in the frenzy of destruction fly into a blazing flame, worlds in the frenzy of destruction enter your mouths. You lick at the worlds around you, devouring them with flaming mouths; and your terrible fires scorch the entire universe . . .[293]

It is also noted that Lord Krishna's true form was a "multi-form, wondrous vision, with countless mouths and eyes and celestial ornaments, brandishing many divine weapons."

Further examples of violence are rife in other Hindu scriptures. As Mark Juergensmeyer noted in *Terror in the Mind of God*:

The simple justification for fighting in battle — killing or being killed in sacred struggle — runs deep in India's religious traditions . . . In India's ancient Vedic times, warriors called on gods to participate in their struggles and to provide divine leverage for victory. The potency of the gods was graphically depicted in mythic stories filled with violent encounters and bloody acts of vengeance.[294]

It is not difficult to find the kind of specific text that would lead to such a belief. The *Rig Veda* (c. 1500 B.C.E.) implores: "May your weapons be strong to drive away the attackers, may your arms be powerful enough to check the foes, let your army be glorious." (1-39:2)

We also find Kali, the Hindu goddess of eternal energy, demanding a violent fealty to the faith: "Lay down your life, but first take a life . . . The worship of the goddess will not be consummated if you sacrifice your lives at the shrine of independence without shedding blood."[295]

Additionally, the myths show how all members of the society must perform the violence for it to be ritualistically effectual, helping to cement the idea of gathering together to commit communal carnage in the name of the sacred. Here are the early underpinnings of war: that sacred violence must be attended by all members of the clan and visited upon someone outside of the group, to be restorative.

René Girard noted one such event in the *Yadjour-Veda* (c. 1400 B.C.E.):

The *Yadjour-Veda* speaks of a sacrificial ceremony in which a god, *Soma*, is to be put to death by the other gods. *Mithra* [the patron divinity of honesty, friendship, etc.] at first refuses to join his divine companions in this act, but he is finally persuaded to do so by the argument that the sacrifice will be totally ineffectual if not performed by all . . . Unanimity is a formal requirement of sacrifice; the abstention of a single participant renders the sacrifice even worse than useless — it makes it dangerous.[296]

Girard continues, in *Violence and the Sacred*, to note that all religious rituals spring from the surrogate victim.

> It could hardly be otherwise, for the working of human thought, the process of "symbolization," is rooted in the surrogate victim . . . archetypal myths tell how all man's religious, familial, economic and social institutions grew out of the body of an original victim. The surrogate victim . . . permits men to escape their own violence, removes them from violence, and bestows on them all the institutions and beliefs that define their humanity.[297]

We can situate this dynamic within the deepest past of the human spiritual narrative, as evidenced in the early Hindu texts. The *Shatapatha Brahmana* (c. 300 B.C.E., although it contains portions that are far older, transmitted orally from unknown antiquity[298]) explains in explicit detail how the original sacrifice of a man led to the fecundity of the Earth:

> In the beginning, the Gods sacrificed a man; when he was killed, his ritualistic virtues deserted him. They entered a horse; the gods sacrificed the horse; when it was killed, its ritualistic virtues deserted it. They entered a cow; the gods sacrificed the cow; when it was killed, its ritualistic virtues deserted it. They entered a sheep; the gods sacrificed the sheep; when it was killed, its ritualistic virtues deserted it. They entered a goat; the gods sacrificed the goat. When it was killed, its ritualistic virtues deserted it and entered the earth. The gods dug for them, and found them in the form of rice and barley. And that is why today we still dig the earth to procure rice and barley.[299]

"Just War"

All religions have developed some form of a "just war" theory, which allows a given party to wage war while still retaining the fiction of being a victim of some aggression, and therefore fighting only in self-defense. In all cases, these theories evolve out of religious thinking and are theologically backed, usually by the scriptures or respected religious leaders in the particular creed.

Hinduism is no different, and as the oldest continually practiced religion, perhaps it set the template that would be followed over the next 5,000 years from the shores of the China Sea to the Potomac River. Dr. Surya Subedi (University of Leeds, England) outlined this Hindu ideal in his article "The Concept in Hinduism of "'just war'"":

> Hinduism is based on a concept known as *dharma*. The essence of dharma is the distinction between good, supporting the cosmic order, and evil, which poses a threat to this order. Accordingly, the preservation of good at the cost of a war was justified in ancient Vedic society . . . The concept

of *dharma* in its original sense means the maintenance of peace and security through the law and order within the larger cosmic order. Thus, the
concept of "just war" in Hinduism is against the evil characters of the day,
whether national or alien. It is based on right and wrong and on justice
and injustice in the everyday life of all mortals, whether Hindus or non–
Hindus. Unlawful and unjust actions, e.g. the denial of the rights to which
one was entitled, gave rise to "just war"s.[300]

The point that Hinduism shares with all other "just war" theories is
that it must take place against the "evil characters of the day," which can
be defined as those specifically in opposition to the geo-political desires
of the leadership of a tribe or nation. Recently we saw George W. Bush
justify his bellicose intentions in this exact same way, and while there
are dozens of specific quotes by Bush equating America's enemies with
"evil" (and therefore justifying the war within his religious beliefs), one
such quote will suffice to stand for the dozens which are extant:

> We are at the beginning of what I view as a very long struggle against evil.
> We're not fighting a nation; we're not fighting a religion; we're fighting
> evil. And we have no choice but to prevail. We're fighting people that hate
> our values, they can't stand what America stands for. And they really don't
> like the fact that we exist. And I want to assure you all that we will fight
> this fight on every front. We will use every resource we have. And there
> is no doubt in my time — in my mind — that in our time, we will prevail.
> There's no doubt.[301]

The reason I am weaving together the streams of sacred violence,
across all religions and all time periods, is to show how endemic this
connection is. It is a human problem — one that haunts us, as the above
quote shows, to this day. Until we appreciate this fact, and react accordingly, any attempts to root out the evil "out there" will be but another
primitive reaction of scapegoating and sacrifice to forge a sacred community out of "us" through religious-based violence against "them."

HINDUS TODAY

Contemporary Hindu adventurism is not hard to uncover, staining
the Indian subcontinent red with righteously spilled blood. An article in
the *Washington Post* addressed one specific instance of Hindu violence, in
this case directed against Christians:

> Babita Nayak was cooking lunch for her pregnant sister when a mob of
> Hindu extremists wielding swords, hammers and long sticks rampaged
> through their village chanting: "India is for Hindus! Convert or leave!" The
> men ransacked dozens of huts, torched the village church, leaving behind
> Bibles and torn down posters of Jesus.[302]

Religious violence within all creeds is often focused on the members of other religious paths, generally those closest at hand. It is not wanton and anarchic violence; it is specifically directed at the other's god, as if the existence of another deity in their geographical space somehow calls their own faith into question.

It is an expression of existential insecurity. As earlier noted, the god of all religions is parsimonious. There is not enough god to go around, in terms of sharing god's benevolence between creeds. Additionally, it is as if the faith of even the most faithful is not quite strong enough. That is to say, faith alone is not enough. Therefore, fealty to a particular god must be proved in two manners: with victory in armed conflict, as well as the eradication of competing faiths. God is great, true — but God never seems to be quite great *enough*, nor can He completely satiate the internal spiritual deficits of His followers. His power must be proven through victory in the basest of human experiences.

An article by journalist Nirmala Carvalho in *Compass Direct* outlined further, and widespread instances of Hindu attacks on Christians:

> By last June [2005] the number of violent attacks recorded by Christian organizations had reached over 200. This number was expected to double by year's end. "This year Hindu extremists have beaten our priests, as-saulted our nuns, broken crosses and urinated on sacred vessels," said Dr. John Dayal, president of the All India Catholic Union. "These acts of des-ecration show the true nature of the attackers." Attacks were reported in Haryana, Rajasthan, Gujarat, Punjab, Uttar Pradesh and the states of tribal central India.[303]

The only way I disagree with Dr. John Dayal is that the acts of dese-cration actually show the true nature of humanity and not just the Hindu attackers.

And lest we become too secure in the belief that the problems that Hindus have is generally with Christians, they certainly have no love for Muslims, either. An article in *Time Magazine*, "Hindu–Muslim Violence Imperils India" explored the clash of these two major religions:

> Ayodhya [Uttar Pradesh state] is at the epicenter of communal hostility stoked by Hindu nationalists in defiance of modern India's founding tradi-tion of secular tolerance. In 1992, the city became the focus of the worst communal violence since India's partition 45 years earlier, when 2,000 people died in clashes after Hindu nationalists tore down the 16th-century Babri mosque. Hindus claim the mosque had originally been built on the site of a temple marking the birthplace of the Hindu deity Lord Rama. Now that same strife threatens to topple the government of Prime Minis-ter Atal Behari Vajpayee. Seventy people were killed in Gujarat province

on Thursday, as Hindu mobs attacked Muslims and torched a mosque and other Islamic facilities.[304]

This is not to say that *only* the Hindus have resorted to violence in this conflict — as the article also noted: "The violence came as retaliation for Wednesday's firebombing by Muslims of a train carrying Hindu activists returning from Ayodhya. Fifty-eight people, many of them women and children, died in that attack." Neither side, though assuredly a "religion of peace" in their own minds, is able to rise above the righteous orgy of violence committed in the name of their god, even when women and children are involved.

Not constrained to attacks against the Abrahamic faiths, there is a violent history between Hindus and Buddhists dating back thousands of years. An article by Dr. M. S. Jayaprakash, a noted history scholar and social activist of Kerala, related in his article "Hindu Violence against Buddhism in India has no Parallel":

> The Hindu ruler, Pushyamitra Sunga [d. 151 B.C.E.], demolished 84,000 Buddhist *stupas* that had been built by Ashoka the Great. It was followed by the smashing of the Buddhist centres in Magadha. Thousands of Buddhist monks were mercilessly killed.[305]

In our times, the civil war in Sri Lanka has taken place between the majority Buddhist population (Sinhalese) and Hindus (Tamil). In fact, it was the Tamil Hindus who popularized the use of the "suicide bomber." From July 1987, when the Tamil separatist movement (LTTE) carried out its first suicide attack, through 2009, it conducted more than 170 suicide attacks, and the suicide attack became a trademark of the LTTE and a characteristic of the civil war. As Lynn Neary reported on National Public Radio, "Sri Lanka's [Hindu] Tamil Tiger rebels didn't invent the suicide bomb, but they pioneered it as a tactic in war."[306]

SIKHISM

It might seem unfair to include what is a very different religion — Sikhism — as a subject covered under the larger umbrella of Hinduism. But Guru Nanak (d. 1539), a Hindu born of the *Khatri*, a warrior tribe from northern India, founded Sikhism. Additionally, the Guru shared many common beliefs with Hinduism, such as *karma*, *dharma*, reincarnation, and meditating on God's name to break the cycle of birth. Founded in the 15th century in Punjab, it is a monotheistic religion, and the fifth-largest organized religion in the world, as well as one of the fastest growing.

Buddhism grew out of Hinduism as well, making the ancient Indian creed similar to Judaism, in that it is progenitor of a trinity of central world religions. Taken together, people of the Abrahamic and Hindu-influenced creeds constitute nearly three quarters of the world's population. All of them have been steeped in the concept of sacral violence.

As with most religions, the initial introduction to Sikhism reveals a beautiful, egalitarian path. Sikh teaching emphasizes the principle of equality of all humans and rejects discrimination on the basis of caste, creed or gender. As defined by the Sikh Missionary Society in the United Kingdom:

> Sikhism stands for human liberty, equality and fraternity. It believes in universal brotherhood, universal peace and prosperity with commitment for selfless service to the entire human race. The Sikh prayer all over the world is not confined to a single community, a nation or a country. It is for wellbeing of the entire human race. It is universal and all embracing. It is not confined to a single caste, color, creed, country or a gender. It does not know man-made barriers or cruel diversities.[307]

However, as is often the case, somewhere between stated beliefs and action, things change. As Mark Juergensmeyer noted: "The history of Sikhism is one of violent encounters."[308] The motivation for its institutional, religiously based violence may be situated in Sikhism's most respected leaders. For instance, the sixth Guru of the religion (Hargobind Sahib, d. 1644) exhorted his followers to combine religion and worldly engagement, including the "sword to hit oppressors."[309]

The most frequently displayed symbol of Sikhism today is the double-edged sword, adding violent iconography to the foundation of this faith. It provides an image of the domestication of violence, and it is worn on lockets, emblazoned on shops and garden gates and stands in front of Sikh *gurdwaras* ("Gateway to the Guru," or a place of worship for Sikhs), "where it is treated with the same reverence as Christians treat their own emblem of destruction and triumph, the Cross."[310]

Like followers of all religious paths, the Sikhs' wrath sometimes knows no bounds. Sohar Singh (d. 1968), an Indian revolutionary, the founding president of the Ghadar Party and a labor rights activist, "spoke eloquently about the role of love in Sikhism," though if others try to kill you, you are warranted in trying to kill them. He claimed that the killings undertaken by militants were always done with a higher purpose and were not simply "killing for killing's sake."[311]

More recently, Jarnail Singh Khalsa Bhindranwale (d. 1984) was inspired by the idea of *miri-piri*, the notion that spiritual and temporal power are linked. This is a fairly common justification given by "just war" theories in all religions, and one that inspires warriors to this day. Brute force successfully applied proves the spiritual power through victory.

Bhindranwale, building on ideas of spiritual warfare, "projected the image of a great war between Good and Evil waged in the present day — 'a struggle for our faith, for the Sikh nation, for the oppressed.' He implored his young followers to rise up and marshal the forces for righteousness."[312] His life ended in a hail of gunfire in the Golden Temple in Amritsar, which he had taken over and fortified with light machine-guns and sophisticated self-loading rifles.

Today, the Sikhs' highest authority, Akal Takht (the designated leader of the Sikh nation), describes him as a "great martyr" of the Sikh community who made the "supreme sacrifice" for the sake of "faith."

Chapter Seven: Buddhism

> The ideas and people encountered in the subterranean realm of Buddhism are the exact inverse of those on the surface. Down below, warfare and killing are described as manifestations of Buddhist compassion . . . The purpose of religion is to preserve the state and punish any country or person who dared to interfere with its right of self-aggrandizement.[313]

Buddhism is not the oldest of religions, having been founded in the 5th century B.C.E. by the Buddha (d. 483 B.C.E.; born to the rulers of the *Shakya* clan, hence his appellation Sakyamuni, which means "sage of the *Shakya* clan"). But in terms of this study, it is the quintessential representation of religious hypocrisy.

Buddhism, more than any other religion, is considered to be a creed founded on peace and nonviolence. As Dr. Mahinda Deegalle (professor at the University of Bath in England; studied at the University of Chicago and Harvard) noted in an article on violence and Buddhism:

> Buddhist teachings maintain that under any circumstances, whether political, religious cultural or ethnic, violence cannot be accepted or advocated in solving disputes between nations. All Buddhist traditions unanimously agree that war cannot be the solution to disputes and conflicts, either. Even for achieving religious goals, violence cannot be justified. A Buddhist cannot imagine a principle of a "'just war'."[314]

Buddhism claims to eschew *all* violent behavior. "The ultimate goal of a person treading the path of Buddhism is the attainment of perpetual inner peace. The Theravada Canonical scriptures contain absolutely no instance in which violence is advocated as a means for achieving it."[315]

Additionally, there is no history or call to forced conversion in Buddhism. Dr. Mahinda Deegalle noted:

> There is not a single example of persecution or the shedding of a drop of blood in converting people to Buddhism, or in its propagation during its long history of 2,500 years. It spread peacefully over all the continent of Asia.[316]

As a layperson, this was certainly my understanding of the Buddhist path, prior to beginning research for this book. Under no circumstances, I thought, could a practicing Buddhist justify even so much as killing a fly — let alone participating in a war. I still have seared into my memory the description of a friend of mine, who later went on to become a Buddhist nun and spend several years in a solitary meditation retreat, of her first visit to Nepal. A college student at the time, she unthinkingly swatted at a fly that was buzzing about her head and was met by the horrified gaze of her host. To kill a living being!

But alas, the deeper I searched into Buddhist history, liturgy and politics, the more I discovered the exact same violent, war-like language and behavior that is evident in all other religious paths on this earth. In fact, despite Dr. Deegalle's insistence that Buddhists have never in their long history practiced forced conversion, Mark Juergensmeyer, in his *Terror in the Mind of God*, shared a vision of Buddhism that aligns itself more with *jihadi* Islam than the non-violent fantasies of quietists everywhere:

> The great expansion of Buddhism in various parts of the world has been credited in part to the support given it by victorious kings and military forces who have claimed to be fighting only to defend the faith against infidels and to establish a peaceful moral order.[317]

As Brian Daizen Victoria noted in *Zen at War*:

> The original message [of Buddhism] was buried under a series of compromises with oppressive political systems in India, China, Japan and elsewhere. In all of these countries, Buddhism has been used as an instrument of state policy for subduing rather than liberating the population.[318]

The Buddhist justification for violence against the "other" is rooted in the underlying premise of the religion's teachings: that the individual human being has no true existence apart from the universal ground of all being, and that this being is similar to, if not the same as, "nothingness." God is represented by a substantive existence so fine that we can neither perceive nor understand it without completely eviscerating all traces of our own selfhood.

The fifth-century Buddhist thinker Houei-Yan encapsulated the fluid thinking that underpins Buddhist justifications for violence and war:

If we admit that the Other and I are identical, and that there is no opposition between our two minds, then from the point of view of the transcendent absolute, which is one, swords that crisscross are neutralized.
There is no conflict between weapons that bang together. Not only does
someone who injures another do no harm to the soul, but there is certainly
no living being that is killable. It is in this sense that, when Manjusri [a *bodhisattva*, or spiritually enlightened being, associated with transcendent
wisdom] took up his sword, he was able to have the appearance of going
against Buddhist morality, but in reality, he was abiding by it.[319]

VIOLENT IMAGERY

Much violent imagery within Buddhism stems from the Indian subcontinent and even dates back to the time of the Buddha. For instance,
Stephen Jenkins (Professor of Religious Studies at Humboldt State University) noted in his article, "Making Merit Through Warfare":

> The Buddha is depicted as an attempted murder victim on multiple occa-
> sions and even as the victim of a conspiracy to implicate him in a murder-
> ous sex scandal (*Jataka* 285) . . . If legend and scripture are any indication,
> the violence of the Indian Buddhist's imagination, and probably the vio-
> lence of their world, was extreme.[320]

This violence in and of itself is not troubling. After all, Buddhism
arose to counteract this aggressive expression. The Buddha was trying to
solve the problem of human violence, so it stands to reason that he must
have seen plenty of it in his time. Also, that someone tried to murder or
conspire against him in no way contradicts his message of nonviolence, it
only makes it more pressing.

However, the line between violence and non-violence was never completely drawn, not even by the Buddha. The oft-quoted story of Buddha
killing one person to save many (the story that came to underpin Buddhist "just war" theory in virtually all Buddhist states) is told in *Upay-
akausalya Sutra* (c. 1st century B.C.E.; The Skill in Means). Brian Peter
Harvey (Co-founder of the U.K. Association for Buddhist Studies), explained the importance of this story in his *Introduction to Buddhist Ethics*:

> Some texts justify killing a human being, on the grounds of compassion
> in dire circumstances. A key text here is the *Upayakausalya Sutra*. This
> says that taking a life is un-reprehensible if "it develops from a virtuous
> thought." A key passage in the text tells of Buddha in a past life as a *bod-
> hisattva* sea captain named Great Compassion who was transporting 500
> merchants. One night, deities inform him in a dream that one of the pas-
> sengers is intent on killing the others and stealing all of their goods. He
> realizes that the robber will suffer in hell for eons for such a deed, as the

merchants are all *bodhisattvas* . . . Accordingly, with great compassion and skill in means, he kills the robber, who is reborn in heaven. A similar story is found in the *Maha-Upayakausalya Sutra*, where the *bodhisattva* feels compelled to kill the scout for 500 bandits, even though he is an old friend, to save the lives of 500 merchants.[321]

The importance of these texts cannot be overstressed, as they became the basis for violent Buddhism, an impetus that is present today in Sri Lanka, Burma and even the United States (as we will see further along). These texts were *Mahayana* scripture, and *Mahayana* Buddhism originated in India and is the larger of the two major traditions of Buddhism existing today.

BUDDHIST LITURGY

The fundamental *Tantric* [scriptural] narrative is one of subjugation, a forced conversion of the non-Buddhists or a taming of the infidels. Conversely . . . the Buddhist *Sangha* [community] looks sometimes like a besieged citadel . . . Buddhists have constantly resorted to the demonization of their rivals, Buddhist or non-Buddhist.[322]

We can find numerous examples of violence in Buddhist scripture and canon. Even in the *Dhammapada* (Path of Righteousness), a text that is ascribed to the Buddha, it is impossible to escape the use of sadistic language to describe the path of this religion of peace.

Having slain mother and father and two *Khattiya* [a royal lineage at the time of the Buddha] kings, having slain a kingdom together with the subordinate, without trembling the *brahmana* goes. Having slain mother and father and two learned kings, having slain the tiger's domain, a fifth, without trembling the *brahmana* goes.[323]

This language is (theoretically) meant as a metaphor. In other versions of this text it is translated as "Having slain mother craving, father self-conceit," making explicit the symbol. Once violent imagery is included in canonical texts, however, the movement from image to action is swift. After all, it is easy to see in a specific, living enemy "mother craving" and "father self-conceit," as the whole point of institutional violence is that it allows us to project our own interior violent tendencies onto an "other" — a scapegoat — and then destroy this part of ourselves through violent acts. By placing this violence, even imagerically, within sacred text, the leap to violent action becomes much easier.

Later Buddhist thinkers situated hostility in the realm of the *bodhisattva*, or enlightened Buddhist practitioner. The *bodhisattva* renounces his own eternal salvation in Nirvana, vowing to help save all human souls. In order to accomplish this compassionate mission, however, Buddhist liturgy sometimes taught that the *bodhisattva* might have to break accepted Buddhist precepts, and humiliate, torture and even kill for the sake of the "lost" person's salvation.[324]

The reasoning generally went that the *bodhisattva* was of such purity as to render his or her motives unquestionable. Therefore, if the *bodhisattva* chooses to kill, it *must* be for the purest of reasons, such as to save someone from themselves, incurring the negative karma on their person while releasing their victim to ultimate realization. A truly selfless act!

Some *Madhyamaka* thinkers (a school of Buddhism, c. 250) proposed that *bodhisattvas* could undertake actions normally considered forbidden, including killing, as long as they remained compassionate while doing so. In the *Sikasamuccaya* (c. 8th century; a compendium of Buddhist doctrine), Santideva says that the very things which send others to hell send a *bodhisattva* to the heavenly *Brahmalokas* (where refined souls exist in blissful contemplation of *Brahma*).

This is hardly out of line with teachings about the Buddha himself. The *Mahaparinirvana Sutra* (c. 200 or earlier, also known as the Nirvana Sutra), a major *Mahayana Sutra* tells the story of the Buddha killing several Brahmins in a previous life, and in so doing preventing them from slandering the *dharma* (natural order of things). The Buddha's murders are presented as growing out of his compassion, to save the evildoers from the *karmic* consequences of their actions.[325]

The *Nirvana Sutra* continues on to exhort Buddhists to "protect the *dharma* at all costs," even if this means committing murder. This echoes teachings in the *Gandavyuha Sutra* (c. 50 B.C.E.), which tells the story of an Indian king who "made killing into a divine service in order to reform people through punishment."[326]

It is important to note that this idea of killing to save a soul (echoing the thinking behind the Christian Inquisition), when coupled with the concept that Buddhist states actually represent the institutionalization of *bodhisattva*-hood on a grand scale, was used to justify whole populations engaging in compassionate killing in defense of the state and the Buddhist values of compassion, peace and love.

The violence in the Buddha's text is hardly the only place where bellicose imagery may be found. Foundational text after foundational text bears the imprint of hatred and slaughter. For instance, Asanga (d. 370), considered a founder of the *Yogacara* school of Buddhism, argued in his *Bodhisattva-bhumi* (Levels of Enlightenment) that compassionate violence offers merit for killing. For Asanga, compassionate killing was an option not just for the realized *bodhisattva*, but also for the civil leader, the king.[327]

Stephen Jenkins explained in his article, "Merit through Warfare and Torture":

> The *Arya-Satyakaparivarta* (The Noble Teachings through Manifestations on the Subject of Skillful Means in the Bodhisattva's Field of Activity) argues that compassionate torture that does not result in permanent physical damage may have a beneficial influence on the character of the victim . . . the *Sutra* says that weapons cannot harm a warrior protected by good *karma*. The unstated implications are that one's victims must be ripe for their own destruction, and that losing suggests a moral failure on the part of the loser.[328]

In the *Saddharmasmrtyupasthana* (c. 692; *Sutra* of Right Mindfulness) "the Lord Yama is depicted as ordering his servants to mutilate and hack to pieces the body of a guilty party, who was destined for this type of *karmic* retribution."[329] The *Jataka Sutra* (c. 100 B.C.E.), concerning the previous lives of the Buddha, "is full of stories of Buddhist warriors, often the Buddha himself in a past life, and occasionally romanticizes their heroic deaths in battle."[330]

The *Jataka Sutra* continues on to note that if a king kills "with compassionate intentions, he may make great merit through warfare, so warfare becomes auspicious. The same argument was made earlier in relation to torture, and the *sutra* proceeds to make commonsense analogies to doctors and parents who compassionately inflict pain in order to discipline and heal without intending harm."[331]

The *Jen Wang Ching Sutra* (c. 200; Benevolent Kings Sutra) represents a conversation between Sakyamuni Buddha and Prasenajit, the king of Kosala (India). In this book of counsel, allegedly from the mouth of the Buddha himself, it is stated that one can escape the *karmic* consequences arising from such acts as killing others by simply reciting this *sutra*. Going further, the *sutra* depicts the Buddha giving detailed instructions to kings on how to best protect their lands from enemies, both internal and external. The advice assures that soldiers involved in any slaughter may be retroactively absolved of the *karmic* consequences of their acts.[332]

The *Milinda Panha* (c. 100; Questions of King Milinda), a highly authoritative *Theravadin* text, argues that punitive violence should be understood as the fruition of the victim's own *karma*. In such a case, the state -sponsored violence was not only a *reaction* to a serious *karmic* deficit in the "other," but also restorative of the grand design, as well as personally healing to the targets of the state's venom.

Of course, these examples (and many more) in no way represent the only, or even main, teaching within Buddhism. There are far more passages that hew to the non-violent precepts which underlie the Buddha's teachings. The point here, however, is to show how easy it is for those who desire to find justifiable violence within Buddhism, to do so.

MORE VIOLENT IMAGERY

Growing out of these scriptural passages was an explosion of violent language attached to the supposedly serene Buddhist path. All religions use the language of war to describe the spiritual path, but it is still surprising to find it so well represented within Buddhism. And I want to stress, again, the importance of this vocabulary of violence in preparing religious followers for what becomes an easy slide from metaphorical violence to literal violence. The hostile language and imagery of spirituality allows lay leaders to fuse the bellicosity of the state with religious and spiritual meaning.

A visit to a Buddhist sanctuary in the Far East often shows the image of Vaisravana, one of the four god-kings, who presides over the north. This deity is represented as an armored warrior . . . for the Buddhists in the north he became a veritable god of war.[333]

Violent portrayals also affected writing on the Buddhist spiritual path. The 18th-century Zen monk Yamamoto Jocho, author of *The Book of Samurai*, wrote:

> Meditation on inevitable death should be performed daily. Every day when one's body and mind are at peace, one should meditate on being ripped apart by arrows, rifles, spears and swords, being carried away by surging waves, being thrown into the midst of a great fire, being struck by lightning, being shaken to death by a great earthquake, falling from thousand foot cliffs, dying of disease or committing *seppuku* [ritual suicide] . . . every day without fail, one should consider himself as dead.[334]

Bernard Faure (Kao Professor in Japanese Religion at Columbia University) noted in *Buddhist Warfare* how this kind of imagery might lead a Buddhist to the practice of violence *as* spirituality:

> Monastic discipline . . . can also be seen as a kind of muted violence against oneself. To show their determination, Chinese monks would sometimes mutilate themselves — including cutting off or burning one or more of their fingers. In extreme cases, self-denial could lead to self-immolation by fire.

The image of the sword also plays an important role in Buddhist teaching and meditation practice. The Chinese master Kuei-Shan Ling-yu (d.

853) referred to the interplay between action and silence as "swordplay." Lin-Chi (d. 866) also used imagery such as "swords," "sword blades" and the "sword of wisdom."[335] The *Nirvana Sutra* exhorts: "Protect the true *dharma* by grasping swords and other weapons."[336]

The master Yuan Wu k'e Ch'in (d. 1135) assured that the sword which kills people and the sword which gives life to people is an ancient custom.[337] Zen master Huang Po (d. 850) expounded on the Sword of Bodhi in his *On the Transmission of Mind*.[338] And Takuan Soho (d. 1645), a major figure in the Rinzai school of Zen Buddhism, described Fudo Myo-o (The commander of the Wisdom Kings) as follows:

> Fudo Myo-o holds a sword in his right hand and a rope in his left. His lips are rolled back revealing his teeth and his eyes are full of anger. He thrusts violently at all evil demons who interfere with Buddha *dharma*, forcing them to surrender.[339]

BUDDHISM AND THE STATE

> The wars of the empire are sacred wars. They are holy wars. They are the [Buddhist] practice [*gyo*] of great compassion. Therefore, the Imperial military must consist of holy officers and holy soldiers.[340]

The leap from the violent language and the various justifications for violence found in traditional Buddhist teachings to actual violence sanctioned by a Buddhist state was a short one. And once Buddhism became a "state" religion, Buddhist violence evolved into yet one more political tool for subjugation and expansion.

Additionally, with Buddhism and temporal power wrapped together (not unlike Catholicism and the various kingdoms in medieval Europe), violence in service to the state could be presented as violence in defense of the "one true religion."

Zhao Puchu (d. 2000; president of the Buddhist Association of China), stated in 1951, concerning China's entrance into the Korean War and the necessity for Chinese Buddhists to support the war effort:

> Buddhists are duty-bound to repay the kindness of the nation and people, and always remind ourselves of this duty through reciting the scriptures every day. Working for the benefit and happiness of people without considering even our lives is the vow of Buddhists.[341]

This dynamic is hardly confined to China, or, as we shall see further along, to Japanese Zen, which historically allied itself with the cult of the Samurai and played an integral role in the Japanese atrocities committed before and during World War II. As Dr. Michael Jerryson (whose primary area of research is on the intersection of religion and violence) noted: "where Buddhism is part of the ideology of statecraft, there is a pervasive tendency for Buddhists to sanction violence."[342]

The perversion of linking Buddhism with state-sponsored murder has been taken to its absolute limits. Paul Demieville (d. 1979; considered one of the pre-eminent "Sinologists" of the 20th century) related one example of the fusion of Buddhism and state sponsored killing in *Buddhism and War*:

> Faqing [c. 515; Ho-pei, China] took the title of "Great Vehicle," and declared the arrival of the new Buddha . . . He had under his command 50,000 men. When a soldier killed a man, he earned the title of first-stage *bodhisattva*. The more he killed, the more he went up the echelon toward sainthood . . . Murder was a charitable act in the crusade against *Mara* (a demonic, virtually all-powerful Lord of evil) . . . The recruits were convinced that they were killing for a "new Buddha."[343]

On one hand, it is tempting to dismiss this as an absurd cult of personality, having more in common with the messianic fervor inspired by the likes of Shabbatai Zevi (d. 1676) or Jim Jones (d. 1978). However, taken more soberly, is this very different from the slaughter outlined in the Jewish Bible, the Christian Crusades, the *jihadi* terrorism of today's Wahhabi Muslim sects and other religiously-inspired (or religiously-justified) mass murders? By the sixth century, there was enough scriptural and historical precedence within Buddhism to justify the absurd claims of the "Great Vehicle," and the dynamic would hardly wane. The 20th century saw examples of the same venomous Buddhist energy from Japanese Zen practitioners, Sri Lankan Buddhists, Pol Pot in Cambodia and others.

"JUST WAR" THEORY

> Buddha Sakyamuni, during religious practice in a former life, participated in a "just war". Due to the merit he acquired as a result, he was able to appear in this world as a Buddha. Thus, it can be said that a "just war" is one task of Buddhism.[344]

Out of the violent impulses coursing through the hidden heart of Buddhism, a concept very similar to the "'just war'" theory of Christianity emerged. Perhaps none was so explicit about this idea as the Fifth Dalai Lama (Ngawang Lobsang Gyatso, d. 1682) of Tibetan Buddhism, who began construction on the majestic Potala Palace. He linked war and the state in a fashion similar to Abrahamic forms of religious justification. As Dr. Derek Maher noted in *Sacralized Warfare*, the Dalai Lama developed the "just war" theory to validate combat fought on his behalf by Gushri Khan and Mongolian allies, 1635-42, for the unification of Tibet.

> [The Dalai Lama] pays great attention to the types of concerns that are encountered in standard just-war theory, elaborated by both Christians and Muslims once they found a need to create governments. The Dalai Lama expended considerable efforts to represent the battles as being responsible reactions to others' improper actions.[345]

Here, we see a normal dynamic: for the purpose of the state, religion and war must be brought in concord. The state is founded on war, this is true, but it also can't be emphasized enough that religion is founded on violence.

JAPAN

> In the Zen sect of Japan, they interpreted the argument for taking another's life as "attempting to bring the other's Buddha nature to life."[346]

This exploration now moves from general Buddhist bloodlust to the specific cultures where it has operated. When I began this study, I assumed that this violent dynamic was confined to one or two cultures (say, Japan and China) and one or two time periods (perhaps the 20th century).

I was wrong.

Although I will start with Japan, as the deep intertwining of Buddhism with the violent *Samurai* (military nobility of pre-industrial Japan) culture is clear and was important as recently as World War II. Buddhism, war and the state have been woven together in virtually all cultures where Buddhism has flourished and even in some, like the United States, where Buddhism is peripheral to statecraft. Ultimately, in no place where Buddhism has been institutionalized as either a state religion or even a religion within a state has it been able to retain its original non-violent character.

EXCEPTIONALISM

Japan represents an especially egregious example of Buddhist justifications for slaughter, torture and restorative violence. Japanese attitudes during the World War II era echo the contemporary American dynamic in disturbing ways.

The idea of Japanese exceptionalism, as it intertwines with the state religion of Buddhism, sounds very much like the American sense of the state and Christianity. A quick comparison between Japanese Buddhist justifications in the period leading up to World War II and a contemporary political thinker will suffice to show how closely related are these two cultures.

In 1934, Shimizu Ryuzan (d. 1943; president of Nichiren Zen sect-affiliated Rissho University) explained:

> The underlying principle of the spirit of Japan is the enlightenment of the world with truth . . . we must lead all the nations of the world into righteousness and establish heaven on earth, where brotherly love and worldwide peace shall prevail and where all men shall be Buddhist saints. There is the true ideal, the spirit of Japan.

This conception of state and religious exceptionalism is hardly sequestered within the Japanese Buddhist spirit. Howard Zinn noted in his article "The Power and the Glory: Myths of American Exceptionalism":

> The notion of American exceptionalism — that the United States alone has the right, whether by divine sanction or moral obligation, to bring civilization, or democracy, or liberty to the rest of the world, by violence if necessary — is not new. It started as early as 1630 in the Massachusetts Bay Colony when Governor John Winthrop uttered the words that centuries later would be quoted by Ronald Reagan. Winthrop called the Massachusetts Bay Colony a "city upon a hill." Reagan embellished a little, calling it a "shining city on a hill."[347]

Zinn goes on to state an obvious fact, yet one that somehow often escapes the vision of God-fearing folks everywhere on their way to the latest war of salvation and liberation:

> Divine ordination is a very dangerous idea, especially when combined with military power (the United States has 10,000 nuclear weapons, with military bases in a hundred different countries and warships on every sea). With God's approval, you need no human standard of morality. Anyone today who claims the support of God might be embarrassed to recall that the Nazi storm troopers had inscribed on their belts "Gott mit uns" (God is with us).[348]

THE SWORD AND THE LOTUS

The sword is generally associated with killing, and most of us wonder how it can come into connection with Zen, which is a school of Buddhism teaching the gospel of love and mercy. The fact is that the art of swordsmanship distinguishes between the sword that kills and the sword that gives life. The one that is used by a technician cannot go any further than killing, for he never appeals to the sword unless he intends to kill. The case is altogether different with the one who is compelled to lift the sword. He had no desire to harm anybody, but the enemy appears and makes himself a victim. It is as though the sword performs automatically its function of justice, which is the function of mercy.[349]

The relationship between Buddhism and the way of the Samurai is not recent, beginning in the 13th century when the Hojo regents (c. 1203–1333) discovered that Buddhist vitality and rejection of life as an object of special craving had much to offer the warrior.[350] From this time on, war and religious observance were separated in Japan by only the thinnest of boundaries.

Later Japanese thinkers could point to an unbroken line of thinkers from the 11th century through World War II, who brought Zen and violence together. The famous Rinzai Zen master Takuan (d. 1645) wrote, echoing other Buddhist justifications for war:

> The uplifted sword has no will of its own, it is all of emptiness. It is like a flash of lightning. The man who is about to be struck down is also of emptiness, and so is the one who wields the sword . . . As each of them is of emptiness and has no "mind," the striking man is not a man, the sword in his hands is not a sword, and the "I" who is about to be struck down is like the splitting of the spring breeze by a flash of lightning.[351]

Monks and War

Japanese Zen monks throughout the ages lauded the warrior's path as a central Zen Buddhist practice, at times even suggesting that there was no better manner of achieving "no-mind" than the practice of dutiful violence. The priest Tannen (d. 1680) related in his daily talks:

> A monk cannot fulfill the Buddhist Way if he does not manifest compassion without and persistently store up courage within. And if a warrior does not manifest courage on the outside and hold compassion within his heart to burst his chest, he cannot become a retainer. Therefore, the monk pursues courage with the warrior as his model and the warrior pursues the compassion of the monk.

Suzuki Shoshan (d. 1655), a Rinzai Zen priest of the same era, claimed that the warrior must absolutely practice *ZaZen* amid war cries. What better place to put meditation into action? He noted that however fond a warrior might be of Buddhism, he should "throw it out" if it didn't work amid war cries.[352]

Hakuin (d. 1768; one of Rinzai Zen's greatest masters) went even further, concluding that the warrior's lifestyle was superior to that of the monk for practicing Zen.[353] Yamamoto Tsunetomo (d. 1719), a Buddhist monk and Samurai warrior, noted a practice he undertook to center his mind: "Last year, I went to the Kase Execution Grounds to try my hand at beheading, and I found it to be an extremely good feeling. To think that it is unnerving is a symptom of cowardice."[354] His assertion that it was an "extremely good feeling" echoes the statements from some warriors of our own era, who assure us that killing is good fun, and even addictive.

Sugawara Gido (d. 1978; Chief Abbot of Hokuku Zenjii Temple) noted: "There is no doubt that all those involved in the Greater East Asia War had disregarded their self-centeredness and . . . attained the path of Truth. If you believe that something is right, that is the path of Truth and you should rush forward toward it."[355]

In writing of the Japanese incursion into China just before World War II, scholar-priest Dr. Hitane Jazan (d. 1954) asserted:

> Speaking from the point of view of the ideal outcome, this is a righteous and moral war of self-sacrifice in which we will rescue China from the dangers of Communist takeover and economic slavery . . . It would therefore, I dare say, not be unreasonable to call this a sacred war incorporating the great practice of a *bodhisattva*.[356]

Scholar-priest Dr. Kurebayashi Kodo (d. 1988), writing of the same incursion, assured that Japanese wars were just because of the "influence of the Buddhist spirit." He also soothed his readers with this thought:

> Wherever the Imperial Military advances there is only charity and love. They could never act in the barbarous and cruel manner in which the Chinese soldiers act. This can truly be considered to be a great accomplishment of the long period that Buddhism took in nurturing [the Japanese Military]. Brutality itself no longer exists in the officers and men of the Imperial Military . . .[357]

A beautiful sentiment, however one that is almost completely independent of reality. As journalist Ralph Blumenthal noted in *The New York Times*:

> While Nazi scientists like Josef Mengele conducted hideous experiments on concentration camp prisoners, their lesser-known Japanese counterparts, led by Gen. Shiro Ishii, were waging full-scale biological warfare and subjecting human beings to ghastly experiments of their own — and on a far greater scale than the Germans. Ping Fan was a camp of plague-bearing fleas, rat cages and warrens for human guinea pigs. Changchun, 150 miles south, was another huge installation for germ tests on plants, animals and people. The Japanese record of atrocities — what victims call "the Asian Holocaust" — is still producing revelations more than 50 years after the end of World War II.[358]

SUGIMOTO

> The reason that Zen is important for soldiers is that all Japanese, espe-
> cially soldiers, must live in the spirit of sovereign and subjects, eliminating
> their ego and getting rid of their self. It is exactly the awakening to the
> nothingness of Zen that is the fundamental unity of sovereign and sub-
> jects . . . In facilitating the accomplishment of this, Zen becomes, as it is,
> the true spirit of the Imperial military.[359]

Although there were many Japanese Zen practitioners who were
Samurai, including the 17th-century Zen monk Yamamoto Tsumetomo
(d. 1719), who wrote *The Book of Samurai* about the fusion of Zen and
the warrior's path, none was more explicit about the marriage of spirit
and war than Sugimoto Goro (d. 1937). He went so far as to propose that
the "national structure of Japan and Buddhism are identical with each
other."[360]

He captured the full feeling of not only his age — the years leading up
to World War II — but also the manner in which Japanese warrior culture and Zen Buddhism were fused together in the popular mind. Quote
after quote of his exudes the spirit of both institutionalized murder and
the mystic's path.

> If you wish to penetrate the meaning of the "Great Duty," the first thing
> you should do is to embrace the teachings of Zen and discard self-attach-
> ment. War is moral training for not only the individual but for the entire
> world. It consists of the extinction of self-seeking and the destruction of
> self-preservation.[361]

He also took great steps to knit Zen together with war and the state,
which helped lead to some of the most horrendous institutional atrocities in recorded history. Sugimoto assured: "Warriors who sacrifice
their lives for the emperor will not die. They will live forever. Truly, they
should be called gods and Buddhas for whom there is no life after death .
. . where there is absolute loyalty there is no life or death."[362]

Perhaps at this point the believer will want to disagree, assert that
these voices in no way represent the true path, they are but mistakes in
the Way and while they cannot be denied, nor should they be held out as
representing a central, or even major, aspect of the spiritual path.

However, in case after case, these very bloodthirsty cries are revered
at the time when it was most important: *during their own contemporary era.*
For instance, Sugimoto's Zen Master, Yamazaki Ekiju (d. 1961) described
Sugimoto's "flowery" death in battle:

> A grenade fragment hit him in the left shoulder. He seemed to have fallen
> down but then got up again . . . he was still standing, holding his sword in

one hand as a prop. Both legs were slightly bent, and he was facing in an easterly direction [toward the Imperial Palace]. It appeared that he had saluted, though his hand was now lowered to about the level of his mouth. The blood flowing from his mouth covered his watch.[363]

As Brian Daizen Victoria notes in *Zen at War*: "In Ekiju's mind, at least, it was his lay disciple's finest moment, when he most clearly displayed the power that was to be gained by those who practice Zen."[364]

ZEN, THE STATE AND A "JUST WAR"

By the 19th century, Japanese Buddhist military objectives were to kill unbelievers and convert their state to Buddhism. As the Zen leaders and lay people of Japan believed that people who were not enlightened (i.e., the enemy) would be reborn, there was, in their mind, no true destruction of life.[365]

This led to Buddhist support for specific military campaigns undertaken by the Japanese government. During the Sino–Japanese War (1894–95), there was almost no peace movement among Buddhists, but numerous Buddhists leaders justified the campaign. They based their support on the contention that Japanese Buddhism was more advanced than other strains in Asia. Mori Naoki expounded on this theme in 1894, in an article entitled "The relationship of Japanese Buddhists to the crisis in China and Korea," in which he presented the battlefield as an arena for the "propagation of the faith" holding high the banner of "benevolence and fidelity."[366]

> By the end of the Russo–Japanese war in September 1905, the foundation had been laid for institutional Buddhism's basic attitudes toward Japan's military activities: 1) Japan's wars are not only just but are, in fact, expressions of Buddhist compassion; 2) fighting to the death in Japan's wars is an opportunity to repay the debt of gratitude owed to both the Buddha and the emperor; 3) the Japanese army is composed of tens of thousands of *bodhisattvas*.[367]

By the early 20th century, a Japanese-Buddhist "just war" theory had been codified and was expounded by Soyen Shaku (d. 1919; the first Zen Buddhist master to teach in the United States):

> War is not necessarily horrible, provided that it is fought for a just and honorable cause, that it is fought for the maintenance and realization of noble ideals, that it is fought for the upholding of humanity and civilization. Many material human bodies may be destroyed, many hearts broken, but from a broader point of view these sacrifices are so many phoenixes consumed in the sacred fire of spirituality . . . War is not a mere slaughter

of their fellow-beings, but they are combating evil, and at the same time corporeal annihilation really means giving a rebirth of the soul.[368]

Zen leaders who supported Japanese militarism did so on the grounds that Japanese aggression expressed the very "essence of Buddha *dharma* and even enlightenment itself."[369] These religious figures went so far as to claim that killing and bomb throwing were done independently of the individual will, and therefore the individual had no choice or responsibility in the matter.[370]

This is an even more problematic line of reasoning than is found in the Abrahamic religions, where at least the holy warrior is personally implicated in his actions. In Buddhism, people are allowed to remain serene in the knowledge that they were not "present" in the acts of violence. And far from being viewed in a negative fashion, they are considered part of the dispersion of the one true faith, as well as responsible for "releasing" the victims for rebirth and future realization.

By World War II, Japanese Buddhist organizations were institutionalizing religious war as *the* best spiritual practice, preparing the country for its orgy of holy violence that began in China (1937) and would go worldwide. An edict from the Association for the Practice of Imperial-Way Buddhism in 1938 set out the specifics of this fusion of worship and war:

> Imperial-Way Buddhism utilizes the exquisite truth of the *Lotus Sutra* to reveal the majestic essence of the national polity. Exalting the true spirit of *Mahayana* Buddhism is a teaching that reverently supports the emperor's work. This is what the great founder of our sect, Saint Nichiren [d. 1282], meant when he referred to the divine unity of sovereign and Buddha.[371]

CHINA

> It is a well-known fact that first of all commandments of the Buddhist creed is "Thou shall not kill," [but] Chinese books contain various passages relating to Buddhist monks who freely indulged in carnage and butchery and took an active part in military expeditions of every description, thus leaving no room for doubt that warfare was an integral part of their religious profession for centuries.[372]

Japan, until the end of World War II, was a warlike nation on par with Germany, so the melding of Buddhism and the way of the Samurai is not at all surprising. But while this might be so — that Japan was particularly adept at fusing war and religion — it was not unique, nor even out of the ordinary for Buddhist countries. A quick trip throughout the nations of Asia and the Indian subcontinent will uncover the violent history of Buddhism across the geographic as well as chronological history of the supposed pacifist creed.

THE TAO OF SLAUGHTER

Buddhism arrived in China in the first century, introduced by traders along the Silk Road. However, there was an ancient, indigenous and peaceful religious practice that it merged with and at times replaced: Taoism. Taoism may be traced to prehistoric folk religions in China, which later coalesced into the Taoist tradition. Lao-Tzu (c. 6th century B.C.E.) is traditionally regarded as the founder of Taoism and his book *The Way of Lao Tzu* is revered as the "bible" of this belief system.

Taoism, like Buddhism, is a creed of acceptance and non-being. Briefly, it may be defined as a way of noninterference with the course of natural events that leads to harmony with the Tao, or universal essence. Echoing the Buddhist abhorrence with worldly striving, Lao Tzu intoned: "There is no greater misfortune than being covetous."[373]

Like Buddhism, however, the Tao was twisted into an accessory to murder, and helped lay the theological groundwork within China for the manner in which Buddhism, after its adoption in the first centuries of the Christian era, would come to underpin Chinese military campaigns up to the Korean War (1950–1953). Early Chinese war theorists such as Ssu-Ma (c. 4th century B.C.E.), Sun-Tzu (c. 6th century B.C.E.) and Huang Shi-Kung (c. 3rd century B.C.E.) all brought militarism together with the Tao to produce a specifically Chinese bellicosity, one which would affect later Buddhist interpretations of religion and war.

A few quick quotes will suffice to show how the practice of Taoism became united with statecraft. Ssu-Ma assured his readers:

> As for the Tao of Warfare: After you have aroused [the people's] *chi* [spirit] . . . encompass them with a benign countenance and lead them with your speeches. Upbraid them in accord with their fears; assign affairs in accord with their desires.[374]

More specifically, Ssu-Ma defined the Tao thusly:

> When the army does not listen to minor affairs, when in battle it does not concern itself with small advantages; and when on the day of conflict it successfully completes its plans in subtle fashion, it is termed "the Tao."[375]

This appears to have more in common with the Florentine political philosopher Niccolo Machiavelli (d. 1527) than the non-violent image of Taoism. Ssu-Ma's fusion of the Tao with war helped soften the earth of

Chinese spirituality for the later incursion of a just violence within Chinese Buddhism.

Sun Tzu averred in his *Art of War*: "one who excels at employing the military cultivates the Tao."[376] And in a passage that echoes the "just war" theory in all religions, Huang Shih-Kung stated in his *Three Strategies*:

> The sage king does not take any pleasure in using the army. He mobilizes it to execute the violently perverse and punish the rebellious . . . weapons are inauspicious implements and the Tao of Heaven abhors them. However, when their employment is unavoidable it accords with the Tao of Heaven.[377]

From these Taoist justifications for institutionalized violence, it was not difficult for the Sino-Buddhists to walk this same theological path. Chinese Buddhism was interlaced with war almost from the outset. The *Jueguan Lun* (c. 2nd century; Treatise on the Extinction of Contemplation) states that if a murderous act is as perfectly spontaneous as an act of nature, it entails no responsibility,[378] a trope seen time and again in Buddhist justifications for violence.

The Emperor Wendi, founder of the Sui Dynasty (d. 604), used another well-known linguistic-spiritual gymnastic for justifying institutional slaughter, as he explained the divine love behind his military campaigns:

> With the armed might of a Cokravartin King, we spread the ideals of the ultimately benevolent one with a hundred victories and a hundred battles; we promote the practice of the ten Buddhist virtues. Therefore we regard weapons of war as having become like incense and flowers (presented as offerings to the Buddha).[379]

During the Tang Dynasty (618-907), there were tantric practices to assure victory on the battlefield. Prayers were offered to the God *Vaisravana* (the chief of the Four Heavenly Kings and an important figure in Buddhist mythology), who would then follow the armies (like a Homeric God) to protect the "true law."[380]

In the sixth century, Chinese Buddhists framed their fight against non-Buddhists as between the Buddha and his nemesis *Mara*, the God of desire and illusion. Chinese monks murdered their foes as part of the larger cosmic battle against this internal enemy.[381] This rationalization hardly waned with time, as in the 15th and 16th centuries Buddhist monks from the *Dhyana* Sect were famous for going to war to serve the homeland.[382]

Violent Imagery

Chinese Buddhism utilized violent imagery and stories to expound on the path. And like all religions, this use of brutal imagery and language helped ease the acceptance of other, more literal interpretations of the Buddha *dharma*, which led directly to Buddhist involvement in wars and other sadistic practices. As David Gray noted in the *Journal of Buddhist Ethics*, "there is a significant body of tantric Buddhist literature that evokes violent imagery or describes violent ritual practices."[383]

An early Buddhist scholar, Buddhajnana (c. 8th century), the founder of an important school of tantric exegesis, composed two works on the fierce deity Heruka. His *Sriherukasadhana* contains the following passage: "[Visualize] a *vajra* generated from [the seed-syllable] *hrih*, which blazes like a destroying fire. From that the compassionate fierce one is born, the great terrifier (*mahabhairava*) bearing a skull garland."[384]

Utilizing the reasoning similar to that of earlier Buddhists, Buddhajnana advanced what would become a very popular interpretation in tantric Buddhist circles. He claimed that Buddhist deities such as Heruka appear in fierce forms, but their ferocity is not believed to be a manifestation of mental afflictions such as anger. Rather, he claimed that these deities' ferocity is rooted in compassion.[385]

The *Mahavairocana-abhisambodhi Tantra* (c. 7th century; first true Buddhist *tantra*) notes: "When subduing hated foes, one should employ the fierce fire."[386] Bhavyakirti (c. tenth century) was an abbot of the Vikramasila monastery in Eastern India whose commentary on the *Cakrasamvara Tantra* (which describes a fierce *homa* rite for the purpose of subduing a rival kingdom) was as follows:

> Then the destruction of all, arising from the *vajra*, is held [to be accomplished] with the great meat. It is the dreadful destroyer of all the cruel ones. Should one thus perform without hesitation the rites of eating, fire sacrifice (*homa*), and sacrificial offerings (*bali*) with the meats of dogs and pigs, and also with [the meat of] those [chickens] that have copper [colored] crests, everything without exception will be achieved, and all kingdoms will be subdued.[387]

He follows this exposition with the usual rationalizing language about how the "ten non-virtuous actions are not necessarily downfalls for [those who have realized] the reality of selflessness."[388]

One last story about a ninth-century Chinese monk Juzhi Yizhi illustrates further the fusion of blood and spirit. Juzhi is famous for the following story, which appears as a *koan* (a story, the meaning of which cannot be understood by rational thinking but may be accessible through intuition) in various collections:

> Gutei raised his finger whenever he was asked a question about Zen. A boy attendant began to imitate him in this way. When anyone asked the boy what his master had preached about, the boy would raise his finger.

> Gutei heard about the boy's mischief. He seized him and cut off his finger. The boy cried and ran away. Gutei called and stopped him. When the boy turned his head to Gutei, Gutei raised up his own finger. In that instant the boy was enlightened.[389]

CHINESE BUDDHISM AND THE KOREAN WAR

> Zhao Puchu [d. 2000] reiterated the importance of a religious follower loving his nation more than his religion. Loving one's nation is primary while loving one's religion is secondary in that the existence of one's religion depends on the existence of one's nation.[390]

In the past century, as China grew from a backward, feudal society into a world power, Buddhist thinkers and spiritual leaders had to keep up or risk their marginalization within the society. And being able to find much precedent within their religion for backing state-sponsored military actions came in handy as they worked with 20th-century Communist leaders to become the de-facto "state religion" in the officially atheist nation.

The new Communist country's first military campaign was the Korean War, which pitted the rising power against the United States, using Korea as the proxy. Religious leaders were strong proponents of the conflict. The Venerable Xindao, addressing 187 monks and nuns, traced his beliefs in restorative violence back to the Buddha himself. He spoke to the *"Committee of Buddhist Circles in Nan Ch'ang for Resisting America and Assisting Korea"* on March 11, 1951:

> The best thing is to be able to join the army directly and learn the spirit in which Sakyamuni, as the embodiment of compassion and our guide to Buddha *dharma*, killed robbers to save people and suffered hardship on behalf of all living creatures. To wipe out the American imperialist demons who are breaking world peace is, according to Buddhist doctrine, not only blameless, but actually will give rise to merit as well.[391]

A bit later, in June of 1951, Buddhists in Jiuquan, in Guansu Province, assured that Buddhists were "family members" of the Chinese nation. As such, they should not hesitate to help in the war effort:

> [We Buddhists] should dispel all misgivings in observing precepts that we would perhaps violate the precept of non-killing if we donate the

airplane or cannons [to the war effort], which are instruments of killing. [We] dare to assure that one who practices the *bodhisattva's* path will take up a knife and kill evil ones so that the good people may live in peace and happiness . . . we are determined to eliminate all evil enemies through "killing for stopping killing."[392]

The Buddhist leader, Venerable Juzan (d. 1984), urged his fellow Buddhists to work with the Communist leadership, arguing that compassion and killing were not necessarily contradictory but dialectically complemented each other. Juzan quoted an oft-used passage from the *Yogacara Bodhisattva* precepts text to demonstrate that one may kill others if the killing is for the sake of saving more lives.[393] He used this basis to justify Buddhist aid to the Chinese state in the Korean conflict:

We Buddhists uphold peace, yet America is the deadly enemy of peace. Therefore, we must reject American imperialism in order to safeguard peace . . . Now, the people of Korea have been severely tortured by imperialist America; assisting Korea will safeguard not only the nation and the world, but also Buddhism.[394]

A recent article in the *Journal of Global Buddhism* by Xue Yu of the Chinese University of Hong Kong, explored the specific relationship between this mid-20th century Chinese Buddhist leader and the Korean War. In it he noted: "I investigate how Juzan urged his fellow Buddhists to work with the Communist leadership, and how he justified government policies on Buddhism by reinterpreting Buddhist doctrines."[395]

Juzan was *not* "reinterpreting Buddhist doctrines." In fact, Xue Yu's statement to this effect is another example of the great problem with scholars undertaking research on their own faiths: they exhibit an unwillingness to acknowledge the fusion of violence and the sacred that lies at the heart of their own faith tradition.

While it is certainly true that the Buddha said: "Thou shalt not kill," it is just as true that in the lore of his own life (as well as past lives) stories may be found of instances when the Buddha himself *did* kill, and justified it in a variety of ways. Additionally, the "reinterpretation" of Buddhist practice, if we are really justified in calling it that, began almost as soon as the Buddha was dead. Certainly, by the middle of the 20th century there was a body of Buddhist ""just war"" theory that could be found in original scripture, exegesis and other Chinese Buddhist texts.

INDIA

India was the birthplace of Buddhism. About 2,500 years ago, Prince Siddhartha Gautama (born in 566 B.C.E.) sat down under a pipal tree in

Bodh Gaya (in the Bihar state in northeastern India) and received the enlightenment that would inspire one of the world's great religions. Bodh Gaya remains the most important Buddhist pilgrimage destination on Earth.

As such, India has a special place in Buddhist history and lore, and it is considered to offer one of the gentlest examples of the spiritual path. Many scholars draw a distinction between the more bellicose Asian version of Buddhism and its Indian manifestation. However, even here, in the birthplace of the religion, we can find many examples of the more muscular, state-oriented spirituality that is so clearly in evidence in China and Japan.

VIOLENCE IN INDIAN BUDDHISM

Buddhist scholar Stephen Jenkins described the world of the ancient Indian ascetic as violent and dangerous:

> Those who lost debates are often described as being swallowed up by the earth, drowning in the Ganges or spitting up blood and dying. It was not uncommon for the stakes to be death or conversion. The threat to split someone's head was typical of intellectual challenges and occurred often . . . in early Buddhist literature. The fact that the threat was taken very seriously is shown [in the *Arya-Bodhisattva-gocara-upayavisaya-vikurvana-nirdesa-sutra*] by Satyavaca's terror and the presence of Vajrapani, who often works violence on the Buddha's behalf.[396]

Jenkins also noted that in another, earlier *sutra*, a non-believer made the mistake of challenging the Buddha to a debate. When he hesitated in answering a key question, Vajrapani threatened to split his head open with a blazing *vajra*, a handheld weapon that later became the primary symbol of the power of compassion.[397]

We find other examples of institutionalized violence in India. As Jenkins, again, noted:

> The location of inscriptions (such as those in Nalanda, the great north Indian monastic university, that glorifies the gore-smeared swords of widow-making Buddhist kings) in a monastic university of vast international prestige suggests that Buddhists, rather than being conflicted or duplicitous, found it appropriate to publicly honor, and so validate military violence.[398]

The *Stanford Encyclopedia of Philosophy* shared another story of a great Indian Buddhist scholar who discovered within Buddhism the seeds of not only contemplation, but also murder and destructive violence.

> An important passage discusses punishment in the Precious Garland (*Ratnavali*), a letter to a king from the great Buddhist philosopher Nagarjuna [c. 200; a Brahmin from southern India who, in some *Mahayana* traditions, is regarded as a second Buddha] . . . To maintain social order, punishment is a regrettable necessity. But the king should not punish out of anger or a desire for revenge. Instead, he should inflict punishment out of compassion, especially compassion for the criminals themselves, whose destructive actions may have condemned them to many lifetimes of suffering.[399]

Not to make too much of a point of it, but the ongoing desire of Buddhists to "save" the lost (designated criminals, miscreants and unbelievers) through corporeal punishment and even murder sounds not unlike the loving ministrations applied by the Inquisition (1480–1834), which applied various tortures to nonbelievers in the hopes of saving them from eternal damnation (see above).

Ashoka

The most important temporal leader within Buddhism is King Ashoka, who represents the prototype of the spiritually realized civil leader. He was an Indian emperor who ruled most of the Indian subcontinent from 269-232 B.C.E. His empire included present-day Pakistan, Afghanistan, Bangladesh, parts of Iran and much of India. After a series of wars of conquest, he embraced Buddhism. He dedicated himself to the propagation of the religion across Asia, establishing monuments marking several significant sites in the life of Gautama Buddha. According to legend, Ashoka was a devotee of *ahimsa* (nonviolence), love, truth, tolerance and vegetarianism.

For our purposes, however, Ashoka is a perfect example of the disconnect within Buddhism or, as Brian Daizen Victoria put it, the surface, non-violent image of Buddhism and the subterranean, hidden darkness within the path. As the original Indian Buddhist lay-leader, Ashoka set the example of how to weave violence into the purportedly non-violent creed.

Although revered as the most important Buddhist king, Ashoka slaughtered 18,000 Jains (an Indian religion that prescribes pacifism and a path of non-violence toward all living beings) *after* becoming *dharma-Ashoka*. Brian Daizen Victoria painted the non-idealized picture of this Buddhist leader:

> Ashoka maintained an army and used force . . . Beyond that, one Buddhist description of his life, the Sanskrit *Ashokavandana* [c. 2nd century], records that he ordered *eighteen thousand* non-Buddhist adherents executed be-

cause of a minor insult to Buddhism on the part of a single one. On another occasion, he forced a Jain follower and his entire family into their house before having it burnt to the ground. He also maintained the death penalty for criminals, including his own wife, whom he executed.[400]

In one sense, it might appear easy to dismiss King Ashoka's peculiarities as simply an outlying example of Buddhism run amok. However, he is revered to this day within Buddhist tradition. As the Venerable Shravasti Dhammika (a distinguished lecturer and Buddhist monk from Australia) recently wrote:

> It is also very clear that Buddhism was the most influential force in Ashoka's life and that he hoped his subjects likewise would adopt his religion. It is also very clear that Ashoka saw the reforms he instituted as being a part of his duties as a Buddhist. The contents of Ashoka's edicts make it clear that all the legends about his wise and humane rule are more than justified and qualify him to be ranked as one of the greatest rulers ... His edicts were imbued with the Buddhist values of compassion, moderation, tolerance and respect for all life.[401]

Reverberations: Violence in Indian Buddhism Today

A recent article concerning a Buddhist rampage explores how the acceptable, though often unacknowledged, violence implicit in the Buddhist path can allow its practitioners license to react to events with wild and violent abandon:

> A Buddhist monk was found dead in mysterious circumstances here Sunday, and in the aftermath of violence by his followers the police have filed a case of murder against a builder and some office-bearers of a Buddhist organization.
>
> When news spread in the afternoon that the monk, Buddhabhanti Badant Sanghraj Thairo, had committed suicide by hanging himself in his tenement at Deonar in northeast Mumbai, Buddhists in the neighborhood took to the streets. Suspecting foul play, they threw stones at vehicles and buildings in the vicinity and torched at least three vehicles. Even as police reinforcements were rushed to control the violence, the angry crowds continued to swell.[402]

Tibet

From India, we move north to Tibet. Certainly, in recent times, no country better represents the oppression that Buddhists can suffer under the yoke of an unjust and irreligious government (in this case, Communist China). Additionally, in the person of Tenzin Gyatso (b. 1935), His

Holiness the 14th Dalai Lama, Tibetan Buddhism has come to represent the potential fusion of non-violence with contemporary geo-politics, as the spiritual leader has unwaveringly preached a patient and non-military reaction to the conflict with his Chinese oppressors.

Alas.

If only this current Dalai Lama was representative of Tibetan Buddhist history. The truth, however, like so much of hidden Buddhism, is far more contradictory. Looking into the Tibetan annals, we find that the country was formed out of violence, and that the power of the Fifth Dalai Lama (Ngawang Lobsang Gyatso, d. 1682) was consolidated through violence and war.

It is stated clearly on the official website of the Tibetan government in exile that the Fifth Dalai Lama founded the *Ganden Phodrang* Government of Tibet in 1642, the first strong, central government in that country's history. What is not noted, however, is the manner in which this came to be. The Fifth Dalai Lama was installed as civil leader of Tibet through warfare.

The war of ascension took place at the instigation of Sonam Rapten, the Regent to the Fifth Dalai Lama. In the winter of 1640, Gushri Khan, the Mongol king, defeated all the Dalai Lama's enemies. The Fifth Dalai Lama was then seated on the throne of the deposed king.

After taking the throne, the Dalai Lama spent the rest of his life rewriting history to fit the war of conquest in with the non-violent philosophy of Buddhism. Immediately after the end of the war, he rushed his *Song of the Queen of Spring* (The History of Tibet by the fifth Dalai Lama, completed in 1643, celebrating the Dalai Lama's coming to power in 1642; he represented this event as a "new spring" in the history of the country) into print "with a journalistic timeliness" to influence the way people perceived the conquest.[403] He suggested in this work:

> Highly advanced Buddhist *yogins* may be able to undertake acts of violence that serve salutary ends without themselves experiencing afflictive emotions. Under certain circumstances, cases of murder, suicide, self-sacrifice, warfare and other types of violence may be regarded as legitimate within Buddhist discourse, so long as they are carried out by people capable of undertaking them without generating harmful mental attitudes.[404]

Derek Maher noted how the religious leader framed the military campaign in "Sacralized Warfare: The Fifth Dalai Lama and the Discourse of Religious Violence":

> The [Fifth] Dalai Lama not only embeds Gushri Khan's military exploits within a Buddhist narrative, but he intends to evoke an identity between

Buddha and the Khan . . . Additionally, the Khan is depicted as a *dharmaja*, or a religious king, a class of sovereign that is regarded as particularly just and righteous because they dedicate their rule to promoting the interests of Buddhism.[405]

Of course, it isn't so easy to scrub the blood from the hands of a murderer, even when the criminal is on your side. Even more so, because the Fifth Dalai Lama was utilizing Buddhist imagery and narratives to justify a victory in what was essentially a sectarian battle between two competing Buddhist sects.[406]

But to the victor go the spoils, and there is no greater booty than control of the historical narrative of an event. Despite the fact that the losers in the war viewed the Gushri Khan's conquests and the political ascendancy of the Dalai Lama as permeated with sectarian agendas, the Dalai Lama was able to reconfigure the entire symbolic universe of the new Tibet, placing the institution of the Dalai Lama at its core,[407] where it remains to this day.

BORN OF VIOLENCE AND VIOLENT STILL

Any Buddhist will tell you that the rules of *karma* would demand that once actors undertake a violent act, they are certain to have this repaid sometime in the future. And so, a devout Buddhist might well view the violence in Tibet in 1959 as simply the *karmic* recompense for past sins.

However, Tibetan Buddhists learned a different lesson from the founding of their country and its justification by the Fifth Dalai Lama in his *Song of the Queen of Spring*. They learned how to validate their own violence when fighting for what they believed in, and wanted.

This can be seen in the recent history of the country. When Tibetan monks originally rebelled against the Chinese Communist occupation in 1959, they used the *Mahaparinirvana Sutra*, (c. 150; considered by English-translator Kosho Yamamoto to be one of the three great masterpieces of *Mahayana* Buddhism) as scriptural evidence to authorize their armed resistance.[408]

Mikel Dunham examined the bellicose role of Tibetan Buddhist monks in his recent book, *Buddha's Warriors: The Story of the CIA-Backed Tibetan Freedom Fighters, the Chinese Communist Invasion, and the Ultimate Fall of Tibet*. In it, he recounted how the "non-violent" Buddhist monks of Eastern Tibet rose as warriors and defenders of the Buddhist faith. Whole monasteries in Kham armed themselves, claiming the mantle of "monk-warrior," and waged war against the Chinese occupiers. As Dunham noted of the *Khampa*:

> Buddhism provided the *Khampa* with a moral code and a sense of oneness with all things Tibetan. The *Khampa* code of conduct while killing an enemy was the same as when picking flowers for the Buddha's altar: proceed with unquestioning devotion, prostrate to the lamas, but stand up for your rights. Whole monasteries armed themselves and went to war.[409]

THAILAND

Buddhism reached Thailand as early as the 2nd century B.C.E., though the form currently practiced in that country (*Theravada* Buddhism) arrived in the sixth century. It was made the state religion with the establishment of the Thai kingdom of Sukhothai (the forerunner to the Thai state) in the thirteenth century. Today, nearly 95% of Thai are *Theravada* Buddhists.

Like other Buddhist countries, Thailand has not remained untouched by Buddhism's violent hand. Thailand has developed a tradition that mimics the Tibetan *Khampa* — the warlike Buddhist warriors of rugged Eastern Tibet — in their own ideal of the military monk.

BUDDHIST APOCALYPSE

In the country's past we find a series of military activities relating to the "millennial accounts," a belief in a messianic return of a figure called *Maitreya*, a *bodhisattva* who is to appear on Earth as a successor of the historic Buddha. Most Buddhists accept the legend of *Maitreya* as a statement about an event that will take place when *dharma* (teachings of the Buddha) will have been forgotten on Earth.

However, like many messianic believers, Thai Buddhists concluded that contemporary woes could lead to the return of *Maitreya* and the coming of ultimate bliss. This return would take place after a period of apocalyptic bloodletting that could be likened, in Christian terminology, to the stories of Armageddon from the Book of Revelation, the last book of the New Testament. Between 1699 and 1959, in eight revolts against Siamese and Thai governments, Buddhist revolutionaries held to a belief that the imminent catastrophes of those conflicts would to be followed by material and spiritual bliss.[410]

MILITARY MONK

Buddhist "just war" theory can be followed through Thai history. In the 1970s, Phra Kittiwuttho (b. 1936; propagated an interpretation of Buddhism that justified centralized authoritarian rule and the use of force to eradicate political threats to the establishment[411]) sanctioned opposing Thai communists on two concepts: 1) the antagonist to the state is a manifestation of *mara*, an embodiment of moral depravity and 2) killing such a manifestation is not the same as killing a human being.[412]

These streams of thought led to an extreme interpretation of Buddhism, an outlier even in terms of a world where Buddhism and violence have often been intertwined. As in Tibet, Thai Buddhism created the "military monk," Buddhist practitioners who are fully ordained monks, while simultaneously serving as armed soldiers. These monks embody the fusion of the militant nation-state and Thai Buddhist principles.[413]

It is interesting to note how very similar dynamics from different religions mimic each other. Thai Buddhism's "warrior-monk" echoes a similar spiritual movement of the Christian faith. Barbara Ehrenreich described such a caste in medieval Europe, a precursor of Thai Buddhism's "military monk":

> It was the Crusades [1095–1291] that led to the emergence of a new kind of warrior, the warrior-monk, pledged to lifelong chastity as well as to war . . . The way of the knight — at least that of the chaste and chivalrous knight — became every bit as holy as that of the cloistered monk.[414]

Michael Jerryson observed in *Militarizing Buddhism: Violence in Southern Thailand*, that the "warrior-monk" ideal has evolved within contemporary Thai Buddhism:

> Since 2002, Buddhist spaces have become militarized by the very existence of military personnel working and living in them . . . military personnel residing at it usually raise the outer walls and stretch barbed wire around the entrance and perimeter. They also convert Buddhist pavilions into barracks, transform sleeping quarters into bunkers and create lookout posts near the entrances.[415]

This is not to say that all military men living within today's southern Thai monasteries are monks, nor that all monks are soldiers, but the nexus between the two is seamless, and there are many that wear both mantles.

Sri Lanka

Historically, the great military conquests of the Sinhalese Kingdoms in Sri Lanka (during medieval times) were conducted in the name of the Buddhist tradition and often with the blessings of Buddhist monks.[416] These religious efforts at temporal victory have not lessened, as contemporary Sri Lanka offers another well-documented case study of religiously sanctioned armed conflict in Buddhism. Recently, a civil war caused the death of hundreds of thousands of countrypersons, with the conflict often framed in sacred terms.

The Sri Lankan people were embroiled in a civil war from 1983 to 2009, a battle that included terrorism, political and economic oppression and open war between Sinhalese Buddhists and Tamil Hindus.

> Members of the Buddhist political party JVP were alleged to have blurred the lines between sacred duty and murder; they traced their justifications back to the Sinhalese mytho-historical chronicle called the *Mahavamsa*. In this work, the Buddhist king Duthagammani wages a sacred war against foreign invaders led by the Tamil king Ejara in the second century B.C.E. In the contemporary Buddhist view, killing the Tamil heathens did not constitute murder because Tamil warriors were neither meritorious nor, more importantly, Buddhist.[417]

History never dies. The *Mahavamsa* chronicle still rankles in Sri Lanka. An article in the Sri Lanka Guardian by a Tamil writer laid the blame for the violent turn to Sri Lankan Buddhism at the feet of this ancient text:

> According to Buddhism, a person ordained as a *Bikkhu* [monk] should practice *Ahimsa* (non-violence), *Karuna* (compassion), *Metta* (affection), and *Maithriya* (loving-kindness) toward fellow humans, (irrespective of race or religion), not only by words but also in his thoughts and action. Unfortunately in Sri Lanka, due to the influence of the *Mahavamsa*, a Buddhist *Bikkhu* is at liberty to engage in racist politics and promote Sinhala-Buddhist chauvinism and hatred, as we see today.[418]

Buddhist religious ceremonies have been co-opted by the military, echoing a similar synthesis in Japan, Tibet, Thailand and other countries. Daniel Kent noted in *Onward Buddhist Soldiers: Preaching to the Sri Lankan Army*, concerning Buddhist religious ceremonies:

> [These] have been commissioned by the army to correspond with a large-scale military operation that was about to begin in the north of the island. The commander of every army base in the country had been ordered to commission sermons during the week leading up to the operation. This entire ceremony had been sponsored by the army in an attempt to bless its soldiers, protect them and grant them success in battle.[419]

MONGOLIA

As was already noted, Mongolian Buddhists played a central role in the founding of Tibet, through prosecuting a war against a Buddhist clan that was a rival to the Fifth Dalai Lama. Gushri Khan, a leader of the *Khoshut Khanate* in Mongolia, defeated the Dalai Lama's enemies (1639–1642), displacing the rival dominant school of the *Karmapas* (one of the four major schools of Tibetan Buddhism). After this military victory, the Fifth Dalai Lama was seated on the throne of the deposed king. He honored Gushri Khan with the title of *King of Tibet*.

Gushri Khan was himself basing his military behavior on the earlier thought of Mongolian Buddhist leaders. As Vesna Wallace noted in *Legalized Violence: Punitive Measures of Buddhist Khans in Mongolia*:

> Khutukhtu Setsen Khung Taiji's (d. 1586; the ruler of the Ordos Mongols) ... conveyed the message that at times it is necessary for a Buddhist ruler to sanction acts of violence for the sake of establishing the *dharma* and for securing inner stability of the state. As attested in the codes of law instituted by later Mongolian rulers, this message echoed for a long time in the minds of Buddhist legislators and the penal systems they established ... the Mongol rulers severely punished those who disobeyed their religious and secular ordinances.[420]

Violence permeated the Mongolian state until the government grew *less* Buddhist, not more. From the middle of the 17th century until the first half of the 20th century, Mongolian Buddhist nobles and monks engaged in violence on behalf of their faith numerous times, and in many variations.[421] Brutal punishments were meted out for the commitment of both civil and religious crime until 1921, when the Mongolian Revolutionary Government (an outgrowth of Soviet secular Communism) was formed.

It should be noted that during this long period of state-sponsored corporeal justice, the penalties were applied after opening eulogies to legislators who were recognized as high incarnate lamas and living Buddhas, praised for their virtue, wisdom and unbiased compassion.[422]

A passage taken from Mongolia's *White History of the Tenfold Virtuous Dharma* (c. 16th century) exhibits the viciousness that could take place not only under the aegis of Buddhist practice, but which might be visited upon the Buddhist monks themselves:

> If a monk breaks his precepts, disrobe him. Tie his hands tightly and paint his face with ink. Place a black flag on his head. Put a robe around him and beat him with a golden stick on his buttocks ... Afterwards, banish him to a faraway place. If one steals, blind his eyes. If one tells a lie, cut his tongue. If one injures the state, take his life.

ET TU, UNITED STATES?

According to the Pew Forum on Religion and Public Life,[423] Buddhism is the third largest religion in America (behind Christianity and Judaism), with as many as 10 million adherents. However, far from offering a peaceful palliative to what is the most militarized nation currently on Earth, American Buddhists embrace the contemporary American ethos and, as so many Buddhists who came before them did, use their religion to serve the state.

Buddhist practitioner Barbara O'Brien noted in *War and Buddhism: Buddhist Teachings on War*:

> Today there are more than 3000 Buddhists serving in the United States armed forces, including some Buddhist chaplains . . . During World War II, approximately half of the troops in Japanese-American units such as the 100th Battalion and the 442nd Infantry were Buddhists.

> In the Spring 2008 issue of *Tricycle*, Travis Duncan wrote of the Vast Refuge Dharma Hall Chapel at the U.S. Air Force Academy. At the dedication of the chapel, the Reverend Dai En Wiley Burch of the Hollow Bones Rinzai Zen school said, "Without compassion, war is a criminal activity. Sometimes it is necessary to take life, but we never take life for granted."[424]

FINAL THOUGHTS

The Florentine political philosopher Niccolo Machiavelli (d. 1527) said: "The great majority of humans are satisfied with appearances, as though they were realities, and are often more influenced by things that seem than by those that are."[425]

This has not changed to our era. An article by journalist Chris Mooney, "We Can't Handle the Truth," explored how we order reality by what we "feel," or what we already believe, independent of the facts, in this case, discussing "belief" versus scientific actualities:

> It's not just that people twist or selectively read scientific evidence to support their preexisting views. According to research by Yale University professor Dan Kahan and his colleagues, people's deep seated views about morality, and about the way that society should be ordered, strongly predict whom they consider to be a scientific expert in the first place — people reject the validation of a scientific source because its conclusion contradicts their deeply held views.[426]

This clinging to one's views can be seen in the context of this study. For instance, one very important source for this chapter was *Buddhist Warfare*, by Michael Jerryson and Mark Juergensmeyer (Oxford University Press, 2010). Even before it was released, however, Buddhist followers were upset with the message — not that they necessarily *disagreed* with it on any factual grounds, just that they didn't *want* to believe it. Michael Jerryson wrote an article in *Religion Dispatches* about the book prior to its release, describing how Buddhists shape reality, as well as how people would rather believe in propaganda than the harsh truth:

> I realized that I was a consumer of a very successful form of propaganda. Since the early 1900s, Buddhist monastic intellectuals such as Walpola Rahula, D. T. Suzuki, and Tenzin Gyatso, the Fourteenth Dalai Lama, have labored to raise Western awareness of their cultures and traditions . . . presenting specific aspects of their Buddhist traditions while leaving out others. In an effort to combat this view and to *humanize* Buddhists, Mark Juergensmeyer and I put together [*Buddhist Warfare*]. It apparently touched some nerves in the academic community *before* its release. Some have objected to the cover [a Buddhist monk holding a gun], which they feel is not an appropriate subject for Buddhism.[427]

We run into this intransigence in the face of Truth time after time. Many faithful are unwilling to accept the violent-sacred observance in their own spiritual path. This version of their creed, often more honest than the image of a religion based in and leading to peace, comes into conflict with the "propaganda" surrounding their creed.

I will state here, once again and clearly: all religions are paths of violence. And, what's more, all religions justify their violence within the context of what they hold most sacred.

CHAPTER EIGHT: WAR AS LOVE

Thus far, this study has been concerned with the historical fusion between God and war, violence and the sacred in all religious paths. If this book ended here, it would be but one more academic investigation, another uncomfortable truth that we could consign to the past and ignore.

But the union of violence and the sacred continues unabated into our own time and culture. By looking more closely at this dynamic as it plays itself out in our contemporary social and political worlds, we can better understand it.

In this section, I will briefly outline how contemporary conflicts are often couched in the religious and spiritual terms that I have been examining. And then, in a longer section, I will examine the American experience since the attacks of September 11, 2001 — and how the country's reaction to these events and subsequent wars are simply more of the same: violence in the name of the sacred. And given how members of all religious paths are steeped in the language, imagery and history of war *as* religion, we can begin to appreciate why politicians and political leaders utilize the language of the sacred to sell war and, even more disturbing, why it successfully resonates within the general society.

ABRAHAM'S CURSE

In 2008, Bruce Chilton wrote a book entitled *Abraham's Curse*, in which he traced much of the sacrificial violence in the Abrahamic faiths back to the event on Mount Moriah (Genesis 22) when God demanded that Abraham sacrifice his son, Isaac — and Abraham concurred. Here, the idea of God's violent rapacity and abject human fealty to this sacral bloodlust was written into the spiritual DNA of Judaism, Christianity and Islam.

While it is vital to situate the contemporary war as love dynamic on its historical foundation, it is just as important to see how this ethos is central to today's conflicts around the world. I touched briefly on this in the previous sections, but now will take a more in depth look at the here and now.

In most bellicose situations, the state (or rebel leaders, in the case of non-state actors) sets itself up as an ultimate truth, one whose geo-political goals are almost always tied to the will of God:

> The moral certitude of the state in wartime is a kind of fundamentalism. And this dangerous, messianic brand of religion, one where self-doubt is minimal, has come increasingly to color the modern world of Christianity, Judaism and Islam . . . there is a danger of a growing fusion between those in the state who wage war and those who believe they understand and can act as agents for God.[428]

Coupled with this is the insidious manner in which the idea of human sacrifice, as an ultimate manner of worship (as first laid out in the Abrahamic story from Genesis), has become intertwined with not only religious worship, but also fealty to the state.

> The rhetoric of sacrifice has been passed on from its religious sources to the lexicon of politically inspired violence . . . Since the end of the 19th century, powerful movements of fundamentalist interpretation — Christian, Jewish and Muslim — have arisen that demand literal sacrifice from their adherents . . . we live in an age of sacrifice.[429]

Sacrificial violence, both suffered by believers and inflicted by them on others, has woven itself deeply into the pattern of Western history. This impulse led to more child sacrifice in the 20th century than in any previous era. In recent times, adolescents and pre-adolescents have joined up with the Lord's Resistance Army in Uganda, the Shining Path in Peru, *al-Qaeda* in Afghanistan and Pakistan, the Aryan Nation in the United States, national fronts throughout Europe and Australia, Maoist guerillas in Asia[430] and even, counting eighteen and nineteen year olds as adolescents, in the United States army, where they are sent to the ultimate sacrifice in the name of God and country.

LOVE, WAR AND SACRIFICE IN THE 21ST CENTURY

Virtually all war *language*, whether describing religious wars or secular conflicts, is laced with religious imagery. One could argue that there is no such thing as a "secular" war, except along the very edges of statecraft, where companies such as Dyncorp, or persons such as Muammar Gadhafi (Libya), or petty princes in Africa and the Middle East collect bands of mercenaries to fight wars. Other than these few and small examples, the vast majority of state -sponsored violence can still be collected under the umbrella of sacred violence, bringing war and God together as the ultimate form of worship.

For instance, Jewish thinking on war and the State of Israel is often deeply affected by the specter of sacral violence. Pulitzer Prize nominated Professor Regina Schwartz noted in *The Curse of Cain: The Violent Legacy of Monotheism*, the linkage between contemporary Israel and the ancient, Biblical precursor:

> The founders and leaders of modern Israel have not thought about their new nation without invoking the ancient one. Their rhetoric is heavily laced with biblical citations. In his opening remarks in the Middle East peace talks in Madrid in 1991, Yitzhak Shamir intoned the psalmist's "If I forget thee, O Jerusalem, let my right hand lose its cunning" and the *Haggadah*'s "Next year in Jerusalem," and he began with an assertion of the complete continuity between the biblical and the present one. The ancient homeland blurs into the national agenda.[431]

The specifics of how this formulation infuses Israeli thinking are not difficult to discern. War correspondent Christopher Hedges noted that he had "heard settlers on the West Bank argue that Palestinian towns, which had been Muslim since the 7th century, belong to them because it says so in the Bible."[432] Jewish citizens in traditional movements throughout Israel have cited the *Torah* to define the political boundaries of today's nation, and the Founders of the state utilized Biblical stories from the Books of Deuteronomy, Joshua and Judges to underpin their arguments for the divinely sanctioned war to birth Israel.[433]

Islam, as we all know, has certainly produced no more peaceful contemporary events than the stories of the *Torah* have. As we have already seen, the Islamic conception of war for religion is based in a deeply rooted understanding of the integration of politics and faith. "The juristic ideal of the unitary *dar al-Islam* (house of Islam) with leadership at once religious and political has impressed itself deeply on historical Muslim polities."[434]

Finding echoes of this in Islamic political activities today — fusing violence and religious obligation — is not difficult. The Muslims who flew the airplanes into the World Trade Centers did so in the service of *Allah*, as have hundreds of other suicide bombers over the past 30 years.

In keeping with the idea of child sacrifice, the age of these religious warriors grows younger and younger — "the Afghan government places the figure of trained child suicide terrorists at 5,000."[435] This represents but one of the countries affected with this disease.

From Osama bin Laden, who said "Peace be upon our Prophet, Muhammad ibn Abdallah, who said, 'I have been sent with the sword between my hands to ensure that no one but God is worshipped',"[436] to the Shia scholar Murtaza Mutahhari (d. 1979): "The *shahid* [warrior in the name of God] can be compared to a candle whose job is to burn out and get extinguished in order to shed light for the benefit of others," Islamic religious leaders have issued calls for sacrifice and murder in the name of God, always based on their reading of their violent religious scripture. At Mutahhari's funeral, the Ayatollah Khomeini praised the scholar, asserting: "Islam grows through sacrifice and martyrdom of its cherished ones."[437]

The perversity in this realm knows few bounds. Christopher Hedges related a story of a Palestinian father who egged his own children on to become martyrs in the name of God, and the Palestinian cause:

> Rayyan gave two of his sons — ages fifteen and sixteen — money to join the youths who throw rocks at Israeli checkpoints. His youngest, Mohammad, was crippled by an Israeli bullet. All three, according to their father, strive to be one thing: martyrs for Palestine. "I only pray that God will choose them," he said.[438]

While it is certainly *de rigueur* these days in the United States to highlight this dynamic within Islam, to the point that the major American news commentator Bill O'Reilly could say, "Muslims killed us on 9–11"[439] on national television and suffer no professional repercussions, the fact remains that Christianity, and specifically American Christianity, is no less prone to sacred violence than Muslims or Jews. And the United States has at its disposal armaments so frightening that it could unilaterally choose to initiate the Apocalypse, as envisioned in its Bible.

In the book *Is Religion Killing Us?*, Jack Nelson-Pallmeyer noted, "Most Christians, including those in the United States, have rejected Jesus's nonviolent power and a nonviolent God while adopting superior violence as Lord and Savior."[440]

I will treat the subject of America's sacred violence in the next section. It should be noted, however, that I am not singling out America or Christianity as in any way special in this war as love dynamic. However, as the United States is currently the largest military actor in the world, it is therefore *de facto* the most dangerous violent force today. It would behoove us to take a more jaundiced look at this country's motivations and behavior, instead of allowing Americans to continue blithely on a destructive path while believing things such as this:

> Most [U.S.] citizens eagerly embraced the explanations of leaders who said we were attacked because of our basic goodness and the base evil of our attackers. We, therefore, can rightfully hate them, hunt them down and kill them in a permanent war against terrorism. God, of course, is on our side.[441]

AMERICA: A CASE STUDY IN SACRED VIOLENCE

> Hypocrisy in America is not a sin, but a necessity and a way of life. It makes possible armories of mass destruction side by side with the proliferation of churches, cults and charities. Hypocrisy holds the nation together so that it can preach, and practice what is does not preach.[442]

There is no country that so worships the fresh, the new and the future, as does the United States. This country has always represented a teleological arrow pointing excitedly to the next invention, the latest technological gadget and the most recent cultural or social creation. Since the first locomotive rumbled west in the middle of the 19th century, the United States has believed that salvation was just around the corner, and if not in the form of the Apocalypse, than perhaps it would come through its ingenious innovations.

The cult of modernity in the United States, however, has in no way altered the God is war dynamic. As Friedrich Nietzsche (d. 1900) stated at the beginning of our frantic age of progress, "calamity lies concealed in the absurd guilelessness and blind confidence of 'modern ideas.'"[443] Technology, God and war sometimes fuse together in the United State into a calamitous modern social stew.

One thing "progress" has done is to advance our means of destruction, to quicken the pace of sacrifice, to invent new and more horrifying manners of proving our love for God with the destruction of the "other," as well as developing gleaming new methods of keeping our sacrificial victims barely alive, short of limbs and eyes and pieces of skull, living testaments to how very deeply we are committed to our God and His blood-lust.

Nietzsche said that anyone who fathoms the calamity concealed beneath our faith in progress and Christian-European morality "suffers from an anxiety that is past all comparison."[444] I concur, as I am up nights tossing and turning, trying to figure out what, if anything, I can do to help stem the orgy of self-destruction that, I fear, bears down upon us from the near future.

So I have written this book, a fittingly impotent act by a man operating outside of the political and cultural mainstream. With this work, I fancy myself joining ranks with a long line of prophets from the Biblical Isaiah to Bill McKibben (b. 1960), who lives in Vermont and bitterly describes the environmental disaster that he warns is about to sweep away several thousand years of human civilization and its progress.

As in all cultures, violence and religion are at the heart of the American psyche. In keeping with the universal idea of sacral violence, the more often Americans go to church, the more likely they are to support the torture of suspected terrorists. In recent polls, people unaffiliated with any religious organization were least likely to approve it.[445] Having removed themselves from the bondage of religious thinking, so-called secular citizens were able to judge actions by their own merits, outside of the grim history of religions' sacred brutality.

The belief that violence is often religiously sanctioned — and the fact, as we saw in the first section of this book, that it can feel spiritually cathartic in the short term for most members of a society — has led the United States to become the single greatest exporter of carnage in today's world.

AMERICA: THE NEW ISRAEL

> Contrary to the American myth and the illusion of American sinlessness, the United States is a country founded on some of the worst crimes against humanity — genocide of Native Americans and enslavement of Africans . . .[446]

Underpinning the sacred violence is the belief that the United States has replaced Israel as God's chosen people. As absurd as this might sound, it is no joke — and the sense of exceptionalism that it engenders is both frightening and dangerous.

Nineteenth-century author Herman Melville captured the particular American spirit:

> We Americans are the peculiar chosen people — the Israel of our time; we bear the ark of the liberties of the world. God has predestined, mankind expects, great things from our race . . . the rest of the nations must soon be in our rear. We are the pioneers of the world, the advance guard, sent on through the wilderness of untried things to break the path into the New World that is ours.[447]

As Melville's quote illustrates, America promotes itself as a religious or mythic entity. In a perverse conflation of nation and God — seen in almost all empires before us, whether it was ancient Rome, 16ᵗʰ-century Spain or Nazi Germany — large numbers of Americans adopt religious attitudes toward their country, overlaying the sacred violence of the Abrahamic tradition on top of the nation-state. The country functions as a type of religion itself, the object of devotion and sacrifice that is normally reserved for God.[448]

A recent survey by the Brookings Institution (one of the oldest and most prominent research organizations in Washington D.C. tracking public policy and views) found that 58% of Americans agreed with the statement: "God has granted America a special place in human history."[449] The country is often portrayed in language reminiscent of Jesus Christ, with political leaders going so far as to identify the nation *with* Christ. The church's teachings of the risen Son of God have been transferred wholesale to the United States. The nation is treated with a reverence that amounts to worship.[450]

Professor Robert H. Nelson (School of Public Policy at the University of Maryland), writing for the PBS website, said:

> In his State of the Union address [January 25, 2011], President Obama offered the latest updating of the American national faith. We are a nation uniquely created, he said, on "common hopes and a common creed." This mission is what "sets us apart as a nation." We . . . must be "not just a place on a map, but the light to the world." John Winthrop [d. 1649; Puritan leader and founding father of Massachusetts] could not have said it better . . . We are hearing again the basic story of America: We have sinned, we will be called to account, we must reform our ways, but God will bless us if we now heed his commands. We are the chosen people.[451]

The Fourth of July becomes a religious holiday for Americans. On Independence Day 2006, President George W. Bush offered this homage to American exceptionalism:

> We offer our gratitude to all the American patriots, past and present, who have sought to advance freedom and lay the foundations of peace. Because of their sacrifice, this country remains a beacon of hope for all who dream of liberty and a shining example to the world of what a free people can achieve. May God continue to bless the United States of America.[452]

All of this talk about America's "light" and its "shining beacon" actually has an ominous subtext to it. For the American "messiah" does not come to inaugurate the Kingdom of God on peaceful clouds of glory. Rather, he comes as one of the Four Horsemen of the Apocalypse (Book of Revelation), using the force of his military, political and economic dominance to subdue the rest of the globe. As Anglican priest Jeremy Young noted in *The Violence of God and the War on Terror*: "This is where the myth of redemptive violence, the idea that evil can only be overcome by force, is particularly influential upon the myth of America . . . the myth of redemptive violence is the real religion of America."[453]

And since America considers itself the standard bearer of truth, and follows closely Augustinian ideas concerning "just war" and his conception of the notion that "error has no right," those who disagree with America are obviously in error. "Because they are wrong and are resisting the onward march of Truth, they have no right to hold onto their beliefs nor to hold America to account for its actions nor to oppose America's God-given right to impose its own convictions upon them."[454]

SACRIFICING FOR GOD AND COUNTRY

The myth of religious America — in which the country has been chosen by God to perfect the world in its image — is endemic in its culture. Many young men and, more recently, women, yearn to sacrifice themselves *as Christ* to the god of nation. After all, to fight a never-ending series of wars in God's name, warriors are needed — and plenty of them. By bringing the sacred, the state and war together, the necessary pool of willing soldiers can be assured.

> The theology of Christ's eternal sacrifice remains, as well as the incentive for martyrs to emulate his ennobling death. Perhaps even more powerfully, [we] capture the rhetoric of Hebrews in a secular form, offering young soldiers the immortality of national remembrance in exchange for their willingness to shed the human blood that alone makes sacrifice effective.[455]

There are thousands of citations one could find to situate this idea within America's mainstream culture, but I will share just one — published in a small-town newspaper in Greensburg, Indiana, reporting on a Memorial Day observance in 2008:

> Memorial Day often brings tears of sadness with swellings of pride to those who have had family members make the ultimate sacrifice in the line of duty. Nowhere was that made more evident than at the annual Memorial Day event at South Park Cemetery. Honoring fallen soldiers, all the way from the Revolutionary War to the current conflict in Iraq, was cause enough for quite a crowd to gather to remember those who had paid with their lives to keep the freedom Americans know alive . . . Sacrifices [are] meaningless without remembrance . . . Pastor Keith Dover (Mt. Moriah Baptist Church, Greensburg, IN) led the group in prayer: "Let us fix our eyes on Jesus, who gives all men, women and children the opportunity to be free," he said. The ceremony's guest speaker, Rev. Jim Splitt (co-Pastor,

First Presbyterian Church of Adrian, MI), then addressed the crowd . . . "But never forget those who made the ultimate sacrifice. Our calling is to honor the sacrifices of our country" . . . The American Legion Ladies' Auxiliary 129 were then asked to place wreaths on crosses representing every war in America's long history. With the memorial wreaths hung and blowing gently in the breeze, the Tree City Harmonizers graced the crowd with their rendition of the Battle Hymn of the Republic. Pastor Dover then offered his benediction: "We ask for blessings over our freedom, nation, families and soldiers."[456]

For the record, the first stanza of the Battle Hymn of the Republic goes thusly:

> Mine eyes have seen the glory of the coming of the Lord:
> He is trampling out the vintage where the grapes of wrath are stored;
> He hath loosed the fateful lightning of His terrible swift sword:
> His truth is marching on.

AMERICAN HISTORY: OUR VIOLENCE IS GOD'S WILL

In America, God and war have a particular kinship: evoking God in the midst of mass killing is inspirational . . . Divine sanction has been used to give meaning to the Constitution's promise of equality, as well as to license genocide . . . This impulse to blend God and war owes much to the American temperament: Americans have always feared one (today, nine out of ten call themselves believers) and loved the other (the United States has fought in dozens of armed conflicts in the nation's two-and-a-third centuries). Not a few old warriors have admitted to thrilling to the words of "Onward Christian Soldiers."[457]

The fusion of God, nation and institutional slaughter goes back to the very beginnings of the nation.

From the very first days of the American colonies, the settlers' belief that they were a chosen people was accompanied by an Old Testament belief that God was a "God of Warre." The image of the ancient Israelites and their battles with their neighbors was used to justify wars against the latter-day "Amalekites," whether Indian or French, and God was held to fight for America in those wars.[458]

From these beginnings, a nearly unbroken line of sacral violence may be drawn down to our current era. In 1640, one New England assembly passed a series of resolutions which included the following: "1) The Earth is the Lord's and the Fullness thereof; 2) The Lord may give the Earth or any part of it to his Chosen People; and 3) We are the chosen people."[459] This certainly gave the proper religious context for the slaughter that was to take place over the next two centuries, as the European settlers considered the Native Americans to be "Canaanites," their land equivalent to Canaan and themselves the new Israelites. Robert Allen Warrior (b. 1963), an Osage Indian and professor at the University of Illinois, noted:

> Many Puritan preachers were fond of referring to Native Americans as Amalekites and Canaanites — people who, if they would not be converted, were worthy of annihilation. By examining such instances in theological and political writings, in sermons and elsewhere, we can understand how Americans' self-image as a "chosen people" has produced rhetoric to justify domination.[460]

By the time of the Founding Fathers (c. 1770s), most of whom were slave owners themselves, an almost never-ending series of military victories and territorial expansion against the Native Americans, French and then the British had proven God's providence and beneficence. To complete the image of America as the new Israel, Benjamin Franklin wanted the Great Seal of the United States to depict Moses, rod lifted, with the Egyptian Army (British Redcoats) drowning in the Red Sea (Atlantic Ocean).[461]

It is hard to deny that the Founding Fathers exhibited a very different subtext to the beginnings of the country than the secular underpinnings that are believed to be enshrined in the Constitution. John Quincy Adams (d. 1848; sixth president of the United States) said at a Fourth of July speech in 1837, at Newburyport, Massachusetts:

> Is it not that, in the chain of human events, the birthday of the nation is indissolubly linked with the birthday of the Savior? That it forms a leading event in the progress of the Gospel dispensation? Is it not that the Declaration of Independence first organized the social compact on the foundation of the Redeemer's mission upon earth? That it laid the cornerstone of human government upon the first precepts of Christianity?[462]

Timothy Dwight (d. 1817), President of Yale University, spoke of the Revolution ushering in an America that would become the "principle seat of that new, that peculiar kingdom which shall be given to the saints most high." Just prior to the Revolution, the American preacher Ebenezer Baldwin insisted that the calamities of war would only help bring about God's plan for the New World,[463] an apocalyptic strain in the American *zeitgeist* that continues to this day.

This manner of thinking did not die with the Founding Fathers and their contemporaries. During the Civil War (1861–1865), both sides claimed the mantle of God, and God Himself was kept busy destroying His enemies on both sides of the Mason Dixon Line.

> The leaders of the Confederacy had no qualms about claiming that God
> had uniquely raised the South up to do His work in the world. Christi-
> anity held an exalted and powerful place in Confederate culture. [At the
> same time] Civil War northern clergy believed that their cause was or-
> dained by God. Part of their mission in this conflict was to punish the
> South for seceding from the United States, a political community that was
> indivisible because it was created by God. But as Northern propagandists
> extolled the Christian virtues of their national Union and the spiritual
> superiority of their society over a sinful South in need of God's repentance,
> the religious and political leaders of the Confederacy were building what
> they perceived to be their own Christian civilization. Indeed, the "Chris-
> tian nation" theme was even more prominent in the South than it was in
> the North. They viewed the Confederacy as a refuge for the godly amid the
> "infidelity" of the Union to which they once belonged.[464]

Even the war's most violent slaughter, Sherman's slow motion, genocidal march to the sea through Georgia in 1864, took on a sacred patina.
On this scorched earth campaign, echoing Old Testament dictums to
completely destroy the enemy, General William Sherman was heartened
to hear many of his 60,000 soldiers break into the Doxology in unison,
singing "Praise God from whom all blessings flow." Flush with the Spirit
himself, Sherman intoned: "Noble fellows! God will take care of them."[465]

Americans certainly didn't learn to disentangle God and war from
the most destructive war on domestic soil in the country's history. At
the start of the Spanish–American War in 1898, U.S. Senator Albert Bev-
eridge (d. 1927; R-IN) took to the floor of the United States Capitol and
assured:

> God has made us master organizers of the world to establish a system
> where chaos reigns. He has given us the spirit of progress to overwhelm
> the forces of reaction through the earth . . . Were it not for such a force as
> this, the world would lapse into barbarism and night. And of all our race,
> he has marked the American people as His chosen nation to finally lead in
> the regeneration of the world.[466]

Among other things, this quote evinces how very little progress we
have made as a species in terms of spiritual issues in the past 5000 years.
This formulation of America the Good fighting against the forces of chaos and dissolution echoes the Babylonian creation myth, where Tiamat
represented the "enemy," the chaos which threatens to destroy the order of the world and Marduk is played by America, the god who will
give security to other nations provided that they accept its leadership
unquestioningly.[467]

William McKinley (d. 1901; 25th president of the United States), president at the time of this particular war, found his solace for the slaughter

in God: "I walked the floor of the White House night after night until midnight. I went down on my knees and prayed to Almighty God for light and guidance." His specific concern was over whether to annex the Philippines. And the Almighty God answered his prayers: "There was nothing left to do but to take them all and to educate the Filipinos and uplift and civilize and Christianize them." Three years later, half a million Filipinos were dead.[468]

In 1906, the battle still raged in the Philippines between the "liberating" American force and the stubborn native population. America, chosen by God to bring light to this world of chaos, could not be stopped, however, and General Leonard Wood (d. 1927) sent the following cable to President Theodore Roosevelt breathlessly recounting his victory over the Filipino Muslims:

> The enemy numbered six hundred — including woman and children — we abolished them utterly, leaving not even a baby alive to cry for its dead mother. This is incomparably the greatest victory that was ever achieved by the Christian soldiers of the United States.[469]

The President's reply extolled the general's "brilliant feat of arms" and the excellent manner in which he had "uplifted the honor of the American flag."[470]

America barely had time to catch its breath from this Far-Eastern adventure when God picked up the phone again: the storm clouds of World War I formed. The clergy joined in the clamor to "kill, kill, kill," assuring that "God is on our side — it is His will that the Germans be killed." Of course, in Germany at the same time, their good pastors called upon their young men to kill the godless allies, to please the very same Christian God.[471]

After World War I, American theologians felt a need to better ground the impetus for war on a solid Christian foundation. After all, the "War to end all Wars" hadn't actually done so — ergo the act of war itself must be re-centered in the spirit life of the nation, so the next war might do what the last was unable. Reinhold Niebuhr (d. 1971; the most influential religious leader of the 1940s and 1950s in American public affairs) built his case for war on Augustine's concept of original sin, arguing that sometimes-righteous force is necessary to extirpate injustice and subdue evil in a sinful world.[472] Not quite as gleeful as past commentators, Niebuhr was considered the pre-eminent sober theologian of his era, and therefore his words carried great weight.

That God smiled upon the American forces was sometimes borne out by the facts on the ground. In addition to piling up military victories through World War II, specific "Acts of God" sometimes aided the military on its march to triumph.

> As General George Patton's columns rolled into Belgium in December 1944, rain and snow slowed the advance, and gave the enemy cover. Patton ordered his chaplain to write a prayer for good weather. The skies cleared for eight straight days; American air power decimated the Nazis. Patton gave his chaplain a bronze star.[473]

Although the Korean War (1950–1953) and then Vietnam War (1961–1975) showed a decided lack of focus on God's part, America regained its spiritual balance with a series of incursions in which He had little choice but to side with His chosen people. Grenada (1983), Panama (1989), a quick bomb strike on Libya (1986) helped rebuild the relationship between the Almighty and the country, leading up to the First Gulf War (1990–1991). Finally having mastered the medium of television, the war played out more like a mini-series or video game than a real-life slaughter, and made it clear that America, once again, was the force against which chaos would collide in its never-ending attempt to undo all of the good that America was wreaking throughout the world.

This self-righteous and God-sanctioned violence has been devastating in the world. Spending ten times more money on the military than on health care between 1940 and 1996,[474] the United States has sallied forth on a destructive course from the Far East through the Middle East, into Africa, Central and South America, leaving very few geographic regions untouched by its bellicose interventions.

Despite constant protestations to be doing God's work and bringing order where once there reigned godless chaos, the fact remains that Americans and their allies typically cause ten to twenty times more combat casualties than American forces suffer.[475] Even more disturbing, these enemy military deaths represent a miniscule fraction of the total slaughter, as in recent wars, civilian deaths have accounted for up to 90% of all fatalities.[476]

Additionally, the American military-industrial complex, engorged with nearly half of the government budget, seeks out other manners of exporting this form of love. The United States is the world's largest supplier of arms, manufacturing almost half of the weaponry sold on the world market.[477] For terrorists and warriors around the world, the United States is the great gun bazaar — and it is not at all unusual for Americans involved in interventions abroad to be killed with American-made weapons.

Lastly, it should be noted what broad support these policies have, from the massive military budget to the history of incursions: between 60% and 85% of the American public support a military action after it begins. For instance, in March 1966, 59% of Americans agreed with American involvement in the Vietnam War.[478] On the eve of the Iraq War (2003), the incursion was supported by 62% of respondents, while the First Persian Gulf War (1991) saw a 79% approval rate in its early stages.[479]

George W. Bush, September 11, 2001, and America's 21st-Century Crusade

> The troubling pattern of grievance followed by violent response justified in relation to faith, God or sacred text is evident in the U.S. response to the terrorist attacks: U.S. leaders peppered their pronouncements of retaliation . . . with references to God. The rhetoric of President Bush and his advisors is eerily similar to that of Osama bin Laden and his supporters . . . Each side poses the conflict as a struggle between good and evil . . . each side justifies the deaths of civilians . . . each believes the grave depravity can only be countered with lethal violence. Each invokes God's name to ground the righteousness of their cause.[480]

During the aftermath of the September 11, 2001 attacks, I and many people around me were astounded by the religious and even spiritual framing that George W. Bush used in describing the American pain and response to the event. Even more so, we were amazed by how it resonated with the American public and how the media kept parroting the absurd framing of light and dark, good and evil, God and Satan. How could people accept and even thrive on such a theistic approach to international politics?

In this final section, I will explore the specific language of God and violence that was used in the decade or so following the heinous incident. What should by now be clear — something that I did not, at the time, understand — was why this faith-based lexicon resonated so deeply and successfully within American culture: because virtually all American citizens, from whatever religious background, grew up in traditions where violence and the sacred were profoundly intertwined. True, the language used in America in the 21st century is primarily that of Christianity, but for Buddhists, Jews, Hindus and even Muslim-American patriots, there is a personal religious history of fusing God and war, which made the language of political leaders acceptable and even successful in framing the institutional violence that the terrorist attacks unleashed.

Earlier ideas of America as the Chosen People influenced contemporary political discourse well before the attacks, leading to a seamless attribution of "God's will" to the military response after the fact. "If we have to use force," Madeleine Albright (U.S. Secretary of State, 1997–2001) asserted, concerning America's bombing raids in Serbia (1999), "it is because we are America! We are the indispensable nation!"

George W. Bush echoed this language, insisting as he prepared the country for its mission against the Taliban in Afghanistan: "Our nation is chosen by God and commissioned by history to be a model for the world." Using the laws of deductive reasoning, U.S. violence was proposed to be an instrument of God's will.[481]

It is also important to note Bush's own fundamentalist views of "Redemption coming only through Apocalypse,"[482] and how deeply even this message resonates with many Christians, due to their conflation of violence and the return of the Messiah, as foretold in the Book of Revelation. Anglican minister Jeremy Young noted in *The Violence of God and the War on Terror*:

> George W. Bush holds a very conservative, even fundamentalist form of Christian belief that anticipates cosmic catastrophe as part of the divine plan for the redemption of the world, a belief shared by many Americans. From the apocalyptic perspective, the prospect of major world conflict is to be welcomed because it is a sign of the end and a preparation for the second coming of Christ.[483]

When combined with the belief that American violence is sanctioned by God, due to the United States' status as the heritors of the original covenant between God and the Jewish people, a dynamic emerges where many Americans believe that *their* violence is not only ordained but also necessary to fulfill God's grand plan.

Political leaders hardly had to lead the public to a conception of sacred violence, as it is so endemic in American culture that the immediate reaction was religious.

> In the weeks after the September [11, 2001] attacks, communities gathered for vigils and worship services. The enterprise of the state became imbued with a religious aura ... The state, and the institutions of state, became for many, the center of worship.[484]

On the first anniversary of the attacks, seven months before the 2003 incursion into Iraq, President Bush said: "Our cause is even larger than our country. Ours is the course of human dignity, freedom guided by conscience grounded by peace. This ideal of America is the hope of all mankind."[485]

The British newspaper The Guardian reported on how deeply held was the President's concept of sacred violence:

> George Bush has claimed he was on a mission from God when he launched the invasions of Afghanistan and Iraq. Nabil Shaath, Palestinian foreign minister said: "President Bush said to all of us: 'I am driven with a mission from God. God would tell me, "George, go and fight these terrorists in Afghanistan." And I did. And then God would tell me, "George, go and end the tyranny in Iraq." And I did.'"[486]

Bush's belief was always framed for the public in a religious manner, which resonated with the understanding of his intended audience: the vast majority of Americans, who are Christian and who grew up in this same tradition of blood sacrifice, American exceptionalism and sacred violence. The President said in his State of the Union Address (January 28, 2003):

> "There is a power, wonder-working power, in the goodness and idealism and faith of the American people." This is a reference to a hymn which proclaims: "the wonder working power" of "the blood of the Lamb who was slain" — in other words, Christ . . . President Bush is suggesting that America is Christ and that its role is to save the world.[487]

Around this same time, Washington Post Columnist Courtland Milloy noted this particular strain of American sacred justice in the President's worldview, as well as the general culture:

> It's been apparent for some time that President Bush sees the world in terms of either/or: good or evil, and this simplicity obviously resonates with many Americans. As one reader [of this column] wrote: "If 3000 or 3 million people, young or old, die to save the lives of Americans, then so be it." In choosing a "world of progress," a lot of Americans apparently believe that war is the way to get there. And a student from the Idaho campus of Brigham Young University-Idaho wrote: "As you can imagine, this campus is strongly pro-war and backs up Bush all the way. Take it from me, fanatic Middle Easterners aren't the only ones who believe in the oxymoron 'holy war'." According to opinion polls, those who subscribe to Bush's view of the world are clearly in the majority.[488]

This points out an important aspect of Bush's religious framing of the war — not that George W. Bush was leading a charge, but that he was simply galvanizing a war-as-love dynamic that lies festering beneath the surface of political society. He didn't need to take responsibility for fusing God, War and American purpose. He was simply giving voice to a central facet lying latent in the American psyche, as it does in the communal lives of all people.

In the end, Bush doesn't have to say he's ordained by God . . . it goes with-out saying. "To me, I just believe God controls everything, and God uses the president to keep evil down, to see the darkness and protect this na-tion," Hardy Billington told me, voicing an idea shared by millions of Bush supporters. "Other people will not protect us. God gives people choices to make. God gave us this president to be the man to protect the nation at this time."[489]

Finally, a virtually unknown incident with then French President Jacques Chirac shows how pervasive was Bush's belief that he was fight-ing a "holy war" and that he represented the forces of good and light against the dark forces as represented by Islam:

In 2003 while lobbying leaders to put together the Coalition of the Will-ing, President Bush spoke to France's President Jacques Chirac. Bush wove a story about how the Biblical creatures Gog and Magog were at work in the Middle East and how they must be defeated. In Genesis and Ezekiel, Gog and Magog are forces of the Apocalypse who are prophesied to come out of the north and destroy Israel unless stopped. The Book of Revelation took up the Old Testament prophesy: "And when the thou-sand years are expired, Satan shall be loosed out of his prison, And shall go out to deceive the nations which are in the four quarters of the earth, Gog and Magog, to gather them together to battle ... and fire came down from God out of heaven, and devoured them."

Bush believed the time had now come for that battle, telling Chirac: "This confrontation is willed by God, who wants to use this conflict to erase His people's enemies before a New Age begins."[490]

BUSH'S MINIONS: YOU'RE EITHER WITH US OR AGAINST US

George W. Bush hardly operated in a vacuum. He surrounded himself with many American Christians who held his same beliefs, and who were willing to use the full power of their offices and oratorical capabilities to make this point. An article in the The Guardian newspaper exhibited the infection that grew around George W. Bush:

One of the top planners of the US war in Iraq gave President George Bush secret intelligence briefs headlined with biblical quotations . . . In the days surrounding the March 2003 invasion of Iraq, US Defense secretary Donald Rumsfeld prepared top secret briefing papers for the president adorned with triumphant images of US military personnel and adoring Iraqis, along with the quotes. The cover of one intelligence briefing shows US soldiers kneeling in prayer, headlined with a selection from the book of Isaiah: "Whom shall I send, and who will go for us? Here I am Lord, send me!" One shows an image of Saddam speaking into a television camera and quotes 1 Peter 2:15: "It is God's will that by doing good you should silence the ignorant talk of foolish men."[491]

The main speechwriter throughout Bush's first term in office, Michael Gerson (who went on to become a columnist for the Washington Post) was:

> an evangelical Episcopalian who said he is reading a biography of the Apostle Paul for "escape," [who] shared Bush's willingness to talk publicly about the centrality of the Christian faith to his life. The result was a president whose public words were laced with Biblical undertones . . . "We have tried to employ religious language in a way that unites people," [Gerson] said. "Martin Luther King Jr. did it all the time during the Civil Rights movement. He was in this tradition, going all the way back to Old Testament prophets, that says God is active in history and, eventually, on the side of justice."[492]

Fluid moral thinking contaminated virtually all followers of this president, as they attempted to wrap God, Jesus and the military together into a 21st -century "Crusade." The following notice seeped out in the alternative press:

> A major defense contractor for the military and Homeland Security claimed that the United States is morally obliged to maintain a permanent presence in Iraq for the sake of God. "If we stay and rebuild Iraq, we will demonstrate to the world that we remain the best force for good in the world," Charles Patricoff, Sr., Contract Manager for Ball Aerospace & Technologies Corp, said. "More importantly, we as Christians can better influence that region for the Kingdom of God."[493]

In another instance, Lt. General William Boykin spoke before an American Christian group, attacking Muslims as "idolaters" and "forces of Satan." He also said that when he found himself in a battle against a Muslim warlord in Somalia, he knew he would vanquish his enemy because, "Well you know what I knew, that my God was bigger than his. I knew that my God was a real God, and his was an idol."[494]

Lieutenant General William Boykin was hardly a peripheral figure, having been a veteran of the elite Delta Force and Deputy Undersecretary of Defense for Intelligence. He was also quoted as saying: "We in the army of God, in the house of God, kingdom of God have been raised for such a time as this," and assured that George W. Bush's presidency was ordained by God.[495] This American Crusader had spearheaded the unsuccessful hunt for high-profile targets such as Osama Bin Laden and Mullah Omar.

From the President's inner circle, the ripples of holy politics expanded outward. Bush had numerous religious advisors, such as Reverend Pat

Robertson, Reverend Franklin Graham and others who helped situate the President's actions within his deep Christian faith, as well as the apocalyptic struggle between Good and Evil.

> The Reverend Franklin Graham, Reverend Billy Graham's son and successor, has repeatedly called Islam an "evil" religion. Christian Coalition founder Pat Robertson described Muhammad as an "absolute wild-eyed fanatic . . . a robber and a brigand . . . a killer." The Rev. Jerry Vines, former president of the Southern Baptist Convention, called Muhammad a "demon-possessed pedophile'."[496]

GOD, WAR AND THE AMERICAN WORLDVIEW

This fusion of God and war in the language and beliefs of America's leaders did not fall on deaf ears. In an article entitled "Praise the Lord and George W. Bush," the Seattle Post-Intelligencer noted how deep religious faith coincided with support for America's war:

> A recent Gallup poll shows that church-going Americans are more likely to support war against Saddam Hussein than are Americans as a whole. According to Gallup, Americans who attend church at least once a week support war to depose the Iraqi dictator by an almost 2-to-1 margin. Americans who never attend church or say religion is not important to them are more evenly divided about the possibility of war . . . Why are religious Americans more prone to support war with Iraq while the more secular are less supportive? Traditional religious people understand that the world is fallen and sinful. War, therefore, is lamentable but sometimes unavoidable if evil is to be resisted.[497]

Even at the level of popular culture and entertainment, we needn't dig too deeply to see the way in which these myths are perpetrated and disseminated. An article about the college football coach (and one-time professional National Football League coach) Jerry Glanville began with this lead:

> Jerry Glanville can pinpoint the instant his life changed forever. In March 2004, on a morale-building trip to Iraq and Kuwait set up by the NFL, he was standing in the last latrine along the Highway of Death when a sentence scribbled on the wall hit him right between the eyes: "I'd rather live a day with the lions than a thousand years with the lambs, the American Soldier." "I thought, Wow, you've got to coach these kids," says Glanville. "They don't question the mission, just, Let's get it done."[498]

Here, we see echoes of St. Augustine, who averred that "a just man, if he should happen to serve as a soldier under a human king who is sacrilegious, could rightly wage war at the king's command, [for following orders] is not contrary to the sure precepts of God."[499] One needn't tweak

St. Augustine's teachings too much to see how sports, religion, unques-tioning fealty to secular goals and war are all wrapped together and pre-sented as heroic in this article that ran in self-appointed "Nation's News-paper," USA Today.

The public is asked — using arguments based in images that it knows from its religious past — to disregard that which makes people most human (their self-critical thought), and either give in to the powerful though spurious spiritual catharsis politicians and war offer — which often is represented as doing God's will — or become (supposedly) sepa-rated from their own "higher" spirit, as well as the nation's community.

For those that waver, the dead soldier is held out as incontrovertible proof of the necessity and worth of the war. After all, how could one "force" the soldier to have died in vain, by questioning the worth of his action? The war becomes worthwhile because someone has died under-taking it, a reversal of the normal assignation of worth which defines an action's merit *before* the risk is actually taken. In a horrifying example of the "sunk costs" theory, the more people who die for a cause, however mistaken, the more valuable the action, no matter what the true human or economic price really is.

Through the sacrifice of human souls for political ends, the sublime nature of war becomes enmeshed with a true God-experience. The very real horrors of war are euphemistically referred to in the language of mys-ticism: "sublime love," "obligation," "good causes," "moral purpose, "save the innocent," "peace" and "sacrifice." The "fog" of war begins in the lan-guage of the powerful, and then overtakes the thought processes of the general population.

This is when the American Christ is honored, the warrior-supplicant who sheds his sacrificial blood for the good of all. Senator John McCain (R-AZ) has been a particularly pernicious purveyor of the war as love construction. Writing as the Republican nominee for president in the nationally syndicated Parade Magazine (the most widely read magazine in America with a circulation of 32.2 million) on July 1, 2008, he stated:

> It is the sacrifices of so many Americans, at home and abroad, in times of peace and times of war, that give meaning to all of us. We are blessed to be Americans, and blessed that so many of us have so often believed in a cause far greater than self-interest, far greater than ourselves.[500]

Memorial Day is a particularly fertile time to cement the bond be-tween nation, God and self sacrifice in war. In that same year (2008), the Washington Post ran an editorial entitled: "In the Profanity of War, a Commitment to Sacred Duty," which included the following passage:

As Lincoln soon came to understand all too well, some of the most basic questions in this high-minded civic religion of lofty ideals and mutual respect and cooperation could, in the end, be settled only by blood. And at Gettysburg, that truth was incorporated into the faith, as Lincoln spoke on farmland that had become a vast cemetery: ground consecrated and hallowed — these were the words he used — by "the brave men, living and dead, who struggled here" and from whose sacrifice all must henceforth strive to bring about a "new birth of freedom" . . . in the more idealistic renderings of the American civic faith before and since, this has been the stated purpose, no matter how imperfectly pursued.[501]

As I write this, with America now embroiled in several military actions in the Middle East, Africa and Latin America as well as various "police" and "peacekeeping" actions (Bosnia/Serbia; North Korea/South Korea; Pakistan, Yemen, Somalia, Israel/Palestine and, according to a recent Department of Defense report, 140 more nations around the globe), the prayers of Americans grow ever more fervent. As Randy Sly (a Vietnam War veteran and Doctor of Divinity) wrote on Memorial Day 2011, in "Memorial Day: Chaplains — A Reminder that We Are One Nation Under God":

There are 1.4 million Christians in the military; wherever they are stationed, the chaplain is there. These chaplains can be found bringing Jesus Christ to their people in desert tents, on the aft deck of a guided missile cruiser, underwater on a submarine, and in post chapels . . . This Memorial Day, let us pause and remember our Chaplains. Let's give thanks for the sacrifice in serving their country as they serve the Lord. Let us especially remember those who laid down their lives for their friends.[502]

It is important to note — and this is a dynamic that I think prevents American society's full appreciation for how deeply intertwined are war and the sacred — that "secular" people are unable to comprehend how prevalent is the connection between war and God, the American flag and the Cross.

This issue was addressed by Mark Tooey in his 2003 article "Praise the Lord and George Bush," which offered a very coherent analysis of why many "mainstream" people in this society are unable to understand the sacred aspect of war, and how deeply ingrained it is for a majority of Americans:

This news [that a majority of religious Americans support the war in Iraq] has failed to capture the attention of most media, liberal and conservative. They continue to chant the mantra that the United States' religious community, excepting the "religious right," is nearly united against the war . . . Why are religious Americans more prone to support war with Iraq while the more secular are less supportive? Secular people, who are less influ-

enced by biblical notions of human sin, are often more idealistic and uto-
pian. In their view, war can be avoided through greater human efforts at
good will and humanitarian outreach. Why the divide between the United States' religious people [who supported the war 2 to 1] and many of
their [religious] leaders [who often did not support the war]? That question is more complicated. But for many church leaders, especially among
the mainline Protestants, the '60s era of anti-war protests was their defining social justice moment. Many of them, and probably more than a few
Catholic bishops as well, continue to view the world through the prism
of Vietnam rather than 2,000 years of Christian history. Their pro-war
lay people may not recall church history. But they might understand the
world and its fallen nature a little better.[503]

Not only the disconnect between mainstream religious leaders —
who are sometimes against war — and their minions — who are over-
whelmingly for it — should be noted, but the deep resonance of religious
faith in American culture must also be appreciated. A recent Gallup poll
noted that 92% of Americans believe in God or a universal spirit. Even
more telling, 63% of Americans consider their holy book "the word of
God,"[504] cementing the violence of God tradition with nearly two-thirds
of American citizens.

In an op-ed in the Washington Post, one soldier explained his coming
to terms with the vital importance of human sacrifice to the nation:

> I came to my decision [to join the army] because my parents along with
> other role models such as my Boy Scout leader instilled in me the concept
> of public service — of becoming part of something greater than myself. As
> a result, I have had the honor to work with incredibly dedicated young
> men and women from all walks of life who are considered blue collar can-
> non fodder in many elite circles . . . Let's all say a prayer of thanks for those
> who serve our country.[505]

There are a few important issues raised in this short passage. First, the
disconnect noted by the author between those who are "instilled [with]
the concept of public service," even to the point of sacrificing their lives
for this "something greater," and the sneering "elite." As we saw above,
the "elite," though they sometimes are represented as a majority in the
mainstream media, are a decided minority in American life.

Another important facet to note is the manner in which these American patriotic values are instilled into the country's youth, via "role mod-
els such as [the] Boy Scout leader." This osmotic manner in which a person is infused with values that, in fact, turn him or her into "cannon fod-
der" is perhaps the most confounding aspect of all. The fusion of sacrifice,
war and love is so endemic in American culture — and all cultures, if the

truth be told — that it is inculcated in the youth in an almost unconscious manner.

Lastly is the sense that by joining the army, one can become part of something "greater" than the self — a yearning that does mimic the spiritual path and the ultimate purpose of religion. However, as has been noted, the two paths — that of the warrior and that of the mystic — diverge when one (the warrior) is asked to be completely un-self critical and the other (the mystic) devotes his life to getting to know him or herself almost entirely through self-reflection. As the Hasidic Rabbi Gershon Chanoch Henich of Radzin (d. 1900) said: "Blessed is he who knows that within and above are synonymous." Or, in the words of the Naqshabandi Sufis: "He who knows himself, knows his Lord."

On the Fringe?

> Christian Identity activists want to merge "religion" and "state" in a new society governed by religious law. They share an apocalyptic view of history and . . . believe that their virulent, militant efforts could threaten the government-imposed evil system and awaken the spirit of the freedom-loving masses.[506]

Christian American terrorism has recent roots, in the battles against abortion providers, the federal government, the United Nations, worldwide Jewry, Blacks, Muslims and other groups that so-called fringe elements consider forces of darkness. However, these homegrown terrorists are hardly out of the mainstream; they simply represent an extension of the norm, the logical conclusion of a lifetime spent in a country where God, justice and American exceptionalism have been propagated everywhere from Boy Scout meetings to Memorial Day and Fourth of July parades. The murders perpetrated by these American holy warriors are often undertaken "as skirmishes in the grand confrontation between forces of evil and forces of good,"[507] echoing the language and motivation of a leader no less important than President George W. Bush.

That Christian American terrorism is a recent phenomenon has to do with a slow-motion backlash to the supposed "libertinism" of the 1960s and 1970s, times when African -Americans were shedding their status as a permanent underclass, ideas of free love were rampant and marijuana was widely used, all of which gave homegrown religious warriors their initial impetus. Add the landmark *Roe* v. *Wade* (1973) Supreme Court decision legalizing abortion into the mix and it became clear to those dedicated to God, country and divine justice that the forces of darkness were winning in America.

> Dominion Theology [is] the position that Christianity must reassert the dominion of God over all things, including secular politics and society. This point of view — articulated by such right-wing Protestant spokes-persons as Reverend Jerry Falwell (d. 2007) and Pat Robertson (b. 1930) — led to a burst of social and political activism in the Christian Right in the 1980s and 1990s.[508]

Of course, activism for the holy warrior often takes the form of violence. Reverend Mike Bray (a former midshipman at the U.S. Naval Academy, and author of the book *A Time to Kill*) comes out of this American Christian worldview, schooled as he was in the Naval Academy, and then drew spiritual and activist sustenance from American leaders such as Ronald Reagan, Pat Robertson and Jerry Falwell. Although he is currently designated a terrorist by the National Memorial Institute for the Prevention of Terrorism, his views are not as far outside the mainstream as we might like to believe.

> Mike Bray's justification of violence against abortion clinics is . . . the consequence of a grand religious vision. His position is part of a great Crusade conducted by a Christian subculture in America that considers itself at war with the larger society. Armed with theological explanations, this subculture sees itself justified in its violent responses to agents of a satanic force.[509]

Before dismissing Bray as a fringe actor, it is vital to remember how closely this dovetails with mainstream American thought on religiously sanctioned violence. Recall that a majority of Americans approve of torture — and the more religious the respondents, the higher their approval rating.

The fusion of God, state and violence as proposed by an endless series of patriotic observances, as suggested by George W. Bush and many other presidents, and as subscribed to by a majority of Americans, leads easily to the positions of right wing Christian movements, which simply represent one conclusion of this social and religious dynamic. And often right wing preachers, like their mainstream counterparts, situate the violence within the Bible:

> The world as envisioned by followers of both Christian Identity and Reconstructionism is a world at war. Identity preachers cite the Biblical accounts of Michael the Archangel destroying the offspring of evil to point to a hidden albeit "cosmic" war between the forces of darkness and the forces of light . . . the struggle is a secret war between colossal evil forces . . . and a small band of the enlightened few.[510]

The scriptural justifications for hostility are explicit. The Reverend Paul Hill who, at the urging of Reverend Mike Bray, murdered an abortion doctor in 1994, had this to say about the act: "My eyes were opened to the enormous impact" of such an event, adding that the effect would be "incalculable." He opened his Bible and found sustenance in Psalms 91: "You will not be afraid of the terror by night, or of the arrow that flies by day." In Hill's religion-soaked thought process, he interpreted this as an affirmation that his act was Biblically approved.[511]

The fluidity between so-called "mainstream" political and religious leaders, such as Jerry Falwell and Pat Robertson, and the thinking of more extreme actors cannot be stressed enough. The difference between the two is a matter of degree — not philosophy. Even so-called progressive pundits, such as Washington Post columnist (and Atlantic Monthly editor-at-large) Michael Kelly wrote after the attacks on September 11, 2001: "American pacifists are on the side of the future mass murderers of Americans. They are objectively pro-terrorist . . . That is the pacifist's position, and it is evil."[512] Overcome by the fervor of the times, he echoed the "with us or against us" language of the American theocracy.

Lastly, ex-Governor of Alaska Sarah Palin, who was the Republican nominee for Vice President in 2008, told ministry students at her former church that the United States sent troops to fight in Iraq "on a task that is from God. That's what we have to make sure we are praying for: that there is a plan and that plan is God's plan."[513]

There is almost no difference between the language of Michael Kelly, Sarah Palin and George W. Bush and those deemed fringe members of society, such as Mike Bray and Paul Hill. And where Bray and Hill murder one at a time, mainstream leaders slaughter tens of thousands in the expression of their cosmic war.

EPILOGUE

> Violence is the dominant religion in the world today. Walter Wink [Professor Emeritus of Biblical Interpretation at Auburn Theological Seminary, New York] says violence "is the ethos of our times" and the "spirituality of the modern world. [It is] accorded the status of a religion, demanding from its devotees an absolute obedience to death. Violence is the real religion of America."[514]

This book was written to explore this question: how religion and violence are intertwined, and why these forces resonate so powerfully together in both the human spirit and contemporary American society. When I began this work, I did not know what, if any, conclusions I would reach. And now, after examining the deep connection between violence and the sacred, in all religious paths and at all times in human history, I have grown sadly convinced that violence, as much as quiet spiritual reflection, gives an ultimate meaning to human existence. They both touch us in the same deep place: at the intersection between being and nothingness, where the original question forms: who am I and why am I here?

Both religion and violence address this issue and, given the deep, animalistic urges that lurk just outside of human consciousness, oftentimes violence answers these questions more immediately and satisfactorily than a non-violent sacred path.

War as Mysticism: Redux

> The eyes of soldiers who carry on the orgy of death are crazed. They speak
> only in guttural shouts. They are high on the power to destroy. They are,
> for a moment, gods swatting down powerless human beings like flies.[515]

I believe that there is no single greater fear latent and unacknowledged within the human soul than the fear of non-existence. For most of us, the dread is an ever-present specter, something just out of reach of our interior monologue that haunts our nights and, as we grow older, overtakes our days, as well.

This primal dread is dealt with in religion through promises of eternal life. Some are able to find solace there. Others simply grow more and more terrified as they age, finally (and thankfully) slipping into insentience before passing away in complete bodily exhaustion. As the Nobel Prize-winning essayist Elias Canetti assured: "The threat of death hangs over all men, and however disguised it may be . . . it affects them all the time." He also noted how this dread morphs so easily into the will to destroy: "It creates in them the need to deflect death onto others. A murder shared with many others, which is not only safe and permitted, but indeed recommended, is irresistible to the great majority of men."[516]

Hugo Grotius (d. 1645, a Dutch jurist who helped lay the foundations for international law) concurred with Canetti, stating that "the end and aim of war is the preservation of life and limb . . . war is in perfect accord with the first principles in nature."[517]

It is here, in the original existential question, that the innate attraction to war and violence sinks its roots. War mimics mystical attainment in many aspects — and mystical attainment is perhaps the surest method of at least convincing ourselves that we have attained some form of permanence, whether this is the case or not. As James Hillman stated in *A Terrible Love of War*: "War belongs to our souls as an archetypal truth of the cosmos . . . a love that no other love has been able to overcome."[518]

As I noted earlier in this study, war *does* offer much of the same spiritual experience as the deepest mystical realization. Although war and mystical attainment diverge at the demand for self-awareness — war asks the participant to quell this need, while spirituality requires the mendicant to lose himself *in* himself, in contemplation of the self — war provides a "poor-man's mysticism," a way of accessing *some* of the highest aspects of the human soul with none of the self-reflection or human loneliness of the mystical path.

War is simply a seduction too great for many people to turn away from, especially when the conception of sacred violence is so successfully rehearsed in all religious traditions. As war correspondent Christopher Hedges noted: "In the beginning, war looks and feels like love."[519]

Coupled with the mystical echoes in war is the manner in which it mimics religious observances, tying this human catastrophe even more closely to the search for God:

> Ceremonies of military service, the coercion by and obedience to a supreme command, the confrontation with death in battle as a last rite on earth, war's promise of transcendence and its sacrificial love, the test of all human virtues and the presence of all human evils, the slaughter of blood victims, impersonally, collectively in the name of a higher cause and blessed by ministers — all drive home the conclusion that "war is religion."[520]

Religion and Violence: A Reconsideration

> Violence will come to an end only after it has had the last word and that word has been accepted as divine. The meaning of this word must remain hidden, the mechanism of unanimity remain concealed. Religion protects man as long as its ultimate foundations are not revealed.[521]

Given the timeless intertwining of the mystic's path and war imagery, the easy manner in which humans turn to bellicosity, and the long history of equating spiritual heroism and the field of battle, we must question whether war is, in fact, natural to the human condition. After all, this dynamic appears across all time periods and in virtually all religious institutions. It appears to be endemic to the human condition, perhaps even necessary to it.

This is not surprising when we consider the ideas undergirding religion. God is parsimonious, and can only have one "chosen people" at a time. Human violence is instituted to prove who is God's beloved — spiritual victory and temporal conquest are viewed as the same.

In addition to this jealous and miserly God, the creation of a social and religious group (us) must be created through the designation of an "other" that is assuredly different from and perhaps even destructive to our own group. This is the enemy, who undoubtedly want to steal God's covenant (as did Isaac with Ishmael in Genesis 16:21 and Jacob with Esau, Genesis 25:33). God's blessing and the comfort of belonging to a group are sealed in the blood sacrifice of both the child-warriors and the "other":

> It is certainly astonishing that all human activities, and even the course of nature itself, are subordinated to the metamorphosis of violence taking

place at the heart of the community . . . The benefits attributed to genera-
tive violence extend beyond mankind to nature itself. The act of collective
murder is seen as the source of all abundance; the principle of procreation
is attributed to it . . . everything beneficial and nutritive is said to take root
in the body of the primordial victim.[522]

We have not come very far at all from the earliest creation myth in
Babylonia, in which the universe was created from the murdered body
of Tiamat, the mother goddess who had birthed the murderer Marduk.

SACRIFICE REVISITED

In his seminal work *Violence and the Sacred*, René Girard proposed
that the origin of symbolic thought, and therefore the beginnings of consciousness itself, could be situated in the act of sacrifice. Collective murder, he proposed, provides the conditions favorable to human thinking.

In sacrifice, and only through this act, can the innate human aggression be channeled and tamed, allowing civilization to thrive around it.
Instead of a pulsing human heart or an imagined god, violence itself lies at
the center of human experience — an almost uncontrollable aggression
that must be visited upon an "other," or else it will turn on itself, render-
ing society itself impossible.

> Polarized by sacrificial killing, violence is appeased. It subsides. We might
> say that it is expelled from the community and becomes part of the divine
> substance . . . Just as the human body is a machine for transforming food
> into flesh and blood, generative unanimity is a process for changing bad
> violence into stability and fecundity.[523]

The dynamic of death leading to life, of the intertwining of genera-
tive violence, human society and the sacred is as old as the earliest human religious narratives. According to the Mesopotamian creation myth,
the universe was created out of a slaughtered mother. In the Abrahamic
faiths, sacrifice is part of a cultural constitution, signed in blood, which
influences religion, culture and politics into our own era. Christianity is
founded on the literal sacrifice of a human. In Islam, an ongoing battle
is waged between believers and infidels. War, civilization and God find
their ground in death and sacrifice.

> Most conflicts are ignited with martyrs, whether real or created. The
> death of an innocent, one who is perceived as emblematic of the nation
> or the group under attack, becomes the rallying point for war. These dead
> become the standard-bearers of the cause and all causes feed off a steady
> supply of corpses.[524]

The public is asked — using an argument based on images that they know from their religious past — to disregard that which makes them most human (self-critical thought). They must either give in to the powerful, and spurious spiritual catharsis offered by war — which is represented as doing God's will — or risk separation from the community.

We are left with only one question: is war truly necessary to the human condition? Are those who find war abhorrent little more than delicate and hopeless dreamers, beating their impotent fists into their breasts while the massive machinery of god and war grinds on through the millennia? Can anything be done to stem the red tide of death spouting from ever-more horrifying war machines?

WILL, VIOLENCE AND GOD'S PURPOSE

> Suppose, finally, we succeeded in explaining our entire instinctive life as the development and ramification of one basic form of will — namely, the will to power; suppose that all organic functions could be traced back to this will to power and one could also find in it the solution of the problem of procreation and nourishment . . .[525]

The human soul is filled with unexcavated urges, unnamed frustrations, a vague yearning for something gone that can never be recaptured. From the Genesis narrative on, the entire human condition is portrayed as one of exile from a mythical paradise, or true home. To be in exile, as is our experience of living, is to be deprived of one's chosen place.[526]

The great medieval Sufi Jallaludin Rumi (d. 1273) captured the longing and desire of this state of exile in this couplet: "I once had a thousand desires, but in my one desire to know You all else melted away." But as we have already variously seen, only a rare individual can practice mysticism of the contemplative sort that leads the yearning and desire at the center of human experience to a life of self-examination, and perhaps even attainment of God consciousness. The vast majority of us, experiencing the same vague sense of "desire for You," or a return to the "mythical paradise," are left with only the pulsing, thrusting "desire" at the heart of the will to live.

The Greek philosopher Plato explored this idea as well, one that has little changed in the past few thousand years of human time:

> The body fills with loves and desires and fears and all sorts of fancies and a great deal of nonsense, with the result that we literally never get the opportunity to think at all about anything. War and revolutions and battles are due simply to and solely to the body and its desires.[527]

The desire at the heart of being, which is necessary from an evolutionary point of view, provides us with the will to live (without this will, the physical universe would simply evaporate). Friedrich Nietzsche said: "Life is simply the will to power,"[528] and this "will to power," I contend, is actually God's will for being, as channeled through His creation.

WAR, GOD AND THE ACT OF CREATION

The original act of nature was not one of love, as some within the religious community contend. Nor, as so many religions assure, is God "merciful, kind and generous." The original act of creation — that of a unitary power, alone, unconscious and unreachable — was one of desperation. It was an act of withdrawal and removal for the sake of self-knowledge. However, the only way that God could create a universe was to create something outside of Himself, which is logically incomprehensible, as God is omnipresent and eternal.

The act of creation initiated the separation, the sense of yearning that we experience as the desire to return to paradise. However, this sense of yearning that we feel is not each of ours individually, but that of God, unitary and alone, still shut off from His own creation by the unbridgeable gap of time, space and dimensionality. For in creating the physical universe, in forming physicality, God fashioned an "other," something that exists outside of His eternal, omnipresent being. And the yearning and desire that we feel is simply that of God, desperately and hopelessly in search of Himself.

Thus, the indescribable and profound sense of longing and will at the heart of being. The German philosopher Arthur Schopenhauer (d. 1860) developed a philosophy expressing this idea, stating: "[T]he inner being of unconscious nature is a constant striving without end and without rest. Willing and striving *is* being, which may be compared with an unquenchable thirst. The basis of all willing is need, deficiency and thus pain."[529]

He went further, explaining the difference that I have been examining, that which separates sacred violence, which captivates the majority of our species, from that interior contemplative monologue that abhors violence, and searches for meaning in reflection, self-awareness and the mystic's path:

> We may call the complete self-effacement and denial of will, the true absence of will . . . the absolute good, and regard it as the only radical cure of the disease of which all other means are only palliatives and anodynes.[530]

The greatest "anodyne" for the disease of will is war, the opposite of "complete self-effacement and denial of will," that which only a select few can attain. Perhaps this, as the mystics assure, *is* the meaning of life, to move God's own will beyond desperation and need, to a place of acceptance, denial of self, an absence of striving.

Only a rare few can make this spiritual leap. What's more, because they have effaced themselves of ego and striving, they have no appreciable effect on the rest of society, though they might well be incontrovertible to the ultimate experience of God, and the meaning of creation.

"Will", for the rest of us, expresses itself through desire. And desire and its basest antidote, temporal power, are most clearly experienced through violence. Through the domination of the other, we can be more certain of our own being. Violence comes to underpin existential meaning for many people. We, the spiritually immature, experience violence as an expression of primal need and the will that rises up from within.

The expression of this will through political power, individual violence or the mass murder of war, however, cannot satiate. It only exacerbates the wound. And so aggression and violence must be expelled in ever-greater explosions, each of which can do nothing to satisfy the will for return that lies at the heart of being, and which we misconstrue, in our spiritual ignorance, as a will to power.

> Desire is attracted to violence triumphant and strives desperately to incarnate this irresistible force. Desire clings to violence and stalks it like a shadow because violence is the signifier of the cherished being, the signifier of divinity.[531]

Violence becomes the basis for our sense of being. That is to say, driven by an unquenchable thirst — that of God's desire for self-knowledge, as channeled through His creation — we are left to satisfy this need in the clearest manner possible: by the expression of power through violence. God's act of creation was based in desperation — a desperate yearning for self-awareness and understanding — and all of us channel this desperation. However, only the most spiritually advanced among us can answer the call through contemplation and self-effacement. The rest, the vast majority, channel our sacred impulses into violence, where they can be viscerally satisfied in a momentary way.

It is the best that most of us can achieve, and it alone allows us to limp along with the semblance of a civilization, instead of dissolving into an anarchic hell, worse than anything most of us can imagine.

LE PLUS ÇA CHANGE

The idea of a maturing human species is fallacious: it does not exist. There are no more or less truly realized human souls now — in Schopenhauer's construction — than there were 500 or 5000 years ago. Carl von Clausewitz (d. 1831; a Prussian general and military theorist), who wrote one of the most important books ever on institutional conflict, *On War*, noted: "[T]he tendency to destroy which lies at the bottom of the conception of war is in no way changed or modified through the process of civilization."[532]

It could well be argued that "modernization" and "advancement" have only made our situation more dire, as we have invented ever-more successful instruments of destruction, which in no way add to our spiritual maturity. The final act of humankind might well be to invent an armament that is no longer dependent on human control, but is simply the will to destroy come to life in a discrete package, without any of the attendant emotions, moral concerns or religious channels to sway its passion to obliterate.

A recent article in the Washington Post pointed to the very real possibility of this outcome for our technological progress:

> [Drones], piloted by people far from the battlefield, represent an approaching technological tipping point "that may well deliver a genuine revolution in military affairs," leading future decision makers to "resort to war as a policy option far sooner than previously."[533]

Even this horrifying advance, however, is surrealistically placed within the ""just war"" theory, situating the drones within the moral universe of the "good" warrior:

> The laws of war call on commanders on both sides of the fight to limit loss of life and that "use of unmanned aircraft prevents the potential loss of aircrew lives and is thus in itself morally justified."[534]

The absurdity and hypocrisy of this statement is frightening, and that the Pulitzer Prize-winning journalist Walter Pincus would allow it to appear without an opposing view in his article points to how very deep runs our collective illness. Drone attacks kill far more civilians than enemy combatants. David Kilcullen (a counterinsurgency adviser to Gen. David Petraeus from 2006 to 2008) and Andrew Exum (a fellow at the Center for a New American Security, and an Army officer in Iraq and Afghanistan from 2002 to 2004) wrote in the New York Times concerning the "kill" rates of drones:

> Press reports suggest that over the last three years [2006–2009] drone
> strikes have killed about 14 terrorist leaders. But, according to Pakistani
> sources, they have also killed some 700 civilians. This is 50 civilians for
> every militant killed, a hit rate of 2 percent — hardly "precision."[535]

While recent asymmetrical wars have increased the civilian death toll
to up to 90% of the war dead, the drone attacks take this grisly statis-
tic even higher — to 98% of all those slaughtered being innocent civilians! And as if this isn't bad enough, we are informed in Pincus's article:
"drones are becoming increasingly automated. With minor advances, a
drone could soon be able to 'fire a weapon based solely on its own sensors,
or shared information, without recourse to higher, human authority'."[536]

Leaving aside the argument over whether human authority is "higher"
than that of the unmanned, autonomous killing machine, the fact remains that we are fast approaching a time when slaughter of civilians *is*
war, and even worse, considered "morally justified," as it protects against
the potential loss of aircrew lives. The final warrior deaths will have been
removed from war, with only the sacrificial "other" remaining, the surrogate victim, the *Pharmakos*, as it was known to the Greeks. In this case,
however, a single representative victim will hardly suffice, and whole
populations will be at risk of ritual destruction.

War the Boundless

> Nobel Prize-winner Konrad Lorenz (d. 1989) contends that there is an
> aggressive instinct embedded in the phylogenetic structure of all species.
> If humans and the lower animals had not developed mechanisms that in-
> hibit fighting — methods like status systems, the love bond and ritualiza-
> tion — their very survival would come into question.[537]

War represents the unbounded will to live, channeled into violence
lying within the human soul, with limits. By directing violence into war,
we protect ourselves from ourselves. There are rules that operate on the
field of battle, and it is only these seemingly arbitrary yet very real boundaries that protect us from our interior chaos and violence. The imposition
of both external law (Geneva Convention, rules of war, civil morals, etc.)
and the internal constraints provided by war's connection to God, religion and the spirit might be the thin line that prevents our civilization
from dissolving in a self-destructive orgy.

> Religion protects man from his own violence by taking it out of his hands,
> transforming it into a transcendent and ever-present danger to be kept in
> check by the appropriate rites appropriately observed.[538]

Given the make-up of our species, the emotional substructure of a unified society cannot be found in love, or even a shared culture, religion or history. Violent unanimity represents the foundation stone of human society. It is violence that allows our species to come together to create families, towns, cities and vast nations. And the sense of community that underpins these human social constructions stems not from a positive identification with the group, but a negative identification against an "other" — an "other" that must be created and then destroyed.

> The emotional foundation of a unified society derives from the collective destruction of a sacrificial victim, a scapegoat or enemy upon whom all together turn on and eliminate. Thereby, the inherent conflicts within a community that can lead to internal violence become exteriorized and ritualized into an enemy. Once an enemy has been found or invented, named and excoriated . . . patriotism and the preemptive strikes of preventative war become opportune consequences.[539]

Without sacred violence, would society be possible?

> Medea, like Ajax, reminds us of a fundamental truth about violence: if left unappeased, violence will accumulate until it overflows its confines and floods the surrounding area. The role of sacrifice is to stem this rising tide of indiscriminate violence and redirect it into proper channels. Sacrifice serves to protect the entire community from its own violence; it prompts the entire community to choose victims outside of itself.[540]

Without war, civilization itself would be impossible.

Without fusing the violence within the human spirit *with* the sacred, the primal aggression that lies at the center of our being would become unmoored, narcissistic, tearing apart the delicate fabric of our social existence and plunging us into an animalistic hell. Worse than animals, really, as man is the only species besides the rat that will turn on its own in unprovoked and unbounded rage. And given our engorged neo-cortex, the possibilities of our violence are far wider than many of us can imagine.

The story of human violence unbridled is as old as the first human children, Cain and Abel. This story also represents the beginning of war, of finding a scapegoat for an unquenchable, interior rage that cannot be suppressed. Here, situated at the very beginning of the human narrative in arguably the most important Holy Book in today's world, we find the beginnings of redemptive violence and the mechanism of the surrogate victim.

The dynamic of necessary, restorative aggression is encoded in our very language. "Sacrifice" and "sacred" come from the same Latin root *sa-*

cra: "sacred rites." In Greek, the *Pharmakos*, a human scapegoat (a slave, a cripple or a criminal) who was chosen and expelled from the community at times of disaster, when purification was needed, signifies at once "poison" and "remedy."[541]

The *Pharmakos* lives on today in the form of every enemy or surrogate victim upon which each nation vents its cathartic violent needs.

> The social activity of organized conflict is a primal form of human activity. Warfare organizes people into a "we" and a "they," and it organizes social history into a storyline of persecution, conflict and hope of liberation, redemption and conquest. The enduring and seemingly ubiquitous images of cosmic war from ancient times to the present continue to give the rites of sacrifice their meaning.[542]

James Hillman, in *A Terrible Love of War*, captured the inescapable centrality of war to civilization:

> War defends civilization, not because war is claimed to be a "just war", or justified war. The just cause lies not in the end — overcoming evil, repelling barbarians, protecting the innocent — but the way the entry into war and the conduct of war maintain the steadfast virtues.[543]

War gives us *to* ourselves in so many ways — channeling aggression; creating an inhumane world within which to find our humanity; bringing an "us" together around the hatred of a shared enemy, or surrogate victim; offering a counterpoint against which the rest of civilization can assure: "we are not *that*." As Rumi said, we know things by their opposite, so war gives us a background against which our "civilization" can stand out.

A CONCLUSION

We are left with the uncomfortable conclusion that the *Pharmakos*, the true sacrificial victim who is expelled from the community in an orgy of violence so that the rest of civilization can survive, is the child-warrior that we send into battle, generation after generation, century after century. For this is the blood upon which civilization is founded — our children and their children meeting on a hallowed ground to consecrate God and humanity at the same time, to provide the rest of us the purification necessary to continue on, to vent the aggressive destruction that wells up within each of us until bursting with the need for release.

Without the warrior, it might be that civilization itself would become impossible. Humanity would devolve into small groups of warring tribes, venting their blind violence on those closest at hand endlessly, until all manner of creative "civilization" became untenable and the human animal was condemned to a culture-less existence of kill or be killed.

Decade after decade we make the decision that Abraham was saved from: to have our children slaughtered to appease God, so that we may live in peace. And if they have the audacity to return from battle alive, or in various pieces, they often are treated as outcasts. Today, one in four homeless people is a veteran, though veterans make up only 11% of the general population. In all of 2006, the National Alliance to End Homelessness estimated that 495,400 veterans were homeless at some point during the year.[544]

They have served their sacred purpose, to provide the purifying need of sacrifice, and their return is an embarrassment, as well as a challenge. Their existence in our midst reminds us of our own internal aggression, something that we had subconsciously foisted off onto them. The sacrifice of our young is a lesser violence, and their return a challenge to our own sense of goodness and restraint.

VIOLENCE AND CHAOS

We are back where we began: to the earliest creation myths, where chaos could only be subdued through violence and murder. The primal chaos, that which represents the unthinkable God before conception, a God driven to the desperate act of creation, always lurks.

I was walking through Washington National Airport when I was arrested by an advertisement, a massive billboard affixed to the wall at the entrance to the airport from the Metro system. Lockheed Martin, the munitions maker, had plastered a huge image of the latest fighter plane on the wall, with text beneath it that read: "Lockheed Martin: Annihilating Chaos." I stood and stared for quite awhile as the streams of people moved past, secure in their belief that they lived in the most advanced age known to humanity, as I myself looked into our deepest, darkest fears, laid bare on an advertising placard.

There are only two manners of "annihilating chaos": religion and violence. And they come together not only in practice, but also in the deepest recesses of the human soul. As Mark Juergensmeyer noted, "Religion, as the ultimate statement of meaningfulness, must always assert the primacy of meaning in the face of chaos."[545]

When I began this study, I had thought that by the end of it I might be able to offer an answer, some hope, perhaps a way out of war and destruction and wanton death. After all, it is the dream of all peace-loving people that war is somehow an aberration, and that harmony will someday reign on earth. But what I have found about war is that it is far more pernicious, and far more necessary to humanity's wellbeing, than I ever could have imagined. In the midst of writing this study, I even joked with a friend that perhaps the teleological purpose of humanity was to invent self-replicating, non-thinking destructive implements — as we have almost achieved — and then die of our own stupidity, brought down by environmental disasters, greed and just plain lack of vision.

I was only half joking, as this outcome might well be in the process of coming true.

The *Upanishads*, one of the oldest religious teachings known to humankind, propose a time before the universe that looked like this:

> There was not then what is nor what is not. There was no sky, and no heaven beyond the sky. What power was there? Where? Who was that power? Was there an abyss of fathomless waters? There was neither death nor immortality, then . . .[546]

For some reason, this "time before time" appeared first to God, and then to humankind, as "chaos."

There is something so terrifying about "nothingness" that God Itself felt compelled to escape it through creation. This represents the desperation at the heart of being; this is the chaos that must continually be destroyed, yet is indestructible.

War and religion both attempt to paper over this abyss, a place so horrifying that God Himself was afraid.

ENDNOTES

1 Girard, René. *Violence and the Sacred* (Patrick Gregory, translator). (Baltimore, MD: Johns Hopkins University Press, 1979), p. 23.

2 Ibid., p. 262.

3 Machiavelli, Niccolo. *The Discourses* (Luigi Ricci, translator). (New York: The Modern Library, 1950), p. 182.

4 Buber, Martin. *Tales of the Hasidim* (New York: Schocken Books, 1991), p. 71.

5 Ibid. pp. 131-132.

6 Quoted in Tumulty, Karen. "Conservatives New Focus: America, the Exceptional." *Washington Post* (November 29, 2010), p. A1, 12.

7 Ibid.

8 Nietzsche, Friedrich. *Beyond Good and Evil* (Walter Kauffman, translator). (New York: Vintage Books, 1966), p. 203.

9 Sun-Tzu. *The Art of War* (Ralph D. Sawyer, Translator). *The Seven Military Classics of Ancient China.* (New York: Basic Books, 2007), p. 157.

10 Ehrenreich, Barbara. *Blood Rites: Origins and History of the Passions of War* (New York: Henry Holt and Company, 1997), p. 227.

11 Kilcullen, David and Exum, Andrew McDonald. "Death From Above, Outrage Down Below." *New York Times* (May 17, 2009), p. WK13.

12 Grossman, Zoltan. "From Wounded Knee to Libya: A Century of U.S. Military Interventions." www. academic.evergreen.edu.

13 Jaffe, Greg. "On a War Footing, Set in Concrete." *Washington Post* (September 5, 2011), p. A1.

14 Hedges, Christopher. *What Every Person Should Know About War.*(New York: Free Press, 2003), p. 1.

15 Hedges, Christopher. *War is a Force that Gives us Meaning* (New York: Public Affairs, 2002), p. 10.

16 Hillman, James. *A Terrible Love of War* (New York: Penguin Books, 2004), p. 17.

17 LeShan, Lawrence. "Why We Love War—And What We Can Do To Prevent It Anyway." *Utne* (January-February 2003), p. 53.

18 Merton, Thomas. *On Peace* (New York: McCall Publishing Company, 1971), pp. 196-197.

19 Salmon, Jacqueline L. "Most Americans Believe in a Higher Power." *Washington Post* (June 24, 2008), p. A2.

20 Primitive religion is a name given to the religious beliefs and practices of those traditional, often isolated, preliterate cultures which have not developed urban and technologically sophisticated forms of society.

21 Quoted in Achenbach, Joel. "Certificate Unlikely to Appease 'Birthers.'" *Washington Post* (April 28, 2011), p. A6.

22 Arendt, Hannah. *On Violence* (New York: Harcourt, Brace and World, Inc., 1970), p. 8.

23 Girard, René. *Violence and the Sacred*, p. 33.

24 Arendt, Hannah. *On Violence*, p. 61.

25 Girard, René. *Violence and the Sacred*, p. 144.

26 Schwartz, Regina M. *The Curse of Cain: The Violent Legacy of Monotheism* (Chicago: University of Chicago Press, 1997), p. 5.

27 Ibid. p. 5.

28 Young, Jeremy. *The Violence of God & the War on Terror* (New York: Church Publishing Inc., 2008), p. 50.

29 www.deathpenaltyinfo.org.

30 www.quickfacts.census.gov.

31 Young, Jeremy. The Violence of God & the War on Terror, p. 53.

32 Nelson-Pallmeyer, Jack. *Is Religion Killing Us?* (New York: Continuum Publisher, 2004), p. 39.

33 Ibid. p. 39.

34 Juergensmeyer, Mark. *Terror in the Mind of God* (Berkeley, CA: University of California Press, 2003), pp. 160-161.

35 Hedges, Christopher. *War is a Force that Gives Us Meaning*, p. 10.

36 Victoria, Brian Daizen. *Zen at War* (Lanham, MD: Rowman & Littlefield Publishers, Inc., 2006), p. vi.

37 Some language and ideas in the paragraph taken from Juergensmeyer, Mark. *Terror in the Mind of God*, pp. 6-7.

38 Girard, René. *Violence and the Sacred*, p. 32.

39 LeShan, Lawrence. "Why We Love War—And What We Can Do To Prevent It Anyway," p. 56.

40 Quoted in Schwartz, Regina M. *The Curse of Cain: The Violent Legacy of Monotheism*, p. 6.

41 Ibid. pp. 10-11.

42 Young, Jeremy. *The Violence of God and the War on Terror*, p. 170.

43 Schwartz, Regina M. *The Curse of Cain: The Violent Legacy of Monotheism*, p. 33.

44 Nelson-Pallmeyer, Jack. *Is Religion Killing Us?* p. 136.

45 Some language and ideas in the paragraph taken from Hillman, James. *A Terrible Love of War*, p. 183.

46 Information in this paragraph from Schwartz, Regina M. *The Curse of Cain: The Violent Legacy of Monotheism*, p. 12.

47 Arendt, Hannah. *On Violence*, p. 68.

48 Hedges, Christopher. *War is a Force that Gives Us Meaning*, p. 171.

49 Broyles Jr., William. "Why Men Love War." *Esquire Magazine* (November 1984), p. 62.

50 Juergensmeyer, Mark. *Terror in the Mind of God*, p. 157.

51 Hillman, James. *A Terrible Love of War*, p. 115.

52 Ibid. pp. 119-120.

53 Quoted in ibid. p. 115.

54 Quoted in ibid. p. 141.

55 Ibid. p. 143.

56 Ibid. pp. 116, 117.

57 Quoted in ibid. p. 119.

58 Ibid. p. 141.

59 Quoted in ibid. p. 80.

60 Ibid. p. 158.

61 Ibid. p. 147.

62 Hedges, Christopher. *War is a Force that Gives Us Meaning*, p. 160.

63 Hillman, James. *A Terrible Love of War*, p. 211.

64 Bazley, Lewis. "Iraq War Veteran Barred from University After Writing Essay About how Addictive Killing Was." *Daily Mail [U.K.] Mail Online* (November 25, 2010), www.dailymail.co.uk.

65 Gourevitch, Philip. "The Life After: Fifteen Years After the Genocide in Rwanda, the Reconciliation Defies Expectations." *New Yorker* (no. 85, vol. 12, May 4, 2009), pp. 40-41.

66 Hillman, James. *A Terrible Love of War*, p. 127.

67 Ibid. p. 9.

68 Ehrenreich, Barbara. *Blood Rites: Origins and History of the Passions of War*, p. 238.

69 Gerson, Michael. "A Searcher with Faith in Mind." *Washington Post* (April 15, 2009), p. A19.

70 Information in this paragraph and Tolstoy quote from LeShan, Lawrence. "Why We Love War—And What We Can Do To Prevent It Anyway," p. 54.

71 Hedges, Christopher. *War is a Force that Gives Us Meaning*, p. 73.

72 Ibid. p. 10.

73 Confucius. The Analects (Arthur Waley, translator). (New York: HarperCollins Publishers, 1992), p. 169.

74 Patterson, David. *Greatest Jewish Stories* (New York: Jonathan David Publishers, 2001), p. 230.

75 Girard, René. *Violence and the Sacred*, p. 266.

76 LeShan, Lawrence. "Why We Love War—And What We Can Do To Prevent It Anyway," p. 55.

77 Hedges, Christopher. *War is a Force that Gives Us Meaning*, p. 45.

78 Johnson, James Turner. *The Holy War Idea in Western and Islamic Traditions* (University Park, PA: Penn State University Press, 1997), p. 131.

79 Hedges, Christopher. *War is a Force that Gives Us Meaning*, p. 9.

80 Hillman, James. *A Terrible Love of War*, p. 2.

81 Girard, René. *Violence and the Sacred*, p. 161.

82 Jaynes, Julian. *The Origins of Consciousness in the Breakdown of the Bicameral Mind* (Boston: Houghton Mifflin Company, 1976).

83 Girard, René. *Violence and the Sacred*, p. 19.

84 Ibid. p. 249.

85 Chilton, Bruce. *Abraham's Curse*. (New York: Doubleday, 2008), p. 34.

86 Ibid. p. 34.

87 Ibid. pp. 24-25.

88 Ibid. p. 17.

89 Ibid. pp. 39-40.

90 Young, Jeremy. *The Violence of God and the War on Terror*, pp. 52-53.

91 Ibid. p. 62.

92 Ibid. pp. 52-53.

93 Girard, René. *Violence and the Sacred*, p. 198.

94 Young, Jeremy. *The Violence of God and the War on Terror*, p. 53.

95 Sandars, N. K. (translator). *Poems of Heaven and Hell from Ancient Mesopotamia*. (London: Penguin Books, 1971), p. 92.

96 Young, Jeremy. *The Violence of God and the War on Terror*, p. 54.

97 Hedges, Christopher. *War is a Force that Gives Us Meaning*, p. 100.

98 Burkert, Walter. *Greek Religion* (John Raffan, Translator). (Cambridge, MA: Harvard University Press, 1985), p. 1.

99 Girard, René. *Violence and the Sacred*, p. 152.

100 Burkert, Walter. *Greek Religion*, p. 127.

101 Hillman, James. *A Terrible Love of War*, p. 83.

102 Burkert, Walter. *Greek Religion*, p. 169.

103 Ibid. p. 37.

104 Ibid. p. 31.

105 Information in the preceding paragraph and quote from ibid. pp. 82-83.

106 Ibid. p. 57.

107 Cortés, Hernán. *Cartas de relación* [originally 1523]. (México: Editorial Porrúa, 2005), p. 26.

108 Reichberg, Gregory M.; Syse, Henrik and Begby, Endre. *The Ethics of War* (Malden, MA: Blackwell Publishing, 2006), p. 19.

109 Burkert, Walter. *Greek Religion*, p. 333.

110 Tyerman, Christopher. *God's War: A New History of the Crusades* (Cambridge, MA: Harvard University Press, 2006), p. 32.

111 Reichberg, Gregory M.; Syse, Henrik; Begby, Endre. *The Ethics of War*, p. 47.

112 Chilton, Bruce. *Abraham's Curse*, p. 131.

113 Hillman, James. *A Terrible Love of War*, pp. 88, 89.

114 Nelson-Pallmeyer, Jack. *Is Religion Killing Us?* p. 28.

115 Julius Wellhausen in von Rad, Gerhard. *Holy War in Ancient Israel* (Marva J. Dawn, translator). (Grand Rapids, MI: Wm. B. Eerdmans Publishing Company, 1991), p. 3.

116 Young, Jeremy. *The Violence of God & the War on Terror*, pp. 40-41.

117   *The Holy Scriptures: According to the Masoretic Text.* (Philadelphia: Jewish Publication Society, 1948), p. 82 (Exodus 15).

118   Ibid. pp. 221-222.

119   Ibid. p. 237.

120   Ibid. p. 238.

121   Ibid. p. 238.

122   Ibid. p. 274.

123   Ibid. p. 275.

124   Ibid. pp. 493-494.

125   Young, Jeremy. *The Violence of God & the War on Terror,* p. 4.

126   Nelson-Pallmeyer, Jack. *Is Religion Killing Us?* p. 34.

127   Young, Jeremy. *The Violence of God & the War on Terror,* pp. 29, 34.

128   Ibid. p. 18.

129   Ibid. p. 19.

130   Chilton, Bruce. *Abraham's Curse,* p. 27.

131   Ibid. p. 44.

132   Ibid. p. 18.

133   Schwartz, Regina M. *The Curse of Cain: The Violent Legacy of Monotheism,* p. 24.

134   Chilton, Bruce. *Abraham's Curse,* p. 49.

135   Sharp, David. "Navy SEAL Honored with Warship Bearing his Name." *Associated Press* (May 5, 2011).

136   von Rad, Gerhard, *Holy War in Ancient Israel,* p. 5.

137   Young, Jeremy. *The Violence of God & the War on Terror,* p. 50.

138   Schwartz, Regina M. *The Curse of Cain: The Violent Legacy of Monotheism,* p. xi.

139   Ibid. pp. x, xi.

140   Nelson-Pallmeyer, Jack. *Is Religion Killing Us?* p. 52.

141   Meir, Rabbi Dr. Asher. "Not All's Fair in War, Part II: Guidelines for Conducting a 'just war'." *Jewish World Review* (Feb. 15, 2006):,www.jewish-worldreview.com.

142   *The Holy Scriptures: According to the Masoretic Text,* p. 237.

143   Solomon, Rabbi Norman. "Judaism and the Ethics of War." *International Review of the Red Cross* (Volume 87, Number 858, June 2005), p. 296.

144   Lustick, Ian. *For The Land and The Lord* (New York: Council on Foreign Relations Press, 1994), p. x. "According to the Book of Esther, the Jews are saved by the king who reverses Haman's evil decree and declares instead that Jews may do unto their enemies what their enemies had intended to do unto them: 'to stand up for themselves, to destroy, to slay, and to annihilate any armed force of any people or province that might assault them, with their little ones and women.' (Esther 8:11)"

145   BBC News. "Graveside party celebrates Hebron massacre." (March 21, 2000), www.BBCnews.com.

146   Quoted in Solomon, Rabbi Norman. "Judaism and the Ethics of War," p. 306.

147   Medzini, Ronan. "Sheikh Jarrah Jews Praise Baruch Goldstein on Purim," *YNet News* (April 3, 2010), www.ynetnews.com.

148 Ehrenreich, Barbara. *Blood Rites: Origins and History of the Passions of War*, p. 227.

149 Juergensmeyer, Mark. *Terror in the Mind of God*, pp. 45-46.

150 Ibid. pp. 58, 55.

151 Ibid. p. 53.

152 Ibid. pp. 48, 49.

153 Information and quote in this paragraph from Bronner, Ethan. "A Religious War in Israel's Army." *New York Times* (March 22, 2009):, p. WK1.

154 Nelson-Pallmeyer, Jack. *Is Religion Killing Us?* pp. 42-43.

155 Reichberg, Gregory M.; Syse, Henrik and Begby, Endre. *The Ethics of War*, p. 115.

156 Johnson, James Turner. *The Holy War Idea in Western and Islamic Traditions*, p. 56.

157 Holmes, Robert. "A Time For War? Augustine's 'Just War' Theory Continues to Guide the West." *Christianity Today* (September 2001), www.christianitytoday.com.

158 Johnson, James Turner. *The Holy War Idea in Western and Islamic Traditions*, pp. 57, 58.

159 Reichberg, Gregory M.; Syse, Henrik and Begby, Endre. *The Ethics of War*, p. 335.

160 Chilton, Bruce. *Abraham's Curse*, p. 9.

161 Ibid. p. 9.

162 Ibid. p. 6.

163 McCain, John. "Eulogy for Pat Tillman." *Fox News: Raw Data* (May 3, 2004), www.foxnews.com.

164 Morgan, Diane. *Essential Islam: A Comprehensive Guide to Belief and Practice* (Santa Barbara, CA: Praeger/ABC-CLIO, 2010), p. 87.

165 In the late 17th century, injured Dutch soldiers fighting for control of Taiwan in 1661 would use gunpowder to blow up both themselves and their opponents rather than be taken prisoner. [Yu Yonghe. *Small Sea Travel Diaries* (Macabe Keliher, translator). (Thailand: SMC Publishing Inc., 2004), p. 196.]

166 Feldman, Noah. "Islam, Terror and the Second Nuclear Age." *New York Times* (October 29, 2006), Magazine.

167 Pape, Robert. "What Really Drives Suicide Terrorists?" *Christian Science Monitor* (December 9, 2010), www.csmonitor.com.

168 Young, Jeremy. *The Violence of God & the War on Terror*, p. 1.

169 Ibid. p. 88.

170 Jose Miranda quoted in Young, Jeremy. *The Violence of God & the War on Terror*, p. 109.

171 Ibid. p. 5.

172 Nelson-Pallmeyer, Jack. *Is Religion Killing Us?* p. 63.

173 Ibid. pp. 62, 98.

174 Quoted in ibid. p. 95. For the full text of the encyclical see: "*Dominus Iesus: On The Unicity And Salvific Universality Of Jesus Christ And The Church*," www.vatican.va.

175 St. Ambrose (d. 397) quoted in Reichberg, Gregory M.; Syse, Henrik and Begby, Endre. *The Ethics of War*, p. 60.

176 Quoted in ibid. p. 63.

177 Quoted in ibid. p. 64.

178 Quoted in ibid. p. 65.

179 Quoted in ibid. p. 66.

180 Wilkins, Brett. "Gallup Poll: 30% of U.S. Christians Approve of Killing Civilians; Muslims and Atheists Most Likely to Reject Violence." *The Moral Low Ground* (August 3, 2011), www.morallowground.com. "The Gallup survey of 2,482 Americans found that 78% of Muslims believe that violence resulting in the death of civilians is never justified. Some 56% of atheists, 39% of Catholics and 38% of Protestants agreed."

181 Young, Jeremy. *The Violence of God & the War on Terror*, pp. 112-113.

182 Johnson, James Turner. *The Holy War Idea in Western and Islamic Traditions*, p. 40.

183 Chilton, Bruce. *Abraham's Curse*, p. 83.

184 Ibid. p. 81.

185 Ibid. pp. 81, 80.

186 Ibid. p. 98.

187 Quoted in ibid. p. 105.

188 Ibid. p. 99.

189 Ibid. p. 103.

190 Hillman, James. *A Terrible Love of War*, p. 191.

191 Austin, Greg, Todd Kranock and Thom Oommen. *God and War: An Audit and an Exploration* (Bradford, England: University of Bradford, Department of Peace Studies, 2003), p. 21.

192 Chilton, Bruce. *Abraham's Curse*, p. 134.

193 Ibid. p. 130.

194 Ibid. p. 133.

195 Ibid. pp. 134-135.

196 St. Augustine quoted in Reichberg, Gregory M.; Syse, Henrik and Begby, Endre. *The Ethics of War*, p. 72.

197 Nelson, Keith L. and Olin Jr., Spencer C. *Why War? Ideology, Theory and History* (Berkeley and Los Angeles, CA: University of California Press, 1980), p. 18.

198 St. Augustine quoted in Reichberg, Gregory M.; Syse, Henrik and Begby, Endre. *The Ethics of War*, p. 83.

199 Johnson, James Turner. The Holy War Idea in Western and Islamic Traditions, p. 79.

200 Reichberg, Gregory M.; Syse, Henrik and Begby, Endre. *The Ethics of War*, p. 70.

201 Joseph Liechty quoted in Young, Jeremy. *The Violence of God & the War on Terror*, p. 125.

202 Dante Alighieri quoted in Reichberg, Gregory M.; Syse, Henrik and Begby, Endre. *The Ethics of War*, p. 202.

203 Parker, Beth Ann and Brock, Rita Nakashima. *Saving Paradise: How Christianity Traded Love of This World for Crucifixion and Empire* (Boston: Beacon Press, 2008), p. 227.

204 Montville, Joseph. "Multiple Religious Belonging: Compassion, Life and Death." (Cambridge, MA: Boston Theological Institute keynote address, February 27, 2009), p. 5.

205 Chilton, Bruce. *Abraham's Curse*, p. 98.

206 Reichberg, Gregory M.; Syse, Henrik and Begby, Endre. *The Ethics of War*, p. 88.

207 Ibid. p. 111.

208 Quoted in ibid. pp. 117-118.

209 Quoted in ibid. p. 123.

210 Quoted in ibid. p. 151.

211 Quoted in ibid. p. 191.

212 Quoted in ibid. p. 213.

213 Quoted in ibid, pp. 247-248.

214 Quoted in ibid. p. 238

215 Quoted in ibid. pp. 248-249.

216 Quoted in ibid. p. 325.

217 Ibid. p. 362.

218 Ibid. p. 189.

219 Reichberg, Gregory M.; Syse, Henrik and Begby, Endre. *The Ethics olf War*, p. 265.

220 Ibid. p. 268.

221 Pope Urban II quoted in ibid. p. 102.

222 Parker, Beth Ann and Brock, Rita Nakashima. *Saving Paradise: How Christianity Traded Love of This World for Crucifixion and Empire*, p. 270.

223 Chilton, Bruce. *Abraham's Curse*, p. 175.

224 Ibid. pp. 173-174.

225 Montville, Joseph. "Jewish-Muslim Relations: Middle East." *The Crescent and the Couch: Cross-Currents Between Islam and Psychoanalysis* (Salman Akhtar, editor). (Lanham, MD: Jason Aronson, 2005), p. 227.

226 Chilton, Bruce. *Abraham's Curse*, p. 177.

227 Ibid. p. 178. Also this passage from a participant in the First Crusade: "Exulting with joy we reached the city of Jerusalem on Tuesday, June 6 [1099] and besieged it in a wonderful manner . . . Day and night we vigorously attacked the city on all sides, but before we made our assault the bishops and priests persuaded all by their preaching and exhortation that a procession should be made around Jerusalem to God's honor, faithfully accompanied by prayers, fasting and alms . . . One of our knights, Letholdus by name, climbed onto the wall of the city. When he reached the top, all the defenders of the city quickly fled along the walls and throughout the city. Our men followed and pursued them, killing and hacking, as far as the Temple of Solomon, and there was such a slaughter that our men were up to their ankles in the enemy's blood." Quoted in ibid. pp. 102-103.

228 Austin, Greg; Kranock, Todd and Oommen, Thom. *God and War: An Audit and an Exploration*, pp. 23-24.

229 Johnson, James Turner. *The Holy War Idea in Western and Islamic Traditions*, p. 39.

230 Ehrenreich, Barbara. *Blood Rites: Origins and History of the Passions of War*, p. 171.

231 Johnson, James Turner. *The Holy War Idea in Western and Islamic Traditions*, pp. 81-82.

232 Reichberg, Gregory M.; Syse, Henrik and Begby, Endre. *The Ethics of War*, p. 153.

233 Marty, Martin E. "Is Religion the Problem?" *Tikkun Magazine* (March/April 2002, Volume 17, Number 2), p. 19.

234 Hillman, James. *A Terrible Love of War*, p. 185.

235 Ibid. p. 185.

236 Steinfels, Peter. "A Catholic Debate Mounts on the Meaning of "just war"." *New York Times* (April 14, 2007), Beliefs.

237 Nelson-Pallmeyer, Jack. *Is Religion Killing Us?* p. 84.

238 Austin, Greg; Kranock, Todd and Oommen, Thom. *God and War: An Audit and an Exploration*, p. 21.

239 Bar, Shmuel. "Jihad Ideology in Light of Contemporary Fatwas." *Research Monographs on the Muslim World* (Washington DC: Hudson Institute, 2006), p. 1.

240 Nelson-Pallmeyer, Jack. *Is Religion Killing Us?* pp. 84-85.

241 Chilton, Bruce. *Abraham's Curse*, pp. 183-184.

242 Montville, Joseph. "Jewish-Muslim Relations: Middle East," p. 224.

243 *The Holy Scriptures: According to the Masoretic Text*, pp. 202-203.

244 Nelson-Pallmeyer, Jack. *Is Religion Killing Us?* pp. 76, 77.

245 *Surah* 4:56-57 quoted in ibid. p. 81.

246 Ibid. p. 75.

247 Quoted in ibid. p. 20.

248 *The Koran* (N. J. Dawood, translator). (New York and Middlesex, England: Penguin Books, 1981), p. 352.

249 *Surah* 7:5 quoted in Nelson-Pallmeyer, Jack. *Is Religion Killing Us?* p. 81.

250 Canetti, Elias. *Crowds and Power* (Carol Stewart, translator). (New York: Farrar, Straus and Giroux, 1984), p. 142.

251 Quoted in Johnson, James Turner. *The Holy War Idea in Western and Islamic Traditions*, p. 65.

252 Islamist Ignaz Goldhizer (d. 1921) in Canetti, Elias. *Crowds and Power*, pp. 142-143.

253 Johnson, James Turner. *The Holy War Idea in Western and Islamic Traditions*, pp. 60-61.

254 Nelson-Pallmeyer, Jack. *Is Religion Killing Us?* p. 90.

255 Chilton, Bruce. *Abraham's Curse*, pp. 185-186.

256 Johnson, James Turner. *The Holy War Idea in Western and Islamic Traditions*, p. 58.

257 Quoted in Canetti, Elias. *Crowds and Power*, p. 155.

258 Nelson-Pallmeyer, Jack. *Is Religion Killing Us?* p. 91.

259 Johnson, James Turner. *The Holy War Idea in Western and Islamic Traditions*, p. 19.

260 Nelson-Pallmeyer, Jack. *Is Religion Killing Us?* p. 1.

261 Juergensmeyer, Mark. *Terror in the Mind of God*, pp. 73, 74.

262 Johnson, James Turner. *The Holy War Idea in Western and Islamic Traditions*, p. 163.

263 Juergensmeyer, Mark. *Terror in the Mind of God*, p. 82.

264 Ibid. p. 80.

265 Johnson, James Turner. *The Holy War Idea in Western and Islamic Traditions*, p. 164.

266 Bar, Shmuel. "Jihad Ideology in Light of Contemporary Fatwas," p. 2.

267 Information in this paragraph from ibid. pp. 12-13.

268 Ibid. p. 1.

269 Ibid. p. 4.

270 Tolson, Jay. "Finding the Voices of Moderate Islam." *US News: Faith Matters* (April 2, 2008), www.usnews.com.

271 Bar, Shmuel. "Jihad Ideology in Light of Contemporary Fatwas," p. 11.

272 Quoted in ibid. p. 11.

273 Ibid. p. 15.

274 Ibid. p. 15.

275 *Bhagavad Gita.* (Barbara Stoler Miller, translator). (New York: Bantam Books, 1986), p. 11.

276 bid. p. 2.

277 W. J. Johnson in *The Sauptikaparvan of the Mahabharata* (W. J. Johnson, translator and editor). (Oxford: Oxford University Press, 2008).

278 *Bhagavad Gita*. p. 3.

279 Ibid. p. 2.

280 Nelson-Pallmeyer, Jack. *Is Religion Killing Us?* p. 139.

281 Ibid. p. 139.

282 *Bhagavad Gita*, p. 34.

283 Nelson-Pallmeyer, Jack. *Is Religion Killing Us?* p. 139.

284 *Bhagavad Gita*, p. 58.

285 Ibid. p. 52.

286 Ibid. pp. 33-34.

287 Ibid. pp. 31-32.

288 Ibid. p. 41.

289 Ibid. pp. 11-12.

290 Ibid. p. 8.

291 Ibid. pp. 12-13.

292 Ibid. p. 1.

293 Ibid. pp. 102-103.

294 Juergensmeyer, Mark. *Terror in the Mind of God*, p. 96.

295 Quoted in Nelson-Pallmeyer, Jack. *Is Religion Killing Us?* p. 18.

296 Girard, René. *Violence and the Sacred*, p. 100.

297 Ibid. p. 306.

298 There are references throughout to a primal mother-Earth worship, un-named snake deities and human sacrifice. There are also recitations of key Vedic-era myths.

299 Quoted in Girard, René. *Violence and the Sacred*, p. 306.

300 Subedi, Surya P. "The Concept in Hinduism of "just war"." *Journal of Conflict and Security Law* (2003, Volume 8, Number 2), abstract.

301 Bush, George W. *Public Papers of the Presidents of the United States: George W. Bush, 2001, Book 2, July 1 to December 31, 2001*. (Washington D.C.: National Archives and Records Administration, Office of the Federal Register, 2003), p. 1308.

302 Wax, Emily. "Christians Face Hindus' Wrath." *Washington Post* (September 15, 2008), p. A16.

303 Carvalho, Nirmala. "A Year of Violence Against India's Catholics." *Compass Direct* (December 19, 2005), www.truthandgrace.com.

304 Karon, Tony. "Hindu-Muslim Violence Imperils India." *Time Magazine* (February 28, 2002), www.time.com.

305 Jayaprakash, Dr. M. S. "Hindu Violence Against Buddhism in India has no Parallel." *Cricket Voice* (May 11, 2007), www.cricketvoice.com.

306 Neary, Lynn. "Tamil Tigers: Suicide Bombing Innovators." *National Public Radio* (May 21, 2009), www.npr.org.

307 www.gurmat.info.

308 Juergensmeyer, Mark. *Terror in the Mind of God*, p. 97.

309 Austin, Greg; Kranock, Todd and Oommen, Thom. *God and War: An Audit and an Exploration*, p. 12.

310 Information and quote from Juergensmeyer, Mark. *Terror in the Mind of God*, p. 163.

311 Ibid. p. 100.

312 Ibid. p. 100.

313 Victoria, Brian Daizen. *Zen at War*, p. XIV.

314 Deegalle, Mahinda. "Is Violence Justified in Theravada Buddhism?" *The Ecumenical Review* (Vol. 55, April 2003), p. 5.

315 Premasiri, P. D. "The Place for a Righteous War in Buddhism." *Journal of Buddhist Ethics* (Volume 10, 2003), p. 154.

316 Deegalle, Mahinda. "Is Violence Justified in Theravada Buddhism?" p. 5.

317 Juergensmeyer, Mark. *Terror in the Mind of God*, p. 114.

318 Victoria, Brian Daizen. *Zen at War*, p. 233.

319 Quoted in Demieville, Paul. "Buddhism and War." (Jerryson, Michael K. & Juergensmeyer, Mark, editors). *Buddhist Warfare* (Oxford, England: Oxford University Press, 2010), p. 43.

320 Jenkins, Stephen. "Making Merit through Warfare According to the *Arya-Bodhisattva-gocara-upayavisaya-vikurvana-nirdesa-sutra*." (Jerryson, Michael K. & Mark Juergensmeyer, editors). *Buddhist Warfare* (Oxford, England: Oxford University Press, 2010), p. 63.

321 Harvey, Brian Peter. *An Introduction to Buddhist Ethics: Foundations, Values and Issues* (Cambridge England: Cambridge University Press, 2010), pp. 135-136.

322 Faure, Bernard. "Afterthoughts." (Jerryson, Michael K. & Mark Juergensmeyer, editors). *Buddhist Warfare* (Oxford, England: Oxford University Press, 2010), p. 222.

323 Carter, John Ross and Palihawadana, Mahinda (translators). *The Dhammapada* (New York: Quality Paperback Book Club, 1992), p. 62 (verses 294-295).

324 Victoria, Brian Daizen. *Zen at War*, p. 225.

325 Information taken from Victoria, Brian Daizen. *Zen at War*, p. 226.

326 Ibid. pp. 226-227.

327 Jenkins, Stephen. "Making Merit through Warfare According to the *Arya-Bodhisattva-gocara-upayavisaya-vikurvana-nirdesa-sutra*," p. 70.

328 Ibid. p. 65.

329 Wallace, Vesna. "Legalized Violence: Punitive Measures of Buddhist Khans in Mongolia." (Jerryson, Michael K. & Mark Juergensmeyer, editors). *Buddhist Warfare* (Oxford, England: Oxford University Press, 2010), p. 97.

330 Jenkins, Stephen. "Making Merit through Warfare According to the *Arya-Bodhisattva-gocara-upayavisaya-vikurvana-nirdesa-sutra*," p. 68.

331 Ibid. p. 68.

332 Victoria, Brian Daizen. *Zen at War*, p. 226.

333 Demieville, Paul. "Buddhism and War," p. 38.

334 Tsumetomo, Yamamoto. *Hagakure: The Book of the Samurai* (William Scott Wilson, translator). (Tokyo, New York, London: Kodansha International, 1979), p. 164.

335 Victoria, Brian Daizen. *Zen at War*, p. 208.

336 Quoted in Victoria, Brian Daizen. "A Buddhological critique of 'Soldier-Zen' in Wartime Japan." (Jerryson, Michael K. & Mark Juergensmeyer, editors). *Buddhist Warfare* (Oxford, England: Oxford University Press, 2010), p. 108.

337 Victoria, Brian Daizen. *Zen at War*, p. 208.

338 Huang Po. *On the Transmission of Mind* (John Blofeld, Translator). (New York: Grove Weidenfeld, 1958), pp. 114-116.

339 Victoria, Brian Daizen. *Zen at War*, p. 217.

340 Sugimoto quoted in Victoria, Brian Daizen. "A Buddhological critique of 'Soldier-Zen' in Wartime Japan," p. 108.

341 Xue Yu. "Buddhists in China during the Korean War (1951-1953)." (Jerryson, Michael K. & Mark Juergensmeyer, editors). *Buddhist Warfare* (Oxford, England: Oxford University Press, 2010), p. 144.

342 Jerryson, Michael K. "Introduction." (Jerryson, Michael K. & Juergensmeyer, Mark, editors). *Buddhist Warfare* (Oxford, England: Oxford University Press, 2010), p. 9.

343 Demieville, Paul. "Buddhism and War," p. 25.

344 Victoria, Brian Daizen. *Zen at War*, p. 93.

345 Maher, Derek. F. "Sacralized Warfare: The Fifth Dalai Lama and the Discourse of Religious Violence." (Jerryson, Michael K. & Mark Juergensmeyer, editors). *Buddhist Warfare* (Oxford, England: Oxford University Press, 2010), p. 88.

346 Demieville, Paul. "Buddhism and War," p. 44.

347 Zinn, Howard. "The Power and the Glory: Myths of American Exceptionalism." *Boston Review* (Summer 2005), www.bostonreview.net.

348 Ibid.

349 D. T. Suzuki quoted in Victoria, Brian Daizen. *Zen at War*, p. 110.

350 Tsumetomo, Yamamoto. *Hagakure: The Book of the Samurai*, p. 13.

351 Sugimoto quoted in Victoria, Brian Daizen. "A Buddhological critique of 'Soldier-Zen' in Wartime Japan," p. 118.

352 Victoria, Brian Daizen. *Zen at War*, p. 219.

353 Ibid. p. 220.

354 Tsumetomo, Yamamoto, *Hagakure: The Book of the Samurai*, p. 103.

355 Quoted in ibid. p. 187.

356 Quoted in ibid. p. 134.

357 Quoted in ibid. p. 133.

358 Blumenthal, Ralph. "The World: Revisiting World War II Atrocities; Comparing the Unspeakable to the Unthinkable." *New York Times* (March 7, 1999), p. 4, Week in Review section.

359 Sugimoto quoted in Victoria, Brian Daizen. "A Buddhological critique of 'Soldier-Zen' in Wartime Japan," p. 107.

360 Quoted in ibid. p. 113.

361 Victoria, Brian Daizen. *Zen at War*, p. 120.

362 Ibid. p. 121.

363 Quoted in ibid. p. 125.

364 Ibid. p. 125.

365 Jerryson, Michael K. "Introduction," *Buddhist Warfare*, p. 9.

366 Information in this paragraph and quote from Victoria, Brian Daizen. *Zen at War*, p. 20.

367 Ibid. p. 30.

368 Ibid. pp. 28, 26.

369 Ibid. pp. X-XI.

370 Ibid. p. 36.

371 Ibid. p. 84.

372 J. J. M. deGroot quoted in Jerryson, Michael. "Introduction," *Buddhist Warfare*, p. 3.

373 Lao Tzu. *Tao Te Ching* (D. C. Lau, translator). (Middlesex, England: Penguin Books, 1983), p. 107.

374 Ssu-Ma. *The Methods of the Ssu-Ma* (Ralph D. Sawyer, Translator). *The Seven Military Classics of Ancient China* (New York: Basic Books, 2007), p. 136.

375 Ibid. p. 137.

376 Sun-Tzu. *The Art of War*, p. 164.

377 uang Shih-Kung. *The Three Strategies* (Ralph D. Sawyer, Translator). *The Seven Military Classics of Ancient China* (New York: Basic Books, 2007), p. 288.

378 Faure, Bernard. "Afterthoughts," *Buddhist Warfare*, p. 213.

379 Quoted in Victoria, Brian Daizen. *Zen at War*, p. 201.

380 Demieville, Paul. "Buddhism and War," pp. 38-39.

381 Jerryson, Michael K. "Introduction," *Buddhist Warfare*, p. 8.

382 Demieville, Paul. "Buddhism and War," pp. 31-32.

383   Gray, David B. "Compassionate Violence? On the Ethical Implications of Tantric Buddhist Ritual." *Journal of Buddhist Ethics* (Volume 14, 2007), p. 244.

384   Quoted in ibid. p. 245.

385   Ibid. p. 246.

386   Ibid. p. 252.

387   Ibid. p. 252.

388   Ibid. pp. 252-253.

389   Mumon. *The Gateless Gate: A Collection of Zen Koans* (1228). (Nyogen Senzaki and Paul Reps, translators of the 1934 edition; in the public domain), #3.

390   Xue Yu. "Buddhists in China during the Korean War (1951-1953)," p. 144.

391   Ibid. p. 145.

392   Ibid. p. 146.

393   Ibid. p. 142.

394   Ibid. p. 139.

395   Xue Yu. "Buddhist Contribution to the Socialist Transformation of Buddhism in China: Activities of Ven. Juzan during 1949–1953." *Journal of Global Buddhism* (Volume 10, 2009), p. 217.

396   Jenkins, Stephen. "Making Merit through Warfare According to the *Arya-Bodhisattva-gocara-upayavisaya-vikurvana-nirdesa-sutra*," p. 62.

397   Ibid. p. 61.

398   Ibid. p. 70.

399   Goodman, Charles. "Ethics in Indian and Tibetan Buddhism." (Edward N. Zalta, editor). *The Stanford Encyclopedia of Philosophy* (Fall 2010 Edition), www.plato.stanford.edu.

400   Victoria, Brian Daizen. *Zen at War*, pp. 197-198.

401   Dhammika. Venerable Shravasti. *The Edicts of King Ashoka*.(Kandy, Sri Lanka: Buddhist Publication Society, 1993), pp. 5, 6.

402   *IANS*. "Mumbai Buddhist monk's death sparks violence." IBNLive, (January 8, 2008).

403   Maher, Derek. F. "Sacralized Warfare: The Fifth Dalai Lama and the Discourse of Religious Violence," p. 84.

404   Ibid. p. 85.

405   Ibid. p. 83.

406   Ibid. p. 83.

407   Ibid. p. 84. "Monasteries were seized and converted, land estates were reassigned to support dGe lugs [the Dalai Lama's sect] institutions, the Karmapa was driven into exile."

408   Victoria, Brian Daizen. *Zen at War*, p. 209.

409   Dunham, Mikel. *Buddha's Warriors: The Story of the CIA-Backed Tibetan Freedom Fighters, the Chinese Communist Invasion, and the Ultimate Fall of Tibet* (New York: J. P. Tarcher, 2004), Introduction.

410   Jerryson, Michael K. "Introduction," *Buddhist Warfare*., p. 8.

411   Biographical material from Jackson, Peter A. *Buddhism, Legitimation, and Conflict: The Political Functions of Urban Thai Buddhism* (Singapore: Institute of Southeast Asia Studies, 1990), p. 148.

412 Jerryson, Michael K. "Militarizing Buddhism: Violence in Southern Thailand." (Jerryson, Michael K. & Mark Juergensmeyer, editors). *Buddhist Warfare* (Oxford, England: Oxford University Press, 2010), p. 189.

413 Ibid. pp. 182, 204.

414 Ehrenreich, Barbara. *Blood Rites: Origins and History of the Passions of War*, p. 171.

415 Jerryson, Michael K. "Militarizing Buddhism: Violence in Southern Thailand," p. 198.

416 Juergensmeyer, Mark. *Terror in the Mind of God*, p. 114.

417 Jerryson, Michael K. "Introduction," *Buddhist Warfare*, p. 8.

418 Devananda, J.L. "The Sinhala (Mahavamsa) Buddhism Revisited." *Sri Lanka Guardian* (December 26, 2009), www.srilankaguardian.org.

419 Kent, Daniel W. "Onward Buddhist Soldiers: Preaching to the Sri Lankan Army." (Jerryson, Michael K. & Mark Juergensmeyer, editors). *Buddhist Warfare* (Oxford, England: Oxford University Press, 2010), pp. 172-173.

420 Wallace, Vesna. "Legalized Violence: Punitive Measures of Buddhist Khans in Mongolia," p. 95.

421 Ibid. p. 91.

422 Ibid. p. 95.

423 The Pew Forum on Religion and Public Life. *U.S.Religious Landscape Survey Religious Affiliation: Diverse and Dynamic* (Washington DC: Pew Forum Web Publishing and Communications, February 2008).

424 O'Brien, Barbara. "War and Buddhism: Buddhist Teachings on War." *Buddhism.* ww.buddhism.about.com.

425 Machiavelli, Niccolo. *The Discourses*, p. 182.

426 Mooney, Chris. "We Can't Handle the Truth: The Science of Why People don't Believe Science." *Mother Jones* (Volume 36, No. 3, May + June 2011), p. 43.

427 Jerryson, Michael. K. "Monks With Guns: Discovering Buddhist Violence." *Religion Dispatches Magazine* (January 12, 2010):,www.religiondispatches.org.

428 Hedges, Christopher. *War is a Force that Gives Us Meaning*, p. 147.

429 Chilton, Bruce. *Abraham's Curse*, p. 12.

430 Ibid. pp. 11, 19.

431 Schwartz, Regina M. *The Curse of Cain: The Violent Legacy of Monotheism*, p. 122.

432 Hedges, Christopher. *War is a Force that Gives Us Meaning*, pp. 26-27.

433 Nelson-Pallmeyer, Jack. *Is Religion Killing Us?* p. 19.

434 Johnson, James Turner. *The Holy War Idea in Western and Islamic Traditions*, p 140.

435 Crimi, Frank. "Jihad's Child Suicide Bombers." *Front Page Magazine* (May, 11, 2011), www.frontpagemag.com.

436 Nelson-Pallmeyer, Jack. *Is Religion Killing Us?* p. 6.

437 Two quotes from Chilton, Bruce. *Abraham's Curse*, p. 190.

438 Hedges, Christopher. *War is a Force that Gives Us Meaning*, p. 69.

439 O'Relly, Bill. "The View." *ABC Television* (October 14, 2010).

440 Nelson-Pallmeyer, Jack. *Is Religion Killing Us?* p. 146.

441 Ibid. p. 114.

442 Hillman, James. *A Terrible Love of War*, p. 197.

443 Nietzsche, Friedrich. *Beyond Good and Evil* (Walter Kauffman, translator). (New York: Vintage Books, 1966), p. 118.

444 Ibid. p. 118.

445 CNN. "Survey: Support for terror suspect torture differs among the faithful." *CNN* (April 30, 2009), www.articles.cnn.com.

446 Young, Jeremy. *The Violence of God & the War on Terror*, p. 144.

447 Quoted in ibid. p. 131.

448 Information and some wording in this paragraph from ibid. p. 128.

449 Tumulty, Karen. "Conservatives New Focus: America, the Exceptional," p. A1.

450 Young, Jeremy. *The Violence of God & the War on Terror*, p. 129.

451 Nelson, Robert H. "Sin, Sacrifice, and the State of the Union." *PBS Religion and Ethics Newsweekly* (January 26, 2011), www.pbs.org. "John Winthrop's (1588–1649) sermon *A Model of Christian Charity*, evidently written on board the ship *Arbella* in 1630, cast the Puritans as the New Israel, the people so manifestly destined to be a light unto the nations that the claim needed no proof: 'We shall find that the God of Israel is among us . . . when He shall make us a praise and glory that men shall say of succeeding plantations, the Lord make it like that of New England. For we must consider that we shall be as a city on a hill. The eyes of all people are upon us.'" www.enotes.com.

452 Bush, George W. "Independence Day Proclamation, 2006." (Found at multiple sources).

453 Young, Jeremy. *The Violence of God & the War on Terror*, p. 143.

454 Ibid. p. 134.

455 Chilton, Bruce. *Abraham's Curse*, p. 89.

456 Hornaday, Joe. "A time to remember the sacrifice: Crowd honors fallen soldiers at South Park." *Greensburg Daily News* (May 26, 2008).

457 Thomas, Evan and Romano, Andrew. "God, War and the Presidency." *Newsweek* (May 7, 2007).

458 Anatol Lieven quoted in Young, Jeremy. *The Violence of God & the War on Terror*, p. 131.

459 Quoted in ibid. p. 130.

460 Quoted in Nelson-Pallmeyer, Jack. *Is Religion Killing Us?* p. 43.

461 Schwartz, Regina M. *The Curse of Cain: The Violent Legacy of Monotheism*, p. 154.

462 John Adams quoted in Baldwin, Chuck. "The Birh of Christ and the Birth of America are Linked." *Editorial Digest* (December 23, 2010), www.editorialdigest.com.

463 Quote and information in this paragraph from Young, Jeremy. *The Violence of God & the War on Terror*, p. 139.

464 Fea, John. "The Confederacy's 'Christian Nation.'" *Confessing History* (April 26, 2011), www.patheos.com.

465 Thomas, Evan and Romano, Andrew. "God, War and the Presidency."

466 Quoted in Nelson-Pallmeyer, Jack. *Is Religion Killing Us?* p. 8.

467 Young, Jeremy. *The Violence of God & the War on Terror*, p. 144.

468 Thomas, Evan and Romano, Andrew. "God, War and the Presidency."

469 Quoted in Victoria, Brian Daizen. *Zen at War*, p. xii.

470 Ibid. p. xii.

471 Butler, Brigadier General Smedley D. *War is a Racket* (Los Angeles: Feral House, 2003), p. 35.

472 Juergensmeyer, Mark. *Terror in the Mind of God*, p. 26.

473 Thomas, Evan and Romano, Andrew. "God, War and the Presidency."

474 Hedges, Christopher. *What Every Person Should Know About War*, p. 4.

475 Ibid. p. 4.

476 Ibid. p. 7.

477 Ibid. p. 6.

478 Lunch, William L., Sperlich, Peter W. "American Public Opinion and the War in Vietnam." *Western Political Quarterly* (March 1979, Volume 32), p. 30.

479 Benedetto, Richard. "Poll: Most back war, but want U.N. support." *USA Today* (March 16, 2003).

480 Nelson-Pallmeyer, Jack. *Is Religion Killing Us?* p. 7.

481 Ibid. p. 112.

482 Hedges, Christopher. *War is a Force that Gives Us Meaning*, p. 85.

483 Young, Jeremy. *The Violence of God & the War on Terror*, p. 178.

484 Hedges, Christopher. *War is a Force that Gives Us Meaning*, p. 146.

485 Young, Jeremy. *The Violence of God & the War on Terror*, p. 138.

486 MacAskill, Ewen. "George Bush: 'God told me to end the tyranny in Iraq.'" The *Guardian* (U.K.) (October 7, 2005), p. 1.

487 Young, Jeremy. *The Violence of God & the War on Terror*, p. 138.

488 Milloy, Courtland. "Why No Outrage Over How We Treat Our Own Citizens?" *Washington Post* (November 18, 2002), p. B1.

489 Suskind, Ron. "Faith, Certainty and the Presidency of George W. Bush." *New York Times* (October 17, 2004), Magazine.

490 Hamilton, Clive. "Biblical Prophesy and the Iraq War: Bush, God, Iraq and Gog." *Counterpunch* (May 22-24, 2009), www.counterpunch.org.

491 Nasaw, Daniel. "Iraq War Briefings Headlined with Biblical Quotes, Reports US Magazine." The *Guardian* (U.K.) (May 18, 2009), www.guardian.co.uk.

492 Allen, Mike. "For Bush's Speechwriter, Job Grows Beyond Words." *Washington Post* (October 11, 2002), p. A35.

493 Thomas, Adam. "Defense contractor openly using God to sell war in Iraq." *Atheist Nation* (August 18, 2007), www.atheistnation.net.

494 Welch, Michael. *Scapegoats of September 11th: Hate Crimes & State Crimes in the War on Terror* (Piscataway, NJ: Rutgers University Press, 2006), p. 56.

495 Information and quotes in this paragraph from Goldenberg, Suzanne. "US defends role for evangelical Christian." The *Guardian* (U.K.) (October 17, 2003), www.guardian.co.uk.

496 Cooperman, Alan. "Christian Leaders' Remarks Against Islam Spark Backlash." *Washington Post* (October 15, 2002), p. A16.

497 Tooley, Mark. "Praise the Lord and George W. Bush." *Seattle Post-Intelligencer* (March 21, 2003), www.seattlepi.com.

498 Steeg, Jill Lieber. "Glanville still shakes things up." *USA Today* (August 30, 2007), p. 3C.

499 Reichberg, Gregory M.; Syse, Henrik and Begby, Endre. *The Ethics of War*, p. 82.

500 McCain, John. "What Is Patriotism? Putting The Country First." *Parade Magazine* (July 1, 2008), www.parade.com.

501 Editors. "In the Profanity of War, a Commitment to Sacred Duty." *Washington Post* (May 26, 2008), p. A16.

502 Sly, Randy. "Memorial Day: Chaplains — A Reminder that We Are One Nation Under God." *Catholic Online* (May 30, 2011), www.catholic.org.

503 Tooley, Mark. "Praise the Lord and George W. Bush."

504 Salmon, Jacqueline L. "Most Americans Believe in Higher Power, Poll Finds." *Washington Post* (June 24, 2008), p. A2.

505 Green, Matt. "Choosing to Serve Their Country." *Washington Post* (November 30, 2002), p. A22.

506 Juergensmeyer, Mark. *Terror in the Mind of God*, pp. 32-33.

507 Ibid. p. 20.

508 Ibid. p. 27.

509 Ibid. p. 36.

510 Ibid. pp. 35-36.

511 Ibid. p. 23.

512 Quoted in Nelson-Pallmeyer, Jack. *Is Religion Killing Us?* pp. 113-114.

513 Terkel, Andrea. "Palin: Iraq is a Task 'from God.'" *Think Progress* (September 2, 2008), www.thinkprogress.org.

514 Nelson-Pallmeyer, Jack. *Is Religion Killing Us?* p. 136.

515 Hedges, Christopher. *War is a Force that Gives Us Meaning*, pp. 171-172.

516 Canetti, Elias. *Crowds and Power*, p. 49.

517 Reichberg, Gregory M.; Syse, Henrik and Begby, Endre. *The Ethics of War*, p. 394.

518 Hillman, James. *A Terrible Love of War*, p. 214.

519 Hedges, Christopher. *War is a Force that Gives Us Meaning*, p. 162.

520 Hillman, James. *A Terrible Love of War*, pp. 178-179.

521 Girard, René. *Violence and the Sacred*, p. 144.

522 Ibid. p. 94.

523 Ibid. pp. 265-266.

524 Hedges, Christopher. *War is a Force that Gives Us Meaning*, p. 144.

525 Nietzsche, Friedrich. *Beyond Good and Evil*, p. 48.

526 Schwartz, Regina M. *The Curse of Cain: The Violent Legacy of Monotheism*, p. 50.

527 Quoted in Hillman, James. *A Terrible Love of War*, p. 23.

528 Nietzsche, Friedrich. *Beyond Good and Evil*, p. 203.

529 Schopenhauer, Arthur. *The World as Will and Idea, Volume I* (Cambridge, MA: The Andover-Harvard Theological Library, 1910), p. 402.

530 Schopenhauer, Arthur. *The World as Will and Representation, Volume 1* (Mineola, NY: Dover Publications, 1969), p. 362.

531 Girard, René. *Violence and the Sacred*, p. 151.

532 Clausewitz, Carl von. *On War* (Anatol Rapaport, editor). (London: Penguin Books, 1968), p. 103.

533 Pincus, Walter. "Debates Underway on Combat Drones." *Washington Post* (April 25, 2011), p. A2.

534 Ibid.

535 ilcullen, David and Exum, Andrew McDonald. "Death From Above, Outrage Down Below," p. WK13.

536 Pincus, Walter. "Debates Underway on Combat Drones," p. A2.

537 Nelson, Keith L. and Olin Jr., Spencer C. *Why War? Ideology, Theory and History* (Berkeley and Los Angeles, CA: University of California Press, 1980), p. 21.

538 Girard, René. *Violence and the Sacred*, p. 134.

539 Hillman, James. *A Terrible Love of War*, pp. 24-25.

540 Girard, René. *Violence and the Sacred*, pp. 10, 8.

541 Pharmakos information from ibid. p. 288.

542 Ibid. pp. 172-173.

543 Hillman, James. *A Terrible Love of War*, p. 204.

544 Associated Press. "Veterans make up 1 in 4 homeless." *USA Today* (November 7, 2007), www.usatoday.com.

545 Juergensmeyer, Mark. *Terror in the Mind of God*, p. 162.

546 *The Upanishads* (Juan Mascaro, editor and translator). (New York and Middlesex, England: Penguin Books, 1984), pp. 9-10.

BIBLIOGRAPHY

Achenbach, Joel. "Certificate Unlikely to Appease 'Birthers.'" *Washington Post* (April 28, 2011): A1, 6.

Allen, Mike. "For Bush's Speechwriter, Job Grows Beyond Words." *Washington Post* (October 11, 2002): A35.

Arendt, Hannah. *On Violence*. New York: Harcourt, Brace and World, Inc., 1970.

Associated Press. "Veterans make up 1 in 4 homeless." *USA Today* (November 7, 2007): www.usatoday.com.

Austin, Greg; Kranock, Todd and Oommen, Thom. *God and War: An Audit and an Exploration*. Bradford, England: Department of Peace Studies, University of Bradford, 2003.

Baldwin, Chuck. "The Birth of Christ and the Birth of America are Linked." *Editorial Digest* (December 23, 2010): www.editorialdigest.com.

Bar, Shmuel. "Jihad Ideology in Light of Contemporary Fatwas." *Research Monographs on the Muslim World* (Washington DC: Hudson Institute, 2006): 1-19.

Bazley, Lewis. "Iraq War Veteran Barred from University After Writing Essay About how Addictive Killing Was." *Daily Mail (U.K.) Mail Online* (November 25, 2010): *www.dailymail.co.uk*.

Benedetto, Richard. "Poll: Most back war, but want U.N. support." *USA Today* (March 16, 2003).

Blum William. *Killing Hope: U. S. Military and CIA Interventions Since World War II*. Monroe, ME: Common Courage Press, 1995.

Blumenthal, Ralph. "The World: Revisiting World War II Atrocities; Comparing the Unspeakable to the Unthinkable." *New York Times* (March 7, 1999): 4, Week in Review section

Bodhidharma. *The Zen Teaching of Bodhidharma* (Red Pine, Translator). San Francisco: North Point Press, 1987.

Bronner, Ethan. "A Religious War in Israel's Army." *New York Times* (March 22, 2009): WK1.

Broyles Jr., William. "Why Men Love War." *Esquire Magazine* (November 1984): 55-65.

Buber, Martin. *Tales of the Hasidim.* New York: Schocken Books, 1991.

Burkert, Walter. *Greek Religion* (John Raffan, Translator). Cambridge, MA: Harvard University Press, 1985.

Bush, George W. *Public Papers of the Presidents of the United States: George W. Bush, 2001, Book 2, July 1 to December 31, 2001.* Washington DC: National Archives and Records Administration, Office of the Federal Register, 2003.

———. "Independence Day Proclamation, 2006." (Found at multiple sources).

Butler, Brigadier General Smedley D. *War is a Racket.* Los Angeles: Feral House, 2003.

Canetti, Elias. *Crowds and Power* (Carol Stewart, translator). New York: Farrar, Straus and Giroux, 1984.

Caputi, Ross. "The Old Man & the Puppy: Eyewitness to the 2nd Battle of Fallujah." *Socialist Action Newspaper* (November 2007): www.socialistaction.org.

Carney, Tom. "Americans, Especially Catholics, Approve of Torture." *National Catholic Reporter* (March 24, 2006).

———. "A Victim of Torture Speaks out on U.S. Apathy." *National Catholic Reporter* (March 24, 2006).

Carvalho, Nirmala. "A Year of Violence Against India's Catholics." *Compass Direct* (December 19, 2005): www.truthandgrace.com.

Chilton, Bruce. *Abraham's Curse.* New York: Doubleday, 2008.

Clausewitz, Carl von. *On War* (Anatol Rapaport, editor). London: Penguin Books, 1968.

CNN. "Survey: Support for terror suspect torture differs among the faithful." *CNN* (April 30, 2009): www.articles.cnn.com.

Cohen, Richard. "America the Conceited." *Washington Post* (May 10, 2011): A17.

———. "Imams of Inanity." *Washington Post* (December 3, 2002): A 25.

Confucius. *The Analects* (Arthur Waley, translator). New York: HarperCollins Publishers, 1992.

Cooperman, Alan. "Christian Leaders' Remarks Against Islam Spark Backlash." *Washington Post* (October 15, 2002): A16.

Cortés, Hernán. *Cartas de relación* [originally 1523], México: Editorial Porrúa, 2005.

Crimi, Frank. "Jihad's Child Suicide Bombers." *Front Page Magazine* (May, 11, 2011): www.frontpagemag.com.

Das, Subhamoy. "What is Namaste?" *Hinduism*: www.hinduism.about.com.

Deegalie, Mahinda. "Is Violence Justified in Theravada Buddhism?" *The Ecumenical Review.* (Vol. 55, April 2003): 1-8.

Demieville, Paul. "Buddhism and War." *Buddhist Warfare* (Jerryson, Michael K. & Juergensmeyer, Mark, editors). Oxford, England: Oxford University Press (2010): 17-58.

Devananda, J.L. "The Sinhala (Mahavamsa) Buddhism Revisited." *Sri Lanka Guardian* (December 26, 2009): www.srilankaguardian.org.

Dhammika. Venerable Shravasti. *The Edicts of King Ashoka*. Kandy, Sri Lanka: Buddhist Publication Society, 1993.

Dunham, Mikel. *Buddha's Warriors: The Story of the CIA-Backed Tibetan Freedom Fighters, the Chinese Communist Invasion, and the Ultimate Fall of Tibet.* New York: J. P. Tarcher, 2004.

Editors. "In the Profanity of War, a Commitment to Sacred Duty." *Washington Post* (May 26, 2008): p. A16.

Ehrenberg, John (& McSherry, J. Patrice; Sanchez, Jose Ramon & Sayej, Caroleen Marji, editors). *The Iraq Papers*. New York: Oxford University Press, 2009.

Ehrenreich, Barbara. *Blood Rites: Origins and History of the Passions of War.* New York: Henry Holt and Company, 1997.

Ehrhart, W. D. *What War Does* (photocopied folio from an unidentified publication): 39-41.

Falwell, Reverend Jerry. "God is Pro-War." *WorldNet Daily Commentary* (January 31, 2004): www.wnd.com.

Faure, Bernard. "Afterthoughts." *Buddhist Warfare* (Jerryson, Michael K. & Juergensmeyer, Mark, editors). Oxford, England: Oxford University Press (2010): 211-223.

Fea, John. "The Confederacy's 'Christian Nation.'" *Confessing History* (April 26, 2011): www.patheos.com.

Feldman, Noah. "Islam, Terror and the Second Nuclear Age." *New York Times* (October 29, 2006): Magazine.

Gerson, Michael. "A Searcher with Faith in Mind." *Washington Post* (April 15, 2009): A19.

Gethin, Rupert. "Can Killing a Living Being Ever be an Act of Compassion?" *Journal of Buddhist Ethics.* (Volume 11, 2004): 167-202.

Girard, Renee. *Violence and the Sacred* (Patrick Gregory, translator). Baltimore, MD: Johns Hopkins University Press, 1979.

Goldenberg, Suzanne. "US defends role for evangelical Christian." *The Guardian* (U.K.) (October 17, 2003): www.guardian.co.uk.

Goodman, Charles. "Ethics in Indian and Tibetan Buddhism." (Edward N. Zalta, editor). *The Stanford Encyclopedia of Philosophy* (Fall 2010 Edition): *www.plato.stanford.edu.*

Gourevitch, Philip. "The Life After: Fifteen Years After the Genocide in Rwanda, the Reconciliation Defies Expectations." *New Yorker* (85, vol. 12, May 4, 2009): 38-49.

Gray, David B. "Compassionate Violence? On the Ethical Implications of Tantric Buddhist Ritual." *Journal of Buddhist Ethics* (Volume 14, 2007): 238-271.

Gray, J. Glenn. *The Warriors: Reflections on Men in Battle.* Lincoln, NE: Bison Books, 1998.

Green, Matt. "Choosing to Serve Their Country." *Washington Post* (November 30, 2002): p. A22.

Grossman, Dr. Zoltan. *From Wounded Knee to Libya: A Century of U.S. Military Interventions.* www. academic.evergreen.edu.

Hamilton, Clive. "Biblical Prophesy and the Iraq War: Bush, God, Iraq and Gog." *Counterpunch* (May 22-24, 2009): www.counterpunch.org.

Harvey, Brian Peter. *An Introduction to Buddhist Ethics: Foundations, Values and Issues*. Cambridge England: Cambridge University Press, 2010.

Hedges, Christopher. *War is a Force that Gives us Meaning*. New York: Public Affairs, 2002.

———. *What Every Person Should Know About War*. New York: Free Press, 2003.

Hillman, James. *A Terrible Love of War*. New York: Penguin Books, 2004.

Hofstadter, Alfred & Kuhns, Richard (editors). *Philosophies of Art and Beauty*. Chicago: University of Chicago Press, 1964.

Holmes, Robert. "A Time For War? Augustine's Just War Theory Continues to Guide the West." *Christianity Today* (September 2001): www.christianitytoday.com.

Hornaday, Joe. "A time to remember the sacrifice: Crowd honors fallen soldiers at South Park." *Greensburg Daily News* (May 26, 2008).

Huang Po. *On the Transmission of Mind* (John Blofeld, Translator). New York: Grove Weidenfeld, 1958.

Huang Shih-Kung. *The Three Strategies* (Ralph D. Sawyer, Translator). *The Seven Military Classics of Ancient China*. New York: Basic Books (2007): 292-306.

IANS. "Mumbai Buddhist monk's death sparks violence." *IBNLive* (January 8, 2008).

Jackson, Peter A. *Buddhism, Legitimation, and Conflict: The Political Functions of Urban Thai Buddhism*. Singapore: Institute of Southeast Asia Studies, 1990.

Jaffe, Greg. "On a War Footing, Set in Concrete." *Washington Post* (September 5, 2011): A1, A8.

Jayaprakash, Dr. M. S. "Hindu Violence Against Buddhism in India has no Parallel." Cricket Voice (May 11, 2007): www.cricketvoice.com.

Jaynes, Julian. *The Origins of Consciousness in the Breakdown of the Bicameral Mind*. Boston: Houghton Mifflin Company, 1976.

Jenkins, Stephen. "Making Merit through Warfare According to the *Arya-Bodhisattva-gocara-upayavisaya-vikurvana-nirdesa-sutra*." *Buddhist Warfare* (Jerryson, Michael K. & Juergensmeyer, Mark, editors). Oxford, England: Oxford University Press (2010): 59-76.

Jerryson, Michael K. (& Juergensmeyer, Mark, editors). *Buddhist Warfare*. Oxford, England: Oxford University Press, 2010.

———. "Militarizing Buddhism: Violence in Southern Thailand." *Buddhist Warfare* (Jerryson, Michael K. & Juergensmeyer, Mark, editors). Oxford, England: Oxford University Press (2010): 179-210.

———. "Monks With Guns: Discovering Buddhist Violence." *Religion Dispatches Magazine* (January 12, 2010): www.religiondispatches.org.

Johnson, Gene. "Palin: Iraq War 'a Task that is from God.'" *Associated Press* (September 3, 2008).

Johnson, James Turner. *The Holy War Idea in Western and Islamic Traditions*. University Park, PA: Penn State University Press, 1997.

Juergensmeyer, Mark. *Terror in the Mind of God*. Berkeley, CA: University of California Press, 2003.

Karmay, Samten Gyaltsen. *Secret Visions of the Fifth Dalai Lama*. London: Serindia Publications, 1988.

Karon, Tony. "Hindu-Muslim Violence Imperils India." *Time Magazine*. (February 28, 2002): www.time.com.

Kent, Daniel W. "Onward Buddhist Soldiers: Preaching to the Sri Lankan Army." *Buddhist Warfare* (Jerryson, Michael K. & Juergensmeyer, Mark, editors). Oxford, England: Oxford University Press (2010): 157-178.

Kilcullen, David and Exum, Andrew McDonald. "Death From Above, Outrage Down Below." *New York Times* (May 17, 2009): WK13.

Kohn, George C. *Dictionary of Wars*. New York: Facts on File, 1999.

Lao Tzu. *Tao Te Ching* (D. C. Lau, translator). Middlesex, England: Penguin Books, 1983.

LeShan, Lawrence. "Why We Love War – And What We Can Do To Prevent It Anyway." (Utne, January-February 2003): 52-58.

Lunch, William L. and Sperlich, Peter W. "American Public Opinion and the War in Vietnam." *Western Political Quarterly* (March 1979, Volume 32): 21-44.

Lustick, Ian. *For The Land and The Lord*. New York: Council on Foreign Relations Press, 1994.

Machiavelli, Niccolo. *The Discourses* (Luigi Ricci, translator). New York: The Modern Library, 1950.

——.*The Prince* (Angelo M. Codevilla, Translator). New Haven: Yale University Press, 1997.

MacAskill, Ewen. "George Bush: 'God told me to end the tyranny in Iraq.'" *The Guardian* (U.K.) (October 7, 2005): 1.

Maher, Derek. F. "Sacralized Warfare: The Fifth Dalai Lama and the Discourse of Religious Violence." *Buddhist Warfare* (Jerryson, Michael K. & Juergensmeyer, Mark, editors). Oxford, England: Oxford University Press (2010): 77-90.

Marty, Martin E. "Is Religion the Problem?" *Tikkun Magazine* (March/April 2002, Volume 17, Number 2): 19.

McCain, John. "Eulogy for Pat Tillman." *Fox News: Raw Data* (May 3, 2004): www.foxnews.com.

——. "What Is Patriotism? Putting The Country First." *Parade Magazine* (July 1, 2008), http://www.parade.com.

McIntosh, Alastair. "A Nonviolent Challenge to Conflict." *Ethics, Law and Military Operations* (David Whetham, Editor). Hampshire, England: Palgrave MacMillan (2010): 44-64.

——. *Hell and High Water: Climate Change, Hope and the Human Condition*. Edinburgh, Scotland: Birlinn, 2009.

Meir, Rabbi Dr. Asher. "Not All's Fair in War, Part II: Guidelines for Conducting a Just War." *Jewish World Review* (Feb. 15, 2006): www.jewishworldreview.com.

Merton, Thomas. *On Peace*. New York: McCall Publishing Company, 1971.

Milbank, Dana. "Obama's Victory Lap." *Washington Post* (May 3, 2011): A2.

——. "War Party Disputes Bush's Stance on Islam." *Washington Post* (November 30, 2002): A4.

Milloy, Courtland. "Why No Outrage Over How We Treat Our Own Citizens?" *Washington Post* (November 18, 2002): B1.

Montville, Joseph. "Jewish-Muslim Relations: Middle East." *The Crescent and the Couch: Cross-Currents Between Islam and Psychoanalysis* (Salman Akhtar, editor). Lanham, MD: Jason Aronson (2005): 217-230.

——. "Multiple Religious Belonging: Compassion, Life and Death." Cambridge, MA: Boston Theological Institute keynote address, February 27, 2009.

Mooney, Chris. "We Can't Handle the Truth: The Science of Why People don't Believe Science." *Mother Jones* (Volume 36, No. 3, May + June 2011): 40-45.

Mumon. *The Gateless Gate: A Collection of Zen Koans* (1228). (Nyogen Senzaki and Paul Reps, translators of the 1934 edition): In the public domain.

Nasaw, Daniel. "Iraq War Briefings Highlighted with Biblical Quotes, Reports US Magazine." *The Guardian* (U.K.) (May 18, 2009): www.guardian.co.uk.

Neary, Lynn. "Tamil Tigers: Suicide Bombing Innovators." *National Public Radio* (May 21, 2009): www.npr.org.

Nelson, Robert H. "Sin, Sacrifice, and the State of the Union." *PBS Religion and Ethics Newsweekly* (January 26, 2011): www.pbs.org.

Nelson-Pallmeyer, Jack. *Is Religion Killing Us?* New York: Continuum Publisher, 2004.

Nelson, Keith L. and Olin Jr., Spencer C. *Why War? Ideology, Theory and History.* Berkeley and Los Angeles, CA: University of California Press, 1980.

Newberg, Andrew and Waldman, Mark Robert. *How God Changes Your Brain: Breakthrough Findings from a Leading Neuroscientist.* New York: Ballantine Books, 2009.

Nietzsche, Friedrich. *Beyond Good and Evil* (Walter Kauffman, translator). New York: Vintage Books, 1966.

O'Brien, Barbara. "War and Buddhism: Buddhist Teachings on War." *Buddhism.* www.buddhism.about.com.

O'Reilly, Bill. "The View." *ABC Television* (October 14, 2010).

Pape, Robert. "What Really Drives Suicide Terrorists?" *Christian Science Monitor* (December 9, 2010): www.csmonitor.com.

Parker, Beth Ann and Brock, Rita Nakashima. *Saving Paradise: How Christianity Traded Love of This World for Crucifixion and Empire.* Boston: Beacon Press, 2008.

Patterson, David, *Greatest Jewish Stories.* New York: Jonathan David Publishers, 2001.

Pew Research Center. "*U.S. Religious Landscape Survey Religious Affiliation: Diverse and Dynamic.*" Washington D.C.: Pew Forum Web Publishing and Communications, February 2008.

——. "Views About Torture Remain Evenly Split." Washington D.C.: Pew Research Center Publications, April 23, 2009.

Pincus, Walter. "Debates Underway on Combat Drones." *Washington Post* (April 25, 2011): A2.

Premasiri, P. D. "The Place for a Righteous War in Buddhism." *Journal of Buddhist Ethics* (Volume 10, 2003): 153-166.

Price, A. F. (and Wong Lou-lam, translators). *The Diamond Sutra and The Sutra of Hui-neng.* Boston: Shambhala, 1999.

Reichberg, Gregory M.; Syse, Henrik and Begby, Endre. *The Ethics of War.* Malden, MA: Blackwell Publishing, 2006.

Salmon, Jacqueline L. "Most Americans Believe in a Higher Power." *Washington Post* (June 24, 2008): A2.

Sandars, N. K. (translator). *Poems of Heaven and Hell from Ancient Mesopotamia.* London: Penguin Books, 1971.

Schopenhauer, Arthur. *The World as Will and Idea, Volume I.* Cambridge, MA: The Andover-Harvard Theological Library, 1910.

——. *The World as Will and Representation, Volume 1.* Mineola, NY: Dover Publications, 1969.

Schwartz, Regina M. *The Curse of Cain: The Violent Legacy of Monotheism.* Chicago: University of Chicago Press, 1997.

Shane, Scott. "Waterboarding Used 266 Times on 2 Suspects." *New York Times* (April 20, 2009): A1.

Sharp, David. "Navy SEAL Honored with Warship Bearing his Name." *Associated Press* (May 5, 2011).

Shasha, David. "War as Social Ritual in Frank Borzage's 'No Greater Glory' and 'The Mortal Storm.'" *Sephardic Heritage Update* (November 23, 2009).

Siasat Daily, The. "Pakistani Christians, Muslims United Against Violence." August 14, 2009.

Sly, Randy. "Memorial Day: Chaplains - A Reminder that We Are One Nation Under God." *Catholic Online* (May 30, 2011): www.catholic.org.

Solomon, Rabbi Norman. "Judaism and the Ethics of War." *International Review of the Red Cross* (Volume 87, Number 858, June 2005): 295-309.

Ssu-Ma. *The Methods of the Ssu-Ma* (Ralph D. Sawyer, Translator). *The Seven Military Classics of Ancient China.* New York: Basic Books (2007): 126-144.

Steeg, Jill Lieber. "Glanville still shakes things up." *USA Today* (August 30, 2007): 3C.

Steinfels, Peter. "A Catholic Debate Mounts on the Meaning of 'Just War.'" *New York Times* (April 14, 2007): Beliefs.

Stroble, James A. "Buddhism and War: A Study of the Status of Violence in Early Buddhism." *University of Hawaii at Manoa* (December 17, 1991): www2.hawaii.edu.

Sun-Tzu. *The Art of War* (Ralph D. Sawyer, Translator). *The Seven Military Classics of Ancient China.* New York: Basic Books (2007): 157-186.

Subedi, Surya P. "The Concept in Hinduism of 'Just War.'" *Journal of Conflict and Security Law* (Volume 8, Number 2, 2003): 339-361.

Suskind, Ron. "Faith, Certainty and the Presidency of George W. Bush." *New York Times* (October 17, 2004): Magazine.

T'ai Kung. *Six Secret Teachings* (Ralph D. Sawyer, Translator). *The Seven Military Classics of Ancient China.* New York: Basic Books (2007): 40-106.

T'ang T'ai-tsung & Li Wei-kung. *Questions and Replies* (Ralph D. Sawyer, Translator). *The Seven Military Classics of Ancient China.* New York: Basic Books (2007): 321-362.

Terkel, Andrea. "Palin: Iraq is a Task 'from God.'" *Think Progress* (September 2, 2008): www.thinkprogress.org.

Thomas, Adam. "Defense contractor openly using God to sell war in Iraq." *Atheist Nation*, August 18, 2007. www.atheistnation.net.

Thomas, Evan and Romano, Andrew. "God, War and the Presidency." *Newsweek* (May 7, 2007).

Thompson, Mark. "The Boykin Affair." *Time Magazine* (November 3, 2003): 31

Tolson, Jay. "Finding the Voices of Moderate Islam." *US News* (April 2, 2008): Faith Matters, http://www.usnews.com/news/blogs/faith-matters/2008/04/02/finding-the-voices-of-moderate-islam

Tolstoy, Leo. *On Civil Disobedience and Non-Violence.* New York: New American Library, 1968.

Tooley, Mark. "Praise the Lord and George W. Bush." *Seattle Post-Intelligencer* (March 21, 2003): www.seattlepi.com.

Tsumetomo, Yamamoto. *Hagakure: The Book of the Samurai* (William Scott Wilson, translator). Tokyo, New York, London: Kodansha International, 1979.

Tumulty, Karen. "Conservatives New Focus: America, the Exceptional." *Washington Post* (November 29, 2010): A1, 12.

Tyerman, Christopher. *God's War: A New History of the Crusades.* Cambridge, MA: Harvard University Press, 2006.

Victoria, Brian Daizen. "A Buddhological critique of 'Soldier-Zen' in Wartime Japan." *Buddhist Warfare* (Jerryson, Michael K. & Juergensmeyer, Mark, editors). Oxford, England: Oxford University Press (2010): 105-130.

———. *Zen at War.* Lanham, MD: Rowman & Littlefield Publishers, Inc., 2006.

von Rad, Gerhard. *Holy War in Ancient Israel* (Marva J. Dawn, Translator and Editor). Grand Rapids, MI: William. B. Eerdmans Publishing Company, 1991.

Wallace, Vesna. "Legalized Violence: Punitive Measures of Buddhist Khans in Mongolia." *Buddhist Warfare* (Jerryson, Michael K. & Juergensmeyer, Mark, editors). Oxford, England: Oxford University Press (2010): 91-104.

Wax, Emily. "Christians Face Hindus' Wrath." *Washington Post* (September 15, 2008): A16.

Welch, Michael. *Scapegoats of September 11th: Hate Crimes & State Crimes in the War on Terror.* Piscataway, NJ: Rutgers University Press, 2006.

Wilkins, Brett. "Gallup Poll: 30% of U.S. Christians Approve of Killing Civilians; Muslims and Atheists Most Likely to Reject Violence." *The Moral Low Ground* (August 3, 2011): www.morallowground.com.

Wu-Tzu. *The Wu-Tzu* (Ralph D. Sawyer, Translator). *The Seven Military Classics of Ancient China.* New York: Basic Books (2007): 206-224.

Xue Yu. "Buddhist Contribution to the Socialist Transformation of Buddhism in China: Activities of Ven. Juzan during 1949–1953." *Journal of Global Buddhism* (Volume 10, 2009): 217-253.

——— "Buddhists in China during the Korean War (1951-1953)." *Buddhist Warfare* (Jerryson, Michael K. & Juergensmeyer, Mark, editors). Oxford, England: Oxford University Press (2010): 131-156.

Young, Jeremy. *The Violence of God & the War on Terror.* New York: Church Publishing Inc., 2008.

Yu Yonghe. *Small Sea Travel Diaries* (Macabe Keliher, translator). Thailand: SMC Publishing Inc., 2004.

Zinn, Howard. "The Power and the Glory: Myths of American Exceptionalism." *Boston Review* (Summer 2005): www.bostonreview.net.

Sacred Books:

Bhagavad Gita. (Barbara Stoler Miller, translator). New York: Bantam Books, 1986.

Dhammapada (John Ross Carter and Mahinda Palihawadana, translators). New York: Quality Paperback Book Club, 1992.

Holy Scriptures: According to the Masoretic Text. Philadelphia: Jewish Publication Society, 1948.

Koran (N. J. Dawood, translator). New York and Middlesex, England: Penguin Books, 1981.

The Upanishads (Juan Mascaro, editor and translator). New York and Middlesex, England: Penguin Books, 1984.

Online Sources:

About.Com: www.about.com
Atheist Nation: www.atheistnation.net
BBC News: www.news.bbc.co.uk
Boston Review: www.bostonreview.net
Catholic Online: www.catholic.org
Christianity Today: www.christianitytoday.com
Christian Science Monitor: www.csmonitor.com
CNN: www.cnn.com
Counterpunch: www.counterpunch.org
Cricket Voice: www.cricketvoice.com
Editorial Digest: www.editorialdigest.com
Encyclopedia Mythica: www.pantheon.org
Fox News: www.foxnews.com
Front Page Magazine: www.frontpagemag.com
Greensburg Daily News: www.greensburgdailynews.com
Guardian Newspaper: www.guardian.co.uk
IBNLive: www.ibnlive.in.com
Jewish World Review: www.jewishworldreview.com
Moral Low Ground: www.morallowground.com
National Public Radio: www.npr.org
New York Times: www.nytimes.com
Parade Magazine: www.parade.com
Patheos: www.patheos.com
PBS: www.pbs.org
Pew Forum: www.pewforum.org
Religion Dispatches: www.religiondispatches.org

Seattle Post-Intelligencer: www.seattlepi.com
Sikh Missionary Society: www.gurmat.info
Socialist Action: www.socialistaction.org
Source Watch: www.sourcewatch.org
Sri Lanka Guardian: www.srilankaguardian.org
Stanford Encyclopedia of Philosophy: www.plato.stanford.edu
Think Progress: www.thinkprogress.org
Time Magazine: www.time.com
Truth and Grace: www.truthandgrace.com
USA Today: www.usatoday.com
US News: www.usnews.com
Vatican: www.vatican.va
Washington Post: www.washingtonpost.com

INDEX